The Process of Writing News

From Information to Story

Brian Richardson

Washington and Lee University

PEARSON

Boston   New York   San Francisco
Mexico City   Montreal   Toronto   London   Madrid   Munich   Paris
Hong Kong   Singapore   Tokyo   Cape Town   Sydney

Editor-in-Chief, Communication: Karon Bowers
Series Editorial Assistant: Suzanne Stradley
Marketing Manager: Suzan Czajkowski
Production Editor: Karen Mason
Full-Service Production: Publishers' Design and Production Services, Inc.
Composition Buyer: Linda Cox
Manufacturing Buyer: JoAnne Sweeney
Cover Administrator: Linda Knowles

For related titles and support materials, visit our online catalog at www.ablongman.com.

Between the time Web site information is gathered and then published, it is not unusual for some sites to have closed. Also, the transcription of URLs can result in typographical errors. The publisher would appreciate notification where these errors occur so that they may be corrected in subsequent editions.

Library of Congress Cataloging-in-Publication Data

Richardson, Brian.
   The process of writing news : from information to story / Brian Richardson.
     p. cm.
Includes index.
ISBN 0-205-45440-2 (alk. paper)
1. Journalism—Authorship. I. Title.

PN4775.R443 2007
808'.06607—dc22   2006043236

Printed in the United States of America

10 9 8 7 6 5 4 3 2 1   CIN   10 09 08 07 06

Photo credits: pp. 7, 11, 45, 46, 54, 82, 117, 118, 138, 164, 174, 240, 248, © *The Roanoke Times*, 2005; pp. 15, 47, 56, 60, 110, 111, 165, 239, 262, WSLS/Newschannel 10 Roanoke, Virginia.

Contents

Preface

To the Student

As a conscientious student and an eager prospective journalist, you are no doubt thinking, "For what I just shelled out for this one measly book, it better be good."

You're right. We had all better be good—you, me, the book. There is a lot of mediocre journalism being passed off as solid work these days, and there is too much at stake for any of us to be complacent about that. Truthful, relevant, reliable information reported in context is the lifeblood of democracy. Whether people get their daily news from newspapers, radio, television or the Web, news empowers them and makes the idea of self-determination meaningful. Whether you wind up spending your career in a newsroom or not, I hope you come away from this book—and this course—understanding how important good journalism and good journalists are in any free society. That's my primary purpose in writing it.

I wrote it with some other purposes in mind too:

1. You should learn to understand writing as a systematic process that is far less mysterious than you might have been led to believe. Not easy, but less mysterious.

2. You should get a good start developing skill in weighing the reliability and relative importance of information.

3. You should get a grasp of the ethical dimension of the decisions you make as a journalist, especially when it comes to weighing benefit and harm.

4. You should begin to develop an understanding of what it means to serve an increasingly diverse public.

5. You should get plenty of practice organizing information and writing news stories clearly and compellingly in three media—print, Web and

broadcast—so that diverse audiences in all three can understand why a story is important to them.

6. You should understand the value of cultivating all these skills.

In each chapter, I address key journalistic concepts at several levels of abstraction. Usually I begin by discussing the importance of a concept in a societal context—why audiences need the particular type of information or journalistic approach. After that, I provide some particular how-tos and characteristics of the skills covered in that chapter. Then I turn to the ethical dimensions of the topic. This is followed by strategies intended to help you in mastering that chapter's challenge.

Finally, you are asked to put the chapter's lessons to work in an exercise or series of exercises. By having you work from the general to the specific, I hope to give you a solid understanding of what you are doing and why you are doing it, as well as extensive practice in developing the skills required of a good journalist.

Nowhere-ville

Life is more than a series of isolated incidents. Things relate to other things; problems continue; issues arise, persist and are sometimes resolved. If we don't know that intuitively, most of us figure it out by the time we are adults. If it is to be helpful, the news is like that too. In this book you will have to deal with ongoing issues, you will keep revisiting some of the same people and you will report events that build on previous events until resolution. Part of good journalism is reminding audiences of how they already know the people and issues you are telling them about.

To give you some idea of the dynamic context in which journalists operate, I have made up an entire community of interrelated people and institutions. The idea has been tried before in journalism teaching. For example, both Auburn University and the University of Florida have used something like it in home-grown lab exercises, and it was the basis for Ken Metzler's *Newswriting Exercises* in the 1980s.

Blue Ridge County, Valleydale and Beausoleil make up a fictitious region in the state of Virginia. The people, places, events and issues described are based on what I encountered as a reporter during years of covering municipal government, courts, education and interesting people. If you cover it as a reporter would, the community will take on a life of its own. Pardon that cliché, but hundreds of my Introduction to Reporting students over the years have borne this out.

Learning the Tools

I know you're eager to get started writing, so I've got an exercise ready for you at the end of Chapter 1. After that shakedown cruise, in Chapter 2 you'll get a reality check of your skill with the journalist's basic tools—words, grammar, punctuation, spelling and syntax. If you're not sure-handed with those tools, your audiences won't understand what you're trying to tell them.

To the Instructor

This book is intended for journalism students in their first writing course. In my department the instructors share an observation about our Introduction to Reporting class: The students say it's about how to write; we say it's about how to think. I have been developing this book in that course over the past six years or so. My intention has been to stimulate students to think appropriately about information, its relative value and reliability and about the ethical dimension of decisions they make as journalists. I also mean for them to learn writing as a systematic process that can be demystified. As I tell them early in the book, the process of writing is fairly simple, but it is never easy.

So the book sticks to the basics. For example, in Chapter 7, on story forms and organizing stories, you will notice that I do not deal specifically with point-of-view narratives or personality profiles. Again, the scope of this book is fundamental, but as the instructor you can adapt the information presented here to take your most talented students, your fastest learners, your fire-in-the-bellies, as far as they are ready to go.

The key to the book is the series of exercises at the end of each chapter. They are intended to give students plenty of practice in writing clearly for three media. They also are designed to challenge students to make difficult decisions about what to put into stories and what to leave out, what should be shared with audiences and what should not. The students are challenged to do all that in the context of people we keep revisiting and an issue that ultimately takes several stories to resolve. I thought it was important that they get an idea of how often things can't be tied up in a bow or settled in one story.

Each of the exercises is designed to reward care, planning and thought, and to punish sloppiness. To that end I have built in misspelled names and inaccurate titles and addresses—mistakes that they can catch and fix by referring to the City Directory at the end of the book. In our courses we respond to fact errors with an F for the assignment; grammar, spelling and punctuation errors result in letter-grade deductions. The way in which you decide to reward accuracy and care is up to you.

At the end of this book, students should feel reasonably comfortable writing for print, broadcast and the Web. It is beyond the book's scope to give them practice in shooting or editing video or writing to tape. But they should understand the visual nature of broadcast media and the premium on brevity. They should be able to write a 30-second RDR (see Chapter 8).

As the instructor, you have the option of augmenting these exercises with real reporting (there are two such assignments built into the exercises), more deadline writing or by adding video elements to broadcast-writing exercises. The book is intended to provide you with both the basis and the flexibility to shape your instruction to the needs of your students.

The accompanying Instructor's Manual includes sample ledes and stories for each of the exercises. I welcome your suggestions for improving these. Even better, I invite you to send me sterling examples your students have written that I can include in later editions or on a companion Web site, credited to the student who wrote it. In your classes, you might choose to prime the pump by sharing one or two of the sample stories before students attempt to write, particularly early on. Or you might choose to let them find their own way, and share the sample stories with them after you return their assignments.

The Instructor's Manual also includes a few tips I have managed to learn the hard way over the years we have been using this approach in our introductory course. There are also transcripts of interviews you may act out in class to give students practice in taking good notes and getting quotes. Again, whether you provide them the transcript before they do the assignment or afterward is up to you.

You will also find a "Year in the Life" chronology, intended to help students develop accurate background for their stories. I recommend sharing one event from the chronology at a time, cumulatively; experience has taught me that if I provide the entire chronology at once, students get confused about how much has happened at any point, and how much their audiences might know. You might also remind them not to look ahead in the book; otherwise they will tend to include as background and context events that haven't happened yet.

Finally, the Instructor's Manual includes a sample final exam developed to test students on as much of the book's content as possible. It is meant to be taken on a three-hour deadline, but, like practically everything else in the book, adjustments can be made to suit your students' needs.

Acknowledgments

I am grateful to my colleagues in the Department of Journalism and Mass Communications at Washington and Lee University for their help, suggestions, and feedback: to Ham Smith and Doug Cumming, who used early drafts of the text with their students; to Claudette Artwick and Bob de Maria, who assisted with the broadcast-writing elements; again to Ham Smith, who wrote the first version of the final exam more than a decade ago and has seen it develop; and to Lou Hodges, emeritus Knight Professor of Ethics in Journalism, who helped clarify my ethical reasoning.

I also thank Executive Editor Mike Riley and the photo staff of *The Roanoke Times* and News Director Shane Moreland, Mike Wright, Matt Dooley, and my former student Juliet Bickford at WSLS-TV Channel 10 in Roanoke, all of whom helped with the photos for the book.

I am also grateful to my students Kristen Youngblood and Kynai Johnson, who with Professor Ted Delaney helped me work through the issues of covering minorities and diversity; and to my student Ann Stewart Banker, who, at a difficult time for her and with admirable courage, helped me write more clearly about interviewing people who have suffered a loss.

I would also like to thank the many reviewers who took the time to evaluate the manuscript and provide valuable suggestions: Darrell Fike, Valdosta State University; Edward Horowitz, Cleveland State University; Hugh Munn, University of South Carolina; Bruce L. Plopper, University of Arkansas at Little Rock; Patricia A. Richards, University of Scranton; Klaus P. Scherler, Spokane Falls Community College; Kenneth S. Sexton, Morehead State University; and Donald G. Spitler, Pulaski Technical College.

Finally, I thank Frances, Aaron and Daniel, who have been patient. Very patient.

Blue Ridge County Map

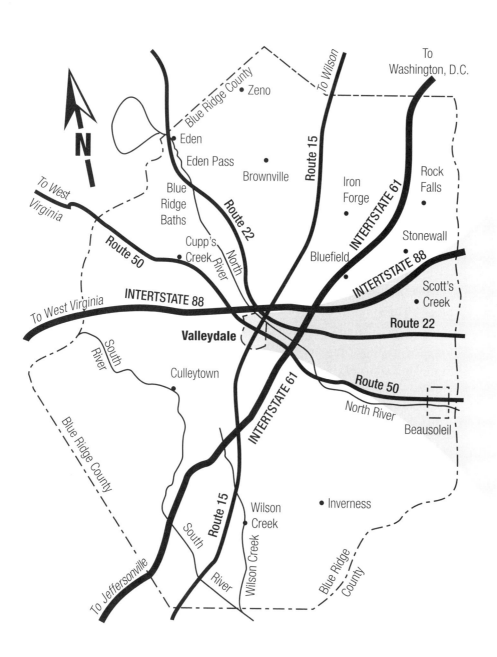

Valleydale

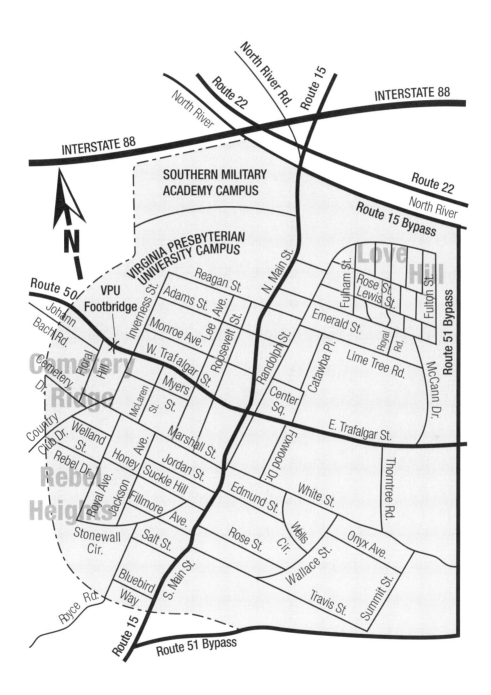

chapter one

Reporters, Communities, and Working in a Converged World

"What's this story about?"

Victoria Baxter takes a deep breath. Even though she hears this question from her city editor almost every day, it always registers a little thump inside. As the *Jeffersonville Herald*'s sole reporter in Blue Ridge County, Tori has to decide every day what is most worth telling her audiences. Some days she will crank out two or even three stories, but most of the time the space in the paper for news—the "news hole"—is at a premium; it's her job to give "downtown" the story that will make the most difference to the most people. She knows that news stories should be about the people involved in events and issues, not just about the events and issues.

"Two members of Valleydale City Council tried to force a vote to fire the city manager last night, but they couldn't, Faith," Tori says. "Three days ago the same two council members had asked the Finance Committee to investigate him, but the committee voted 2 to 1 to ignore their request. We wrote about that."

"Is this the guy who was going through the messy divorce?" Faith Palmer asks.

"No, that was the fire chief, Skeeter Wofford," Tori replies. "These two council members are mad at City Manager Prentice because they say his budget has irregularities that he won't explain. But they won't give us any details."

"That the only thing the council could find to do last night?" Faith asks.

"I think what's important here is that these two keep trying to get rid of the guy, without any solid evidence," Tori says. "Nobody will tell me yet what's really behind this. But I guarantee we haven't heard the end of this thing."

"Okay, Tori," Faith says. "Ten inches. And remember to do a reader for broadcast, and give us a summary as soon as you can for the Web site. Anything in the Web versions we should link to?"

"I'll let you know," Tori says.

A Paradox

Before we go any further, let's acknowledge that something's a little off-center. This is a funny way to start a newswriting textbook. In this chapter and the ones that follow, I've created a reporter, a newspaper, a TV station, a county, a couple of cities, a bunch of local officials, two universities, some students and a slew of issues and events that touch them all. There is a name for that: fiction—in this case, pretty threadbare fiction. Nothing wrong with that—except that this book is meant to be an introduction to doing journalism: weighing factual information and turning it into news stories. Do you see the problem yet? Of course you do: News is not fiction. Reporters are not allowed to make stuff up. People—thousands of them at a time—rely on journalists for truthful information, information they can depend on to make decisions about their lives. It's a sacred trust, recognized by the U.S. Constitution and anchored in truth telling. It's especially important in a world where audiences are inundated with suspect information from suspect sources, spin doctors, strident on-air and online bullies, and outright liars. So how are we going to learn to be good reporters and writers by spending a whole semester dealing with fictitious places, made-up people, events that never happened?

First, Tori Baxter is a composite, not a fantasy; she shares characteristics with any number of young reporters I have known, although I hope to God she is better at her job than I was when I was starting out. She also runs into many of the same issues and situations that living, breathing reporters encounter every day. The paper she works for is part of a rapidly changing communications industry, as are all contemporary news outlets. And the community she covers features the same kinds of conflicts, tragedies, good guys and bad guys that affect hundreds of real communities across the United States each day.

Second, I could confine this book to a series of how-to lessons accompanied by the real-life experiences of reporters. But when it came down to doing it for yourself, you'd have two choices. The first would be to rely on a series of real-world-based but unrelated exercises. The problem with that approach is that, in real communities, events and issues that are newsworthy are often related. You wouldn't get used to dealing with contextual issues if all your exercises were based on discrete, unrelated events. The second option would be for you to go out into your community and find stories and track people down. You will do that in any decent beat-reporting class, of course—probably pretty soon—but for ground-level journalism students, it's a tall order. And the variety of stories produced would make it difficult for a teacher of beginners to stay focused on individual students' progress. (I do hope you will get at least one chance to kick over the traces—to go out into your community and cover at least one "live" story—before you get to the end of this book. In later chapters I provide some opportunities for you to do that.)

Now here's the irony, I think: Using made-up "facts"—about events, issues, people, an entire community—enables us to make sure you're getting them right. Your teacher can check your reporting against the information you are given in each exercise, and your attention to names, addresses and spellings against the City Directory in the Appendix. And you can learn something about how connected the people, events and issues in a community typically are, whether you live in Boston, Boca Raton, Bakersfield or Bellingham. If you learn to be careful reporting on the fictional community in this book, including understanding how events and issues may be related, I'm betting that you'll use that same care when you get to cover a story or a beat in your own community. If you don't stray from the "facts" you're given here, you won't stray from the ones you get anywhere else.

Plan of the Book

The first several chapters of this text focus on principles and critical elements of doing news, whether you are working for print, the Web, or broadcast. We next look at how to structure your stories for each of those three media. Then, in subsequent chapters, you will learn to write about different kinds of events and issues, based on the kinds of reporting most reporters do most often. I approach writing as a process, and you will become familiar with what I consider key elements of that process. I'll expand on this idea later, but for now you should know that in each chapter you will work on recognizing who your audience is, knowing the community you are covering, making news judgments based on the impact that the information you gather will have on your audience, reflecting on the ethical component of every decision you make and every story you write as a journalist, and developing your skills as a writer in a converged world—one in which reporters are increasingly expected to tell a story effectively for print, broadcast and the Web.

I begin each chapter by laying out the basic information in conventional textbook-presentation format. I will try to get you thinking about the kind of ethical challenges the topic might present. Then I will assist you in putting all that information to work: first by presenting strategies you can use in your reporting and writing, and then by giving you at least one exercise comprising facts and background about a particular event or issue. You will be asked to write at least one news story for each exercise, and you may be called upon to write the story for print, the Web and broadcast. It will be up to your instructor to decide which stories you will write for a particular medium, and which you will write for all media. As we go forward and your skills improve, you will be called on to do some assignments on deadline—completing a story in one class period—much as reporters must do every day. The story assignments will get more and more complex, requiring you to refer to earlier stories in order to provide your readers with appropriate background about connected events and ongoing issues. Again, the fictional community I've created provides the context for those events and issues.

Now let's get back to Tori Baxter and her work.

A Young Reporter

Tori Baxter loves her job. She likes the opportunity it gives her to stay in close touch with many diverse people, to learn every day, to write, and to make a difference in people's lives. It's not only vital and challenging work; on most days it's also great fun. We'll talk more about Tori's job shortly.

Tori has been covering Blue Ridge County, Valleydale, and Beausoleil since she joined the *Herald* 18 months ago. She's three years out of journalism

For many young reporters, like Lindsey Nair of *The Roanoke Times,* journalism is as rewarding as it is challenging.

school. What she learned in J-school and in her internship was that to become a better reporter and writer, you have to write a lot of stories. After graduation, she took an entry-level job at a small daily paper in western Carolina. Hammering out three and four stories a day at that little paper gave her a lot of experience meeting deadlines. Unfortunately, it also got her into some bad habits.

Tori wants to move from the *Herald*'s bureau in Blue Ridge County to Jeffersonville, but jobs on the city desk there are pretty competitive. People with twice as much experience as she has are dying to work "downtown" because of Jeffersonville's quality of life and the paper's reputation. The *Herald* won a Pulitzer Prize several years ago for exposing corruption in coal mine inspections. The two writers who dug out that story moved on to *The Philadelphia Inquirer*. Tori believes she is good enough to go that far, but there are dues to pay first. So for now, she is a one-person bureau on the northern edge of the *Herald*'s circulation area.

The Community

Blue Ridge County, Valleydale, and Beausoleil have a total population of about 37,000, but the three have distinct, autonomous governments. (See Box 1.1.) It took Tori, like most reporters from out of state, a while to understand that while people who live in Valleydale and Beausoleil are geographically within the borders of Blue Ridge County, technically they are not citizens of the county. Unlike in most other places in the United States, in Virginia residents who live in cities pay taxes to their city but not to the surrounding county. This, and the fact that the three governments don't cooperate much, is pretty important background for some of Tori's stories.

Blue Ridge County stretches from the western slope of the famous Blue Ridge, for which it is named, across the Valley of Virginia. The county line nudges the first ridges of the Allegheny Mountains to the west. Real estate developers and promoters of tourism like to say that the county is in the Shenandoah Valley. But Tori knows that the Shenandoah Valley actually lies miles north.

Box 1.1

LOCAL GOVERNMENTS AT A GLANCE

Blue Ridge County

Board of Supervisors: Five elected members; one member elected chair by the others

County Administrator: Full-time professional hired by the Board of Supervisors

Valleydale

Mayor: Elected separately from City Council members. Presides at meetings; votes only to break a tie

City Council: Six elected members

City Manager: Full-time professional hired by City Council

Beausoleil

City Council: Six elected members; mayor elected from among the council by the other members

City Manager: Full-time professional hired by City Council

Like local officials everywhere, county leaders are hoping to attract clean industry and tourism dollars. Because Interstates 88 and 61 intersect at the center of the county, heavy traffic passes through the area day and night, both north–south and east–west. Other than that, though, Blue Ridge County is pretty remote. Jeffersonville is 55 miles to the southwest; Wilson, a city of about 35,000, is 40 miles northeast.

Valleydale is the most important city in the county, although Beausoleil residents bristle when they hear that. Valleydale is a pretty, restored 19th-century hamlet of 7,000, a number that includes 3,500 college students. It is home to both Virginia Presbyterian University (VPU) and Southern Military Academy (SMA). The tourism people like to call it the Shrine of the South, because several Confederate war heroes either lived there or are buried there. It's gotten more notice recently because SMA began admitting women for the first time in 1997, which attracted international media attention. That was a boon for Tori, who led the *Herald*'s coverage of the story all year. As a result she got numerous Page 1 bylines, a lot of exposure on the air and from the wire services, and a couple of awards from the Virginia Press Association.

But because of the intense coverage of SMA, she has not paid enough attention to other events and issues in Valleydale, Beausoleil, and Blue Ridge County during the past year. Beausoleil, a struggling blue-collar city of 7,000, is six miles from Valleydale at the base of the Blue Ridge. Its residents are insular and fiercely independent. Even the pronunciation of the town's name— "Bee-oo-slee" (rhyming roughly with "loosely")— sets it apart, and locals are quick to recognize strangers by the way they mangle it. Beausoleil has a new flood wall that cost almost $60 million. It was built to protect the people from the North River and the creeks that feed it. Five times in the last 30 years those creeks have overflowed, and flood damage caused old-fashioned "smokestack" industries virtually to abandon the city. Beausoleil has had modest success in the last few years luring new businesses, but while employment figures keep creeping upward, low-wage jobs remain a problem. A new high school was completed a year ago, but money to pay off the construction debt has been tough to find.

The Blue Ridge County community is like hundreds of other small communities nationwide. But it is unusual in one important respect: There is little racial diversity in the county, in Valleydale or in Beausoleil. The one significant African American community is in Valleydale. Some of the community's African American families have lived in the town for five generations or more, but full assimilation remains a problem for them. There is a small group of black professionals, including faculty members from both universities, but many in the black community are working-class, and affordable housing is a challenge. Most live in a small section of town called Love Hill, where many dwellings are substandard. Adding to the problem is a recent move by some investors to buy up low-cost housing in the area to rent to VPU students at several times what local families can afford to pay. That has created a housing crunch. Partly because she is African American herself, Tori is aware of the problems facing many of Valleydale's black citizens. But she believes that any good reporter, no matter what her race or ethnicity, must pay attention to all of the residents making up her community of coverage, and the issues affecting them.

Tori likes to find out who and what make a community work, and to tell their stories, from the people who run City Hall, to the sanitation workers on garbage trucks, to the numerous community volunteers who serve on the boards of all sorts of nonprofit agencies.

The Audience

The *Herald* has a huge coverage area, stretching more than a hundred miles down the valley from northern Blue Ridge County to Steubenburg, 50 miles southwest of Jeffersonville. The paper has a paid circulation of about 100,000 and is read by about twice that number each day. Only a few thousand of those readers live in the Blue Ridge County area. Readers in each of the newspaper's many communities are interested primarily in what their own local governments and communities are up to, so most of those readers have little interest in Beausoleil's problems, or whether Valleydale will fire its city manager. Most of Tori's stories make it into only the North Region edition, which circulates in Blue Ridge County and Madison County, the county southwest of Blue Ridge on the way to Jeffersonville. It's only when the people whom Tori covers do something of interest to all the *Herald*'s readers that her stories make the "main sheet," the sections of the paper that are sent to all subscribers. Southern Military Academy's coeducation was one such story. A lot of people found it compelling.

Convergence

Even though Tori has been out of journalism school only a few years, the job of many reporters has changed substantially since she began to learn her craft. Like practically all daily newspapers now, the *Herald* has its own online edition, accessible on the World Wide Web. The paper maintains a small separate staff to produce the online edition, but all the reporters contribute to it. The online staff is so small that they do not have time for much rewriting, so Tori is often asked to write an early version of her story for immediate distribution on the Web.

The *Herald* also owns Channel 5, one of the two TV stations in Jeffersonville, and while the station maintains its own staff of broadcast reporters, trained to shoot and edit video, there are no broadcast reporters assigned to Blue Ridge County. For marketing and competitive reasons, the station recently expanded from a 30-minute to a one-hour evening newscast, without hiring additional staff. Tori is often asked to rewrite her print stories for broadcast, usually in the form of 30-second "readers," or RDRs. Because TV stations don't do "zoned" broadcasts, stories that go on the air have to appeal to all the station's viewers, and airtime to cover a vast area is at a premium. So Tori must be brief, especially when she has no video to accompany her stories. In its online and broadcast presence, the *Herald* is following the lead of a number of big newspapers, including the *Chicago Tribune,* the *Tampa Tribune,* the *Orlando Sentinel* and the *South Florida Sun-Sentinel.*

A number of news organizations now use their Web sites to converge audio, video and print news, offering their audiences multimedia and interactive features.

When something happens in Blue Ridge County that is newsworthy enough for the TV station to send a reporter and videographer, Tori is asked to share her reporting with them. And she has been told that within the next year she will be cross-trained to shoot and edit her own video. The day is at hand when her little office in Valleydale will contain an editing suite and satellite mini-uplink so she can do broadcast as well as print stories from there. Already, the *Herald*'s Web site contains both print stories and video stories "streamed" to the Web by the TV station.

The phenomenon is called convergence, and nothing Tori learned in J-school prepared her for it. Broadcast and print were considered separate tracks, and while advanced-reporting students learned how to find and download data on the Web, the university had not yet begun online publishing. Tori knows that if she is to move downtown, cross-training will put her a jump ahead of older print reporters who have more experience but no broadcast training. Again, in this book, you will work on learning the basics of print, broadcast, and Web writing.

A Journalist's Responsibilities

Faith Palmer, Tori's city editor, is all for convergence, even though she broke into the business in an era when newspaper people didn't take TV reporters seriously. But Faith also knows that the front-end skills required of good journalists—solid, persistent fact-gathering and interviewing, disciplined thinking, careful analysis, sure-handed ethical reasoning and clear, concise writing—won't change, no matter what the delivery systems for news look like in the next decade and beyond. Faith is a demanding taskmaster, but Tori has developed tremendous respect for her. In several important respects, the paper Tori worked for in North Carolina was not a good place to learn. It was unimaginative in its coverage, it didn't like to rock the boat with local officials, and it was insensitive to the needs of many of its readers, particularly those from minority communities.

Faith has taught Tori about her responsibilities as a journalist. One of the first things she disabused her of was the idea Tori had brought from North Carolina that reporters don't make news, they just gather and report it. What reporters gather, Faith told Tori, is information. They make it into news. There is nothing inevitable about the news people get; what people learn about is a function of decisions that reporters and editors make. Every day, Tori learns of only a fraction of what is going on in her coverage area. She can work only a small part of that into stories. What people read is pretty much up to her judgment. There is nothing wrong with that, but to make those decisions responsibly, Tori must abide by a set of professional ethics and an understanding of the role journalists have in our society. These are not things that journalists talk about a lot, but Tori has come to learn that good journalists are responsible journalists. Ethical considerations are part of every decision she makes, whether she acknowledges them consciously or not.

Core Values

Most journalists share several core values that arise from journalism's primary functions in a democratic society. (See Box 1.2.) These primary functions are:

1. *To serve as a watchdog* over government and other powerful institutions, including education, religion, and the economy, to help keep them accountable to those they serve;
2. *To educate* audiences;
3. *To serve as a mirror* of society and culture;
4. *To act as a bulletin board* for events and issues.

Box 1.2

JOURNALISM'S PRIMARY FUNCTIONS

1. *Watch over powerful institutions*, including government, education, religion, the economy, and the mass media.
2. *Educate* readers, listeners and viewers.
3. *Mirror* trends, issues and values in society.
4. *Provide a bulletin board* for the community.

The values journalists embrace to fulfill those functions (see Box 1.3) include:

1. *Independence.* Audiences have to trust the information they receive if they are to use it to make important decisions. They need to know that the journalist who provides it is free of any influences that could compromise the reliability of the information.

JOURNALISM'S CORE VALUES

1. *Independence.* Journalists remain free of influences that could compromise the faith their audiences have in them.

2. *Fairness.* Journalists try to give all stakeholders in stories fair representation.

3. *Truthfulness.* Journalists place facts in appropriate context, and try to separate truth from fiction, embellishment and lies.

4. *Respect.* Journalists are sensitive to their sources and their audiences. They strive never to cause avoidable harm, and to minimize harm when they cannot avoid doing harm.

2. *Fairness.* Because they are often the only source of information for audiences, journalists try to be fair in gathering it, weighing it and reporting it.

3. *Truthfulness.* To be able to trust information, audiences need to know that the journalist is trying her hardest to make sure the information is true. Audiences are inundated with information from advocates of particular causes or positions, particularly since the advent of several cable television "news" channels that are arguably thinly disguised political or ideological platforms. Audiences need to be able to turn to someone who can separate truth from fiction, embellishment and outright lies. Telling the truth includes placing facts in the appropriate context.

4. *Respect.* Journalists know that they wield great power, and that with that power comes the potential to do great harm. To give audiences information they need, it is often necessary to cause a certain amount of harm. For example, journalists invade the privacy of some people involved in events or issues so that audiences have access to essential information. Journalists must treat both their audiences and the people they cover with respect, striving never to cause harm if it can be avoided, and to minimize harm when it cannot.

News Matters

Acknowledging that journalists have important responsibilities to their audiences is not to say that journalists cover only what affects people in measurable ways—their jobs, their pocketbooks, their sense of security. Some stories make it into the paper or on the air because they are what reporters and editors call "a good read"—they engage us, they make us pay attention to the story until the end.

What Faith Palmer has taught Tori is that those news elements she learned about in high school and college—proximity, timeliness, consequence, magnitude, conflict, human interest, unusualness and so forth—all raise this question: Why do we say those elements make a story worth telling? Every time Faith asks Tori or any of her other reporters "What's this story about?" she and the reporter know she is asking, "Why should anybody care? Why should we ask them to spend their time on this story?" The answer she is looking for, each time, is "Because it affects them," and she expects her reporters to show how.

Faith teaches her reporters that stories affect people in at least two ways. They can have rational impact: Say the city council passed a tax increase last night. How much will it cost the average homeowner next year? What will the money pay for? Stories can also have emotional impact: A 3-year-old child

Journalists are responsible for covering events and issues that affect their audiences. When gas prices rise, reporters try to discover the impact.

drowned in a backyard swimming pool last night. How can we show audiences that accidents are about people, and are not merely statistics? Even though practically none of the *Herald*'s readers knew the child, or his family, or anything about the neighborhood where he lived, the paper reports it because it affects people emotionally. It makes them aware of their shared humanity, of where their values converge and diverge.

Not all stories that hit home emotionally are sad or tragic. Some provoke different responses from different readers. Take a story that Tori wrote a week ago:

> BLUE RIDGE COUNTY— The chief of the local volunteer fire-rescue squad is burned up about some pictures of her that her colleagues posted on the World Wide Web.
>
> Cecelia "Sissy" Baxter has asked County Administrator Rufus Stallard to find and fire the firefighters who posted pictures of Baxter, drenched and in a T-shirt, taken at a benefit car wash two weeks ago.
>
> "I've fought discrimination and sexism every step of the way to get where I am," Baxter said Tuesday. "Now I get taken advantage of when I go out on my day off to raise money for the department. This is sick."
>
> A series of six pictures was posted on an amateur candids page of a popular men's magazine's Web site. Baxter, second runner-up in the Miss Virginia Pageant in 1990, is shown under the headline "She Can Light Our Fire Anytime."
>
> Stallard promised to investigate the incident.

Other stories move us because they show people at their best.

> VALLEYDALE— Virginia Presbyterian University senior Meagan LeBlanc, who dived into a burning home last October to pull a toddler to safety, was honored by City Council Thursday for her bravery.
>
> LeBlanc, a 21-year-old from Detroit, was given a key to the city for her rescue of 2-year-old Chandra Jefferson, who lived next door to LeBlanc.
>
> LeBlanc is already something of a hero locally. In January, three months after the rescue, she was lauded by the president during his State of the Union message for developing a privately financed economic recovery plan for a blighted Washington, D.C., neighborhood.
>
> She devised that initiative as part of a summer internship with VPU's poverty studies program.

Many stories have both rational and emotional impact. The coming of women to SMA was more than just the tale of how short the women would have to wear their hair, or whether the bathrooms could be modified for them, or whether they were tough enough to do pull-ups and weather verbal abuse from upperclassmen. Those details became the focus of much reporting, because journalists were trying to show how such a profound change affected the daily lives of those who were a part of it. When it's difficult to grasp the magnitude of change, sometimes reporters can help audiences understand by showing it in small chunks.

Good newswriters know the importance of *showing* people how stories will affect them. "Show me, don't tell me," is advice Faith gives Tori and her other reporters almost every day. Again, though, the reason SMA coeducation was a big story was not haircuts and bathrooms and pull-ups. There were issues involved that challenged both journalists and audiences to think about values such as fairness: Should an institution that is supported by taxpayers be allowed to exclude applicants because of their sex? Should it be allowed to continue as a male-only military institution because male applicants would have no opportunity for getting that kind of education elsewhere in the state?

There were also emotional issues involved: Should thousands of alumni who feel a deep attachment to SMA have to see it change fundamentally? Would any woman in her right mind want to subject herself to the rigors that first-years go through? Should the government be able to get that involved in anybody's life?

Journalism Ethics

It is important that Tori and her paper—and the Web site and the television station she is increasingly reporting for—have a defensible rationale for doing news. The way they go about deciding what to report is a function of their sense of professional responsibility and their ethics. As you work your way through this book, always keep in mind why we are doing a particular story. How will it serve our audiences? Do we as newspeople have a legitimate reason for doing the often intrusive work we do?

You probably already know that journalism ethics has been getting a lot of public attention lately, mostly because of some whopping transgressions by some reporters. For example, while he was a reporter with *The New York Times*, Jayson Blair plagiarized material for some stories and simply made up material for others—quoting people he had never talked to, among other things. During the 2004 presidential election campaign, as questions arose about President Bush's National Guard service 35 years before, CBS News aired a story that called his service into question. It turned out that the documents CBS had relied on could not be authenticated. Other instances of plagiarism, relying on false information, or sloppy reporting have also come to light recently.

Lou Hodges, retired Knight Professor of Ethics in Journalism at Washington and Lee University, argues that in several of those cases there were no real ethical dilemmas or issues at stake. They were cases of reporters knowing right from wrong and simply yielding to temptation—doing the wrong thing for personal aggrandizement or gain. But most journalists don't yield to temptation; they don't plagiarize, lie or fabricate. Still, they are faced with ethical dilemmas nearly every day. Why?

Because giving audiences the information they need to make decisions about their own lives often involves putting values in conflict. For example, audiences often need information about private individuals that those individuals would rather not have disclosed. So the reporter has to weigh the relative importance of two ethical principles—providing people information that will help them be self-determining, and respecting an individual's right to privacy. Professor Hodges says the toughest ethical decisions—and the ones that honest, conscientious reporters face most often—involve trying to resolve those competing or conflicting principles. The challenge is to look for not the perfect outcome but the relatively better one, not the one that will cause no harm, but the one that will minimize harm while providing the maximum benefit to your audience. Those decisions take care, deep and rigorous thought, and collaboration—talking things over with your editors and others. Because there is an ethical dimension to practically every decision a journalist makes, and because of the enormous consequences those decisions can have, I will try to get you thinking about ethics in each chapter of this book. I hope this leads to some lively classroom discussions.

It's important to distinguish ethics from the laws governing journalists. For one thing, because journalism enjoys First Amendment protection, journalists have few legal constraints. So it is possible to behave irresponsibly, to lie, fabricate, plagiarize and cause unnecessary harm, without violating any laws. Depending on the law alone in setting your ethical limits is a guaranteed way to behave unethically. By relying only on constraints imposed from outside, we become ethically lazy and deny our own sense of duty and responsibility.

There is another problem with relying only on the law for our ethical standards. While journalists, just like other citizens, are duty-bound in nearly all circumstances to obey the law, unjust laws have existed historically. The leaders of the American civil rights movement come to mind, courageous individuals who chose to break unjust segregation laws and accept the consequences until the laws were changed. Recently, some courts have ordered reporters to reveal the names of their confidential sources. Some reporters have refused, most notably Judith Miller of *The New York Times*, who was jailed for her refusal to cooperate. In such cases, a journalist is faced with an ethical dilemma: Obey the law, or accept the consequences of believing that an independent press that monitors the judicial system serves the public better than a press that becomes an investigative tool of that system. Miller determined that her moral obligation was to disobey the court's order. After serving almost three months in jail, Miller reached an accord that resulted in her cooperating with the order.

Thinking about ethics does not mean that reporters should shy away from controversy, or that they should always be able to keep everybody happy. If those were our only goals, we could not serve our audiences. Many times, Tori Baxter encounters people who are suspicious of reporters, people who are offended at any invasion of their privacy, or people who are defensive because Tori is writing a story about something bad that happened. Sometimes there are other reasons as well, having to do with people's preconceived notions or prejudices. For example, a county supervisor from a rural, all-white district simply refuses to talk to Tori because she is African American.

Nobody called Tori with a tip about the Web pictures of the fire-rescue chief. A worker at a local Internet service provider tipped her about the Web site where the photos were posted. Sissy Baxter was willing to talk to her, but when Tori tried to get reaction from county supervisors, she got an earful from Boone District's Cleveland McNitt about media transgressions and nosy reporters trying to sell newspapers. McNitt, owner of the biggest auto dealership in Blue Ridge County, threatened to pull his ads from the *Herald* if the story ran. When Tori was in North Carolina, her paper sometimes yielded to such pressures. The *Herald* never has. In the end, McNitt kept the ads in.

Tori also had to deal with a plea from Baxter not to include in her story the address of the Web site that contained the photos. After a newsroom discussion in which Tori participated by phone, the *Herald* withheld the address of the Web site from Tori's story, and did not link to it in the online version. That discussion would sound familiar to any reporter in a real newsroom. Again, practically every day, they are called on to do some moral reasoning about the appropriateness of what they are doing.

Objectivity

Thanks to Faith Palmer's guidance, Tori has come to realize that *objectivity* is a term some journalists still use loosely. They claim never to take sides in a story, and not to care about the outcome of an event or issue. Obviously, that's not the case. Reporters who write about plane crashes and what caused them seldom take the attitude that they don't care whether the plane crashed or not. No story about John F. Kennedy Jr.'s death struck a tone like, "What the hell. He flew the plane; he had it coming," or "Tough luck, rich boy." (Fred Friendly, a former producer at CBS News, once said there was no such thing as two sides to a story about a starving child.)

In his book *Public Journalism and Public Life* (1997), Davis Merritt, a veteran newspaper editor, makes a distinction between objectivity and detachment. When Dr. Jonas Salk was seeking a vaccine against polio, Merritt says, he was hardly detached from the issue. Salk wanted desperately to protect people from a disease that was crippling thousands every year. But he knew he had no chance to succeed unless he gathered and evaluated his data objectively. Simply wanting one formula to work would not make it so. By weighing his data carefully, he ultimately got the information he needed to develop an effective vaccine. If Salk hadn't cared deeply at the outset about saving people from polio, though, he never would have gotten to a vaccine.

What reporters do strive for is to use a methodology that honors their values and helps keep their covenant with their audiences: They want to be fair, balanced and thorough in gathering and reporting information, so that audiences know they can depend on news media for the information they need. When audiences understand that information, they can act on it as they choose to. Jack Fuller, publisher of the *Chicago Tribune,* says reporters must be neutral in their inquiry, but not necessarily in the expression of their findings.

Framing

Tori knows that most stories have more than two sides, so limiting herself to a representative quote from "both" sides usually is a disservice to her audience and the people involved in the stories. When we look for only two polarized opinions to put into a story we also leave little room for our audiences to understand a story and form an opinion about it or react to it. Most of us are not at one extreme or the other on an issue. We recognize our own ambivalence about the difficult decisions involved in almost any issue. We place ourselves somewhere along a continuum, with absolute advocacy at one end and absolute opposition at the other. Journalists who don't "frame" their stories with that in mind fail in their duty to audiences. While conflict is one way to frame a story, it is not the only way and often not the best way. One way to think of framing is in terms of the context we provide for information.

Tori also knows that she has a duty to point out when someone is lying. Rather than settle for "he said, she said" reporting, she must try to show her audiences when she knows one statement is true and one is false.

When Tori decides to do a story, it's usually because she cares about it. But she has to examine why she cares about it, because she knows that just because something interests her it does not necessarily interest or affect her audience. Tori measures how much she cares about a story by knowing who her audience is, and knowing how the information will affect that audience. She keeps both in mind when she is reporting and writing. It is her job to show her audiences, in a coherent manner, the elements of the story that will convey why they will care about it.

Your Job

Gathering the information that is of interest to and affects your audience is a challenging job, often frustrating and full of false starts, leads that don't pan out, and reluctant or downright hostile sources. It's probably too big a job for beginning reporting students to wrestle with. Evaluating, organizing and writing information in a way that will make sense to a broad audience is enough of a challenge for beginning newswriters. So, as already explained, in this book, information will be given to you. Your job is to decide which of it is important and how to present it in a way that will show your audience why it is important. The book will take you through most of a year in the life of the Blue Ridge County/Valleydale/Beausoleil community. As the term progresses, you will find that many of the stories you do will be related to ones you wrote earlier, and that there will be more stories ahead about the same issues.

Getting It Right

News is a journalist's account of events and issues that affect many people in significant ways. But news is told in stories, and as I said at the beginning of this chapter, stories should be about people. When we put a human face on a story, with people's quotes and opinions, we increase the possibility of making errors: Stories that don't quote people never misquote people, but they are weak stories.

Most people, most of the time, *believe in* their news media; that is, they recognize and understand the importance of the role of news in our society. Whether they *believe* their news media is a different question. Sometimes it's unavoidable that someone loses faith in a news organization. When a story about a controversial issue achieves balance, advocates of one position may feel slighted. In Miami, Florida, for example, a small but vocal part of the Cuban American community has chosen not to assimilate in the same highly successful way that most of their neighbors have. They consider themselves, essentially, a government in exile, waiting for the day when Fidel Castro is overthrown and they return to Cuba in triumph. To these people, any story in *The Miami Herald* that is not vehemently anti-Castro in tone is proof that the paper and its reporters are dupes of communism. As long as *The Herald* strives for fairness in its coverage of Cuba, it will alienate that small segment of the population. That attitude was underscored a few years ago in the controversy over 6-year-old Elian Gonzalez, the boy who was taken to the United States by his mother but, upon her death, was eventually returned to his father in Cuba after a lengthy diplomatic tug-of-war.

Most of the time, though, when people don't believe their news media it isn't because we are perceived as being biased. It's because we make stupid, avoidable mistakes. We misspell names and words. We get addresses wrong. We misquote or take quotes out of context. We use bad grammar or punctuation. People think that if they can't trust us on the basics, they can't trust us to get the "big stuff"—complex events and issues—right. Some people see their local news media as staffed by people whose primary goal seems to be to take the next step up the career ladder; they do not trust the news organization's commitment to the local community and its people. A study several years ago by the American Society of Newspaper Editors found such negative attitudes among audiences. Whether or not these beliefs reflect the truth, they are understandable.

Even though she had a slow start, the hours are long and entry-level pay is lousy, Tori Baxter thinks that being a reporter is the best job in the world. While there is a lot of routine and her responsibilities are awesome, every day is a little different, advancement can be quick and spectacular, and she gets paid to be a perennial student of life. And, as we said earlier, it's almost always fun.

Strategies

Here are some strategies as you prepare to work your way through your first several assignments (see Box 1.4):

Box 1.4

STRATEGIES FOR GETTING STARTED

1. Familiarize yourself with the City Directory in the Appendix.

2. Learn to use your City Directory to verify spellings, addresses, middle initials and so forth. Errors have been built in to many of the exercises.

3. Identify people properly in your stories.

4. You will encounter the same people in several exercises. Keep an eye out for them. Real reporters are called on to revisit an emerging issue repeatedly.

5. A reporter may need several stories to find out and tell her audience everything that audience needs to know. Keep reminding your audience of what has happened so far.

6. Ask your instructor for an ongoing summary of significant events in the life of the Blue Ridge County/Valleydale/Beausoleil community.

7. Make sure to brush up on your grammar, spelling and punctuation skills. The test in Chapter 2 will give you an opportunity to check them.

8. When you write, think of your audience first. Mass audiences are different from specialized audiences. How much explaining will you need to do?

1. Take a look at the City Directory at the back of the book. It lists everyone who is mentioned in the newswriting exercises. There are also entries for businesses. The directory is alphabetized by last name, or by business or institution name. With people, that is followed by the first name. Then, in parentheses, the directory lists a spouse or partner's name, and the spouse or partner's occupation. That is followed by the occupation of the first person named, and the address of that person. In the case of businesses or institutions, the name of the proprietor, owner, or head is listed before the address. Here is an example:

BEAUCHAMP, Ottis (Sherri), pipe fitter, 1912 Sycamore St., Beausoleil

From looking at this listing, we know that Ottis Beauchamp is a pipe fitter who lives with his wife, Sherri, at 1912 Sycamore St., Beausoleil. (See Box 1.5 for other examples.)

Box 1.5

EXAMPLES OF CITY DIRECTORY LISTINGS

BAXTER, Cecelia "Sissy" (Howard, mechanic), county fire-rescue chief,
311 Forbes Rd., Blue Ridge County

BAXTER, Victoria "Tori," reporter, 379 Flower Lane, Blue Ridge County

BEATTY, Effie, assistant manager Valley Bank, 1395 Rebel Dr.

BEAUCHAMP, Ottis (Sherri) pipe fitter, 1912 Sycamore St.,
Beausoleil

BENSON, Todd (Marya, teacher), principal, Ridge View Elem.,
181 South River Rd., Stonewall

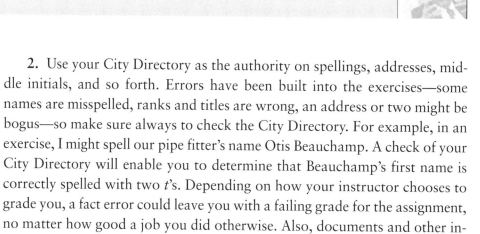

2. Use your City Directory as the authority on spellings, addresses, middle initials, and so forth. Errors have been built into the exercises—some names are misspelled, ranks and titles are wrong, an address or two might be bogus—so make sure always to check the City Directory. For example, in an exercise, I might spell our pipe fitter's name Otis Beauchamp. A check of your City Directory will enable you to determine that Beauchamp's first name is correctly spelled with two *t*'s. Depending on how your instructor chooses to grade you, a fact error could leave you with a failing grade for the assignment, no matter how good a job you did otherwise. Also, documents and other information may contain spelling, grammar and usage errors. Be sure to look for and correct those kinds of errors before they wind up in your story.

3. Remember that identifying people in your stories is critical. In almost all cases, we owe it to our audiences to tell them whom we are writing about and whom we are quoting. There are some exceptions, which we'll cover in later chapters, but proper identification is the rule. Your City Directory gives you enough information to provide the basics of identification—name, address, occupation. How else you describe people depends on how and why they show up in your story.

4. In this book you will encounter the same people again and again. That's because I have created both an ongoing issue involving the city manager and City Council and a series of events surrounding a VPU student, Meagan LeBlanc, and her friends. This happens to real reporters: They are called on to revisit an emerging issue repeatedly, and many times they find a link in a series of events that might not have appeared related at first.

5. Often, because events continue to unfold and information is revealed in stages, it takes several stories for a reporter to tell her audience everything that audience needs to know. By dealing with the ongoing issues and events in these exercises, you will get practice looking for context and framing stories appropriately.

6. To help you with context and framing, and so that you can provide appropriate background in your stories, your instructor can give you an on-going summary of significant events in the life of the Blue Ridge County/Valleydale/Beausoleil community over the time period covered in this book.

7. We'll continue your training in Chapter 3 by looking at how news-people go about deciding what's important. But first, wrestle with Exercise 1. Then in Chapter 2 we'll test your skill with the English language.

8. Audience first. Think about who your audience is when you are trying to create understanding. For example, in an essay written to impress your English professor with how much you have learned about Jane Austen, you will start with a set of assumptions about what someone with a Ph.D. in 19th-century British literature already knows about Jane Austen, what terms you can assume she will understand, and her level of interest in your topic. In writing a news story for a mass audience or an e-mail to a friend, or in constructing an oral account for a young child, though, you start with an entirely different set of assumptions about who your audience is, what it knows already, and what words will be most effective.

Exercise 1

Same Story, Different Audiences

Write a narrative of three or four short paragraphs about the 9/11 attacks at the World Trade Center and the Pentagon for each of the following: A daily newspaper audience in Jeffersonville; your best friend, whom you are e-mailing; and a 5-year-old child, who must hear your account read aloud. Consider the appropriate content, tone and word choice for each audience. Finally, try to write your narrative as a 30-second story a television news anchor would read. Time yourself reading the story aloud.

Assume that it is still September 11, 2001, and that the people you are giving the information to are not aware that the attacks have happened. Hint: If you need some background on the events of that day, try a Web search.

chapter two

Using Tools with Skill

The aim of this chapter is to determine your strengths and weaknesses in using the language. When it comes to helping diverse mass audiences understand unfamiliar information, journalists have three primary obligations:

1. They must get the facts right.
2. They must place those facts in a true and appropriate context.
3. They must craft a story that makes clear what happened, what is at issue, and what is at stake for the audience.

The Task

We are the people—often the only people—our audiences rely on for that. To be sure, we use images—moving and still—to help tell the story, but it is the words we choose and the way we string them together that make facts and images clear and put them in the appropriate context. So it's crucial that we use words correctly, and that the intended meaning of those words is well understood.

While some slang, colloquialisms and informal constructions might be familiar to you and your friends, they might cause confusion or misunderstanding for many who read and watch news stories. Remember that our goal, in each story, is to help mass audiences understand what is happening and what is at stake for them. In his book *The Stories of English*, linguist David Crystal celebrates the myriad varieties of English being spoken and written today. But he also acknowledges the value of standard usage: "The role of a standard language, whether it is used nationally or internationally, is to enable the members of a community to understand each other. Everyone needs to learn it, in the interests of efficient and effective communication" (p. 6). Because words are the tools we use to craft stories, we must become experts in using those tools.

There are at least two challenges in learning to write well. The first is that learning to write well takes discipline, hard work, and a lot of practice. But one thing we can do that is a little easier is to avoid writing badly.

The second challenge is that some people use words not to make things clear and help people understand, but to obfuscate and create confusion. As reporters we must learn to recognize those efforts and get to the truth. Not everyone uses language with evil intent; some people are just lousy at it or careless.

Fortunately, avoiding writing badly and cutting through other people's obscure language often take the same skills of recognition. In your own writing and in working with the writings of others, you can eliminate poor grammar, confusing punctuation, misspellings, clichés, redundancies, bureaucratese and other forms of obfuscation. You will take a test on grammar, spelling and punctuation later. First, though, let's consider a few examples of redundancies, wordiness and bureaucratese (see Boxes 2.1 and 2.2).

Some city employees are referred to as "urban transportation specialists." You and I might recognize them as bus drivers. These workers occasionally encounter "pavement deficiencies"—potholes. A tax on airline tickets is sometimes called a "passenger facility charge." Nobody wants to hear that he or she has a bossy child, so teachers sometimes say such children "display leadership charisma." Unruly children display "negative attention-getting behavior." Instead of reading, some schoolchildren are now said to "interact with print."

Box 2.1

BUREAUCRATESE

Some public officials, military leaders, and educators would rather people not know what they are up to, or have them think that their jobs carry special importance. Some examples of the language they use, and the translations:

Term	What It Means
achieved nonmastery	failed
agricultural specialist	farmer
career offender cartel	Mafia
chronologically gifted	old
custodial engineer	janitor
health care professional	nurse or doctor
pavement deficiencies	potholes
servicing the target	bombing
socially marginal	a loose cannon
urban transportation specialist	bus driver
waste management technician	garbage collector

I heard a TV weatherman several years ago warn of an impending "major frozen-precipitation event," when I thought it was just going to snow. An intern at a newspaper I worked for tried to tell his readers that someone had "drowned for 20 minutes." Another person was "electrocuted to death." Police reports often refer to vehicles that are "yellow in color" (yellow), "traveling at a high rate of speed" (speeding), or "traveling in a northwesterly direction" (headed northwest). Fire is often said to "totally destroy" a building (*destroyed* is sufficient; there are no degrees of destruction, only of damage). Employees who misbehave are sometimes "temporarily suspended" (suspended), before they are allowed to "resign voluntarily" (resign; if it's not voluntary, it's a firing). Finally, decades ago advertisers recognized the power of a gift to entice consumers. But then they had to distinguish their gift offer from the other guy's. By the beginning of the 21st century, we were being offered "a complimentary free gift at no cost to you. You pay nothing." Really.

Box 2.2

REDUNDANT REDUNDANCIES AND WORDINESS

Using more words than necessary is a good way to confuse audiences. For some sources journalists deal with, that's the goal. Don't let them get away with it.

Long Version	*Short Version*
advance planning	planning
armed gunmen	gunmen
at this point in time	now
canceled out	canceled
city of Valleydale	Valleydale
completely unnecessary	unnecessary
complimentary free gift at no cost to you	free
cooperate together	cooperate
electrocuted to death	electrocuted
exactly identical	identical
few in number	few
general consensus of opinion	consensus
traveling at a high rate of speed	speeding
high-speed chase	chase
large in size	large (or big)
necessary requirement	necessary
postpone until later	postpone
recessed into	recessed
still remain	remain
temporarily suspended	suspended
totally destroyed	destroyed
true facts	facts
widow of the late	widow of
yellow in color	yellow

Exercise 2

Grammar, Spelling, Punctuation

Take the following quiz. Some of these shouldn't give you much trouble. Others might, because bureaucrats, spokesmen, public officials, ad copywriters, sports broadcasters and journalists regularly screw them up. Too often, professionals don't give you much in the way of role models.

When you have finished the quiz, go on to find the correct answer and explanation for each. If you cheat you won't learn as much. Consider how you complete the quiz to be your first ethical challenge as a journalist, because the more you learn, the better you can serve your audiences.

Questions

1. She is older than (he, him).
2. Researchers have detected the presence of a nonlethal (bacteria, bacterium) at the Army base.
3. Aspirin has no (affect, effect) on viruses.
4. No data (has, have) been lost.
5. The new building will be located at this (sight, site, cite).
6. Her questions were intended to (elicit, illicit) useful answers.
7. Had someone else said it, everyone would have laughed and (went, gone) on with life.
8. We cannot succumb to threats (comma, semicolon, no punctuation) however (comma, no comma; semicolon) we can let every voice be heard.
9. The editor had trouble deciding which (course, coarse) of action to take.
10. Mary chose to (forgo, forego) the offer of legal (counsel, council).
11. The water was treated with chlorine and smelled (bad, badly).
12. The organizers were disappointed at the small (amount, number, quantity) of supporters.
13. The school's president announced his (eminent, imminent) retirement.
14. When the train wrecked, rescuers (sprung, sprang) into action.
15. The media (has, have) not served (their, its) audiences well.
16. Mother went camping with Ruth, Maynard and (I, me, myself).
17. Everyone who has an interest in cultivating roses in (his, her, their) garden will be fascinated.

18. She is the one (whose, who's) coming to dinner.

19. I usually (lie, lay) on the sofa to watch baseball.

20. His message appeals to people (that, who, whom) see the world in simple terms.

21. She said she had (lay, laid, lain) there for an hour before anyone found her.

22. The Southern Military Academy library has far (less, fewer) books than the Harvard library.

23. That lawyer gave the newspaper wise (counsel, council) in (their, its) (liable, libel) suit.

24. Food is in short supply because (there's, there are, they're) so many people.

25. Neither Jim nor Martha (like, likes) crab cakes.

26. Meagan LeBlanc jumped (off, off of, from) the cliff to save the child.

27. A leader can do many things to try (and, to) buffer negative consequences.

28. Was the (family's, families) privacy invaded?

29. He was charged with drunk driving after swerving and hitting a car coming (towards, toward) him.

30. Hunter was living with his girlfriend (comma, no comma) Topping (comma, no comma) who was also injured in the accident.

31. He had to choose (between, among) four alternatives.

32. The death of the Queen Mother (effected, affected) her deeply.

33. Then they found the other girls (comma, no comma) who were in (their, there, they're) beds sleeping.

34. His arraignment has been set for tomorrow morning (comma, no comma) at which time he could (loose, lose) his freedom.

35. He was (arrested for, charged with) selling drugs to a (miner, minor).

36. This needs to be resolved by you, (I, me), and (he, him).

37. Was it (she, her) (who, whom) he was referring to?

38. Just as I (lay, laid, lie) down, the chicken started clucking because she had (lay, laid, leid) an egg.

39. When the hotel dining room caught fire, the guests were evacuated (without injury) to the parking lot (without injury).

40. A dromedary is different (than, from) a Bactrian camel.

41. (It's, Its) pretty clear that the organization wants nothing to stand in (its, it's, their) way.

42. She said she (will, would) go if it doesn't rain.

43. The first time I did my laundry in college I (shrunk, shrank) all my jeans.

44. She said after the accident that she was feeling (alright, all right).

45. According to the police report, the prisoner (snuck, sneaked) out of the van when the driver stopped for gas.

46. He stops for an ice-cream cone on the way home almost (every day, every-day).

47. The streaker (dived, dove) into the bushes when he saw a campus security guard coming.

48. At one minute past midnight (comma, no comma) the police spokesman said (comma, no comma) the convicted murderer was executed.

49. The senator said (hopefully, he hoped) a budget would be passed soon.

50. If McNab (throws, had thrown) the ball a yard (farther, further), that play (goes, went, would have gone) for a touchdown.

Answers

1. **She is older than he.** What you are really saying is "She is older than he *is*." Because *he* is the subject of the clause *he is*, the subjective case is used. *Him* is objective. You wouldn't say, "*She is older than him is.*"

2. **Researchers have detected the presence of a nonlethal bacterium at the Army base.** Bacterium is singular; bacteria is plural. That's Latin for you. Chances are the researchers found more than a single bacterium, but to take away the indefinite article and say, "*Researchers have detected the presence of nonlethal bacteria*" creates confusion, because it could mean more than one strain of bacteria.

3. **Aspirin has no effect on viruses.** Remember that most of the time *effect* will be a noun and *affect* will be a verb.

4. **No data have been lost.** Another pesky Latin word. *Data* is plural. *Datum* is singular. Increasingly, though, *data* is being used with singular verbs.

5. **The new building will be located at this site.** *Sight* is the ability to see. *Cite* is to call to someone's attention or to recognize formally. *Site* is a location.

6. **Her questions were intended to elicit useful answers.** *Illicit* means unlawful or not permitted. *Elicit* means to bring forth.

7. **Had someone else said it, everyone would have laughed and gone on with life.** You're really saying, "Everyone would have laughed and *would have* gone on," so *gone* is correct here.

8. **We cannot succumb to threats; however, we can let every voice be heard.** In the first case, independent clauses have to be separated by a comma and a conjunction or by a semicolon; a comma alone won't do it. In the second case, you need a comma to avoid confusion. Without the comma, we're saying we can let every voice be heard in whatever way possible.

9. **The editor had trouble deciding which course of action to take.** *Course* refers to an option or path; *coarse* is a texture.

10. **Mary chose to forgo the offer of legal counsel.** Let's take these two backwards: First, *counsel* is advice; *council* is a body that meets to deliberate. Second, if you chose *forgo*, good for you. Practically nobody recognizes that *forego* means to go before; *forgo* means to do without. Note: Some dictionaries now allow *forego* as an alternative spelling of *forgo*, but that just confuses things, doesn't it?

11. **The water was treated with chlorine and smelled bad.** A lot of people choose badly because *bad* is often used ungrammatically ("We played bad," Coach Hockenmeister said.) But in this case we need *bad*, the adjective, because it modifies *water*, the noun, not *smelled*, the verb. If we say the water smelled *badly*, we mean that the water has a poorly developed sense of smell.

12. **The organizers were disappointed at the small number of supporters.** Use *number* with things you can count (like people); use *amount* with things you measure (like rain). Generally, leave *quantity* out of journalistic writing. It's stilted.

13. **The school's president announced his imminent retirement.** *Eminent* means distinguished; *imminent* means about to happen.

14. **When the train wrecked, rescuers sprang into action.** *Sprang* is the simple past tense of spring; *sprung* is the past participle: *had sprung*.

15. **The media have not served their audiences well.** You need subject-verb agreement: *Media* is a plural noun; it should be a hanging offense to misuse it. Because it is plural, it must take both the plural verb *have* and the plural pronoun *their*.

16. **Mother went camping with Ruth, Maynard and me.** This one should not be a problem when you think that what is really being said here is "*with Ruth, with Maynard, and with me.*"

17. **Everyone who has an interest in cultivating roses in his garden will be fascinated.** You can also say "*cultivating roses in her garden,*" but then you run into the sexist assumption that all gardeners are women. Because use of the male pronoun as the generic singular sounds so hidebound and

archaic, and the use of *his or her* is so clumsy, we are tempted to use the plural pronoun *their* as a substitute. But *everyone* is singular; it can't take the plural pronoun *their*. Try this as a solution: *"Everyone who has an interest in cultivating roses will be fascinated,"* or *"People who have an interest in cultivating roses will be fascinated."* (And remember, when you're tied in knots grammatically, the best solution could be just to cut the string. Rewrite the sentence.)

18. **She is the one who's coming to dinner.** *Whose* is a possessive pronoun; *who's* is a contraction of *who is*.

19. **I usually lie on the sofa to watch baseball.** *Lay* is a transitive verb; it takes a direct object: *"Watch the chicken lay an egg."* *Lie* is intransitive; it takes no object: *"I like to lie in bed every morning."* Where it gets confusing is that *lay* is also the simple past tense of *lie*: *"I lay down for an hour before dinner."* Hey, if it was easy anybody could do it.

20. **His message appeals to people who see the world in simple terms.** *Who* is a personal pronoun; personal implies that it has to do with people. *That* is an impersonal pronoun; it refers to things: the train *that* derailed.

21. **She said she had lain there for an hour before anyone found her.** More fun with the *lie/lay* business. You already know that you need the intransitive verb *lie*. But in this case you need not the present tense *lie* nor the simple past tense *lay*; the presence of the verb *had* means you need the past participle: *lain*.

22. **The Southern Military Academy library has far fewer books than the Harvard library.** As with *number* and *amount*, you use *fewer* with things you count, *less* with things you measure.

23. **That lawyer gave the newspaper wise counsel in its libel suit.** One at a time: As you saw in question 10, *counsel* refers to advice. Next, *libel* is a legal term meaning to harm someone's reputation by a statement; *liable* means likely or inclined to. And a newspaper is a singular noun, not collective, so it takes the singular pronoun *its*. (Note: remember that *its* is the possessive form of *it*. We don't use an apostrophe here because *it's* is a contraction of *it is*.)

24. **Food is in short supply because there are so many people.** *People* is a plural noun, so you need the plural subject and verb *there are*. *They're* is a contraction of *they are*.

25. **Neither Jim nor Martha likes crab cakes.** The *neither/nor* construction tells us we are considering Jim and Martha as separate subjects. So each singular subject must take the singular verb *likes*.

26. **Meagan LeBlanc jumped from the cliff to save the child.** *Off of* is redundant; *off* is acceptable, but it could imply that Meagan was already off the cliff when she jumped. *From* clears up the ambiguity.

27. **A leader can do many things to try to buffer negative consequences.** The intended meaning is that the leader will make *an attempt to buffer*. To say a leader can try and buffer gives the sentence compound verbs: The leader *will try* and *will buffer*.

28. **Was the family's privacy invaded?** Because privacy is a right belonging to the family, *family* must take the possessive, indicated by the apostrophe. Had we intended to refer to the privacy of more than one family, we would need *families' privacy*.

29. **He was charged with drunk driving after swerving and hitting a car coming toward him.** The preposition *toward* is singular. Interestingly, in British English it ordinarily is plural: *towards*.

30. **Hunter was living with his girlfriend, Topping, who was also injured in the accident.** When used as internal punctuation, commas come in pairs, one before, one after. The use of commas here says Hunter has one girlfriend, and her name is Topping. Without the commas we would be saying that he had more than one girlfriend, so the name Topping would become essential to the meaning of the sentence and would not be set off by commas.

31. **He had to choose among four alternatives.** Use *between* when you have two options; use *among* when there are three or more.

32. **The death of the Queen Mother affected her deeply.** Again, in most cases *affect* is a verb and *effect* is a noun.

33. **Then they found the other girls, who were in their beds sleeping.** Again, use of the comma here restricts the meaning to one set of other girls, who happened to be in their beds. Without the comma, the sentence means that there were two batches of girls in bed. For the second choice we want the plural possessive pronoun *their*.

34. **His arraignment has been set for tomorrow morning, at which time he could lose his freedom.** Set off the second clause with a comma because it is incidental to the primary idea in the sentence, the time of his arraignment. For some reason, *loose* and *lose* are often confused. They shouldn't be; one means not tight; the other means to forfeit or misplace.

35. **He was charged with selling drugs to a minor.** Let's take the strictly grammatical problem first. A *minor* is someone younger than legal age; a *miner*

is someone who removes valuable elements from the earth. We use *charged with* instead of *arrested for* because of the implications involved. *Arrested for* implies that he committed the crime, so he was arrested. But in our legal system we value the presumption of innocence; a defendant is presumed not guilty until guilt is admitted or proven in court. We should stick with what we know to be true: that he was *charged with* a crime, not that he committed it.

36. **This needs to be resolved by you, me and him.** All three pronouns are objects of the preposition *by*, so all three must be in the objective case. We wouldn't say *by you, by I, and by he.*

37. **Was it she whom he was referring to?** If you turn the structure of the two clauses in this sentence around, it becomes clear that the first pronoun needs to be subjective, the second objective: *It was she* (she is identical to and renames the subject *it*) and *he was referring to whom (whom* is the object of the preposition *to).* By the way, it is usually okay to end a sentence with a preposition.

38. **Just as I lay down, the chicken started clucking because she had laid an egg.** Okay, one more time and we can lay this one to rest. *Lay* in this usage is the simple past tense of the intransitive verb *lie*, and *laid* is the past perfect of the transitive verb *lay.*

39. **When the hotel dining room caught fire, the guests were evacuated to the parking lot without injury.** We risk a misplaced modifier here, the prepositional phrase *without injury.* If we put it before *to the parking lot* it means the parking lot wasn't injured. That's probably not what we mean.

40. **A dromedary is different from a Bactrian camel.** *Different* almost always takes the preposition *from* rather than *than.*

41. **It's pretty clear that the organization wants nothing to stand in its way.** In the first instance, *it's* is the appropriate contraction for *it is.* In the second, *organization* is not a collective noun, so it takes a singular pronoun. Remember that the possessive form of *it* is *its.*

42. **She said she would go if it doesn't rain.** The issue here is called sequence of tenses, and it's something practically everybody screws up. When the second verb depends on the main verb (she *would go* is what she *said*), it must obey the tense of the principal verb. But because *if it doesn't rain* does not depend on *she said* (it will rain or not despite what she said), it does not have to follow the tense of the main verb.

43. **The first time I did my laundry in college I shrank all my jeans.** I don't care how many movies you have seen that talk about what somebody

shrunk. Getting the tense wrong for this verb is goofy. *Shrank* is the simple past tense of *shrink*.

44. **She said after the accident that she was feeling all right.** While some dictionaries now accept *alright*, *all right* is preferred. *All right* is also the choice of the Associated Press Stylebook, a guide most journalists and news organizations use.

45. **According to the police report, the prisoner sneaked out of the van when the driver stopped for gas.** *Sneaked* is preferred, although many dictionaries now acknowledge *snuck*. The Associated Press Stylebook says not to use *snuck*.

46. **He stops for an ice-cream cone on the way home almost every day.** Practically everyone is abusing this one lately. In this usage, it must be two words because *every* is an adjective modifying the noun *day*. *Everyday* is one word only when it acts as a single adjective: Thunderstorms became an *everyday* occurrence that July. In that case, *everyday* is one adjective modifying the noun *occurrence*.

47. **The streaker dived into the bushes when he saw a campus security guard.** *Dove* is not the preferred past tense of *dive*.

48. **At one minute past midnight, the police spokesman said, the convicted murderer was executed.** Because the execution happened at one minute past midnight, we need to set the attribution off by commas. If we had meant that the police spokesman made the statement at one minute past midnight, we would not need commas.

49. **The senator said he hoped a budget would be passed soon.** Everybody seems to be using *hopefully* to mean *I hope, we hope, he hopes*, and so forth. But *hopefully* is an adverb; it cannot substitute for a subject and a verb.

50. **If McNab had thrown the ball a yard farther, that play would have gone for a touchdown.** *"If McNab throws . . . that play goes . . ."* has come into common usage because sports broadcasters are incapable of handling anything more complex than the present tense. But because we are describing an event that might have happened, we need the conditional tense both times. You need "farther" because we're dealing with physical distance. Use "further" when you're talking about a figurative distance: *He couldn't take his argument any further.*

Box 2.3

STRATEGIES FOR USING TOOLS WITH SKILL

1. Choose words on whose meaning practically everyone agrees.

2. Avoid slang, colloquialisms and informal constructions. They may be unfamiliar to many in a mass audience.

3. Words are the tools you use to craft meaningful stories. Become an expert in using those tools.

4. Develop the discipline to work hard and practice writing a lot.

5. Avoid writing badly by learning to recognize poor grammar, confusing punctuation, misspellings, clichés, redundancies, bureaucratese and other forms of obfuscation.

Strategies

To find out how you did: First, tally the number of correct answers. Then, multiply by two. (Remember that some sentences have two or three sets of choices, so a perfect score would be 134.)

If you scored 120 or better, you're pretty handy with your principal tool, the English language. If you scored 100–120, you know the language fairly well, but you might brush up on certain skills. If you scored below 100, be honest with yourself, give yourself a pep talk, and ask your instructor to point you to some easily digestible grammar books that will help you develop your skills. One suggestion is Paula LaRocque's *The Book on Writing: The Ultimate Guide to Writing Well.* A little extra work now will pay handsomely later.

What Is News?

In this chapter we examine how journalists go about deciding what is news. Most people recognize what news is, even if they are hard-pressed to give a coherent definition of it. Almost every day, by way of greeting our friends, we tell them about something that we witnessed or that happened to us.

"I just saw something totally gross. This guy threw up right in front of the Union."

"I just got my LSATs. 167. Yessss!"

Neither of these occurrences is going to make Tori Baxter lunge for the phone to call her editor in Jeffersonville. But both had an effect in your life. In the first case, the emotional impact of seeing somebody toss his cookies affected how your day started. As a result of seeing it, you will need a little while to settle into your B hour class. In the second, the rational impact of a good LSAT score is obvious: It will help you determine the course your life will take.

News Defined

News is like that on a large scale. As stated in Chapter 1, *news is a journalist's account of events and issues that affect many people in significant ways.* Instead of sharing with our friends information that affects only us or them, we as reporters are looking to share with a *mass audience* information that will affect all or most of that audience in a significant way. Again, that effect can be rational, emotional or a combination of both. In this chapter we will look at how journalists go about deciding what is news on any given day, and how you can begin making those decisions yourself.

Mass Audiences

Let's take a minute to identify some characteristics of mass audiences (see Box 3.1). First, obviously, they comprise *large numbers*. But even that statement can be deceptive. For a Valleydale regional weekly newspaper the mass audience may be on the order of 5,000 people. For the *Jeffersonville Herald* it might be 100,000. For the TV station affiliated with the *Herald* it might be twice that number. But for the *CBS Evening News* or CNN.com, it would be millions.

The fact that mass audience sizes can vary markedly leads us to a second characteristic: Even though each member might not realize it, members of mass audiences *share many interests*. These broad interests frequently are defined by community: The 5,000 people who read the Valleydale weekly newspaper share their citizenship in the city. They all pay taxes to the city in one form or another,

Box 3.1

CHARACTERISTICS OF MASS AUDIENCES

1. *Mass audiences are large.* They range from a few thousand to many million.

2. *Members of mass audiences share many interests.* Examples are fans of the Boston Red Sox and constituents of a particular member of the U.S. Congress.

3. *Mass audiences are diverse* in age, gender, race, ethnicity, religion, level of education, life experiences, political affiliation, temperament and any number of other characteristics.

4. *Mass audiences come to news stories with those differences.* Those differences help shape how people respond to news stories.

and they are bound by the same local laws. Many have children in the public schools. The readers of the *Jeffersonville Herald* share broader characteristics: They are nearly all residents of Virginia, governed by its General Assembly and governor, subject most days to pretty much the same weather. The millions of people who watch the *CBS Evening News* share even broader interests: They are nearly all Americans or live in the United States. They are governed by the same federal system and led by the same president. They share many of the same worries about terrorism.

Third, while mass audiences share broad interests, *they are diverse* as well—in sex, age, race, ethnicity, religion, education, experience and temperament. There is much diversity even in some small communities. For example, while Valleydale is not especially diverse racially, even the comparatively few readers of the local weekly range broadly in age, comprise men and women and rich and poor (although low-income people do not make up a large proportion of newspaper readers in many communities), and reflect different political affiliations.

Finally, as we talked about in Chapter 2, mass audiences *come to news stories with wide differences in background, context and expertise for those stories.* And no one—no matter how smart, well educated or voracious a consumer of news—will already be familiar with every story he or she sees.

Elements of News

The impact of events or issues on mass audiences is a function of several factors, and newspeople use an almost universal template to help them determine the significance of those events and issues: *Who* was involved? *What* happened and *what* is at issue? *When* did it happen? *Where* did it happen? *Why* did it happen and *why* is it an issue now? *How* did it happen and *how* did we get into this situation? (See Box 3.2.) These so-called five Ws and an H are probably familiar to you if you took journalism courses in high school or worked on your school paper or radio station. They are no less important for being hackneyed.

Most often, journalists use these elements in some combination to determine whether an event or issue is worth reporting. For example, if Valleydale mayor Delmer Hostetter falls and tears cartilage in his knee, it's doubtful even the local Valleydale weekly newspapers would report it. Neither the *who* nor the *what* carries much impact. But when then-President Clinton fell and hurt his knee in 1997, only a week or so before a summit meeting with Russian

Box 3.2

FIVE WS AND AN H

Journalists try to answer the same fundamental questions in nearly all stories. Depending on the story, some of those questions are more important than others.

1. *Who* was involved, and *who* was, is or will be affected?

2. *What* happened or *what* is at issue?

3. *When* did the event take place, or *when* did the issue become important?

4. *Where* is the action in the story taking place, or *where* do the people affected live?

5. *Why* is the event or issue important, or *why* did someone behave as he or she did?

6. *How* did the event come to pass, *how* did the issue evolve, or *how* will the audience become involved?

President Boris Yeltsin, the *who*, the *what* and the *when* yielded enough impact to merit reporting the incident, because the fitness of the most powerful man in the world affects us all. Most of us get to choose to keep an injury reasonably private. The president of the United States did not have that option, because there was a legitimate question about whether the injury would affect his performance at the summit. As it turned out, most observers—whether they worked for broadcast, print or online media—thought it did. Clinton had just had knee surgery, he was confined to a wheelchair, and he was in obvious pain. The image he conveyed to the rest of the world was not that of the confident, take-charge leader he wanted to project.

Some events affect a large but not universal audience. If the knee injury happened to Shaquille O'Neal on the eve of the NBA finals, for example, basketball fans all over the world would feel the impact—emotionally, at least; rationally if they were planning to bet on the outcome of the series. For others who don't care about basketball, the injury would mean nothing.

Professional Responsibilities and Duties

Our definition of news as events and issues that affect large audiences in significant ways should help us understand why journalists recognize at least two steps in making decisions about news. The first step is whether to try to gather information in the first place. The second involves how—or whether—we will give that information to audiences as stories. You will probably recognize some overlap in those two decisions, but because the goal of this chapter is to get you thinking about what kind of information is important to your audience, let's examine each step in turn.

In *deciding whether to gather information*, Tori Baxter thinks first about her audience. Say she has gotten a tip that a member of Valleydale's City Council is having an extramarital affair. Does her audience need to know that? Is there any reason for her even to check out the rumor? If she were to pursue the rumor, and it turned out to be true, would it make any difference—that is, would it affect the performance of the council member's official duties?

Journalists must also think about how they allocate their resources. If Tori takes the time to chase down the rumor about the City Council member's affair, what other story or stories will her audience not read or see? Is nailing down one story worth giving up another? As you might imagine, Tory's editors at the newspaper and producers and assigning editors at the television-news operation also make constant decisions about allocation of

Section editors at *The Roanoke Times* discuss stories at their daily news meeting. In almost all newsrooms—print, broadcast or Web—editors and producers gather regularly to talk about the day's news and how prominently stories will be displayed.

Reporters find information that becomes news in many places besides City Hall or the local courthouse. *Roanoke Times* reporter Joshua Garner walks among Jacob sheep at a farm that specializes in rare livestock.

resources. If the superintendent of schools in an outlying county calls a news conference to announce results of the district's latest state-mandated testing, for example, is it worth it for a station to send out a reporter and videographer, whose time commitment in getting to the event and gathering the necessary information is half a day, not to mention the time it takes to turn that information into a story? Again, what stories will the station miss because it decided to allocate two people to the news conference? Is the story they got worth more than the ones they might have missed?

The second step in making news decisions—how or whether to give information to audiences—is often a collaborative process in newsrooms. Like most reporters—broadcast, print or online—before she writes a story, and often before she has even gathered much information for it, Tori almost always talks with her assigning editor about the approach she will take. She and her editor will talk about the key information the story will contain and how that information will be organized and presented to Tori's audience. To get an understanding of what that conversation might entail, look again at the dialogue between Tori and her editor at the beginning of Chapter 1, and think about the discussion of framing and objectivity included in that chapter.

At least once a day, the section editors and top editors of a newspaper will gather for a news meeting. In television news operations, producers and the news director will have a similar meeting. The purpose of these news meetings is to figure out the relative importance of the day's stories. Those decisions will be reflected in how much space the stories are given and where they are placed in the newspaper, on the Web site or in the news broadcast.

It's important to remember that reporters and editors hear many tips and get a lot of preliminary information that they don't pursue, because they have judged it to be irrelevant to or inappropriate for their audience, or not worth the resources they would have to invest. But if there is any doubt about the importance of information, journalists will usually do at least some preliminary fact-gathering. If they do not make the attempt, they will never know whether the information would have been worthwhile for their audiences to know—unless they see it featured by a rival news outlet. If they gather some facts, they can then make an informed decision about whether to continue to pursue the story, and then about whether to share it with audiences or let it go.

Deciding what is news—and how to show it to audiences—is often a team project for television reporters.

Ethics

We need always to keep in mind our professional responsibilities as journalists when we make decisions about what is news. Often, that is expressed ethically as our *duty* to our audiences, or what we *owe* our audiences. For example, we can argue that any information we get about a prominent person will have some impact on audiences. But many times that impact is merely titillating or voyeuristic. Some publications and TV shows are committed to showing audiences every scrap of personal information they can gather about Jessica Simpson or Michael Jackson. Even legitimate news organizations continually wrestle with how much of a public figure's life has a substantial impact on audiences. Gathering and publishing personal information always involves an invasion of privacy. Our responsibility as journalists is to decide whether it is a *justifiable* invasion of privacy. For example, when Jackson was charged with child molestation and faced a criminal trial, he moved from a constant presence in the pages of lurid tabloid "newspapers" and salacious video gossip shows to mainstream news media, although his lengthy trial was downplayed by many of the latter.

To use another example, this one involving a public official rather than a celebrity, most Americans responding to surveys said that whether then-President Clinton had an affair with Monica Lewinsky was between him, Lewinsky, and Hillary Rodham Clinton. But many cared deeply about whether Clinton lied about his relationship with Lewinsky under oath—a felony. Newspeople were left with difficult choices about how to report on aspects of the president's private life that affected his public performance and hence our own lives.

Even when an event involving a public person has no impact on the public welfare, journalists wrestle with whether the event, because the person is part of the public consciousness, is news. The Kennedy family's prominence in American life and culture for half a century determined the quality and quantity of coverage given John F. Kennedy Jr.'s death in a plane crash in 1999. No news organization debated the importance of the story to the American audience. There was plenty of discussion, though, about the line between satisfying public curiosity and inexcusably invading the Kennedy family's privacy.

We live in a society that believes in and tries to practice self-governance and participatory democracy. Newspeople take their marching orders from the firm belief that access to comprehensive, trustworthy information is essential if people are to make effective decisions about how they ought to be governed and about how other institutions of society ought to work. We hear the word *empowerment* a lot these days, and its connotations make some of us uncomfortable. But when newspeople fulfill their duty to their audiences, they give people some control over their own lives. We can argue, then, that news empowers audiences. That result provides justification for much of what journalists do, but the process of gathering information and turning it into stories should be guided by care and careful thought.

Strategies

Now then, how does all this flag-waving translate into the decisions newspeople make every day? (See Box 3.3.) In this chapter, we have looked at the *elements* that go into those decisions, at the mechanics and the ethics of that process. As you work through the exercises below, try to apply those criteria to the choices you must make. You will choose which of several potential stories need to be in the paper or on the air today, and in what order of *relative* importance.

Remember, to make those decisions, we must first determine *who our audience is.*

Box 3.3

STRATEGIES FOR DECIDING WHAT IS NEWS

1. Think about your audience. Who are its members? What needs and interests do they share? How will they be affected?

2. Does your audience need to know the information you have gathered? Or is it fun to know, but not essential?

3. What resources must you spend to get this story? Is there another story you should devote those resources to instead? What other story might you be giving up to get this one?

4. What *elements* of this story should you emphasize for your audience—*who, what, when, where, why* or *how*? Which ones most make it news?

5. What is the relative importance of this story compared with the others your newsroom is working on today? Where will it go in the paper or on the newscast or Web site?

6. Would sharing this story with a mass audience show good ethical judgment?

Exercise 3A

A Warm-Up

Either as a class discussion or among your friends, talk about whether Michael Jackson's trial on child molestation charges should have been covered by the news media. Did it fit the criteria discussed in this chapter for deciding what is news, including ethical considerations? Were there elements of the story that audiences did not need to know about? Compare what you remember of television, Web and newspaper coverage of the story. Do you think one medium covered the story more responsibly than the others? Try the same discussion about President Clinton's affair with Monica Lewinsky (there are hundreds of stories on the Web if you need to refresh your memory). Does the difference between President Clinton's and Michael Jackson's professions and public responsibilities make any difference in your discussion?

Exercise 3B

What's News Today?

Assume you are Tori Baxter, and that the following events occurred or were revealed in Blue Ridge County, Valleydale or Beausoleil within the past 24 hours. You have to decide their relative importance to the audience for the Jeffersonville Herald's Blue Ridge County, Valleydale and Beausoleil edition of the paper, for that evening's television news broadcast and for the Web site. Remember that stories affect audiences both rationally and emotionally, and that the long-term emotional impact of some stories is more profound than the short-term rational impact of others.

Hint: Consult the City Directory for information about the people involved. You might find it useful in making your decisions. Remember also that newspaper people and online journalists have the choice of putting several stories on the front page, but that it is still necessary to rank them because readers' eyes customarily go to some parts of the page before others. Radio and TV journalists can present only one story at a time, so stories have to be ranked sequentially.

Once you have ranked the stories, write a one-page analysis showing your rankings and why you ranked the stories as you did. If you think your decisions would be different for the different media, explain why. Assume that we learned about all of these events today.

1. A light plane plummeted into a field in northern Blue Ridge County during a thunderstorm. Both occupants of the plane were killed. Sheriff's deputies have not released their names, pending notification of next of kin.

2. Beausoleil City Manager L. E. "Skeet" Thurston announced that a group of investors is "very interested" in building a golf course on city property, a project that could create 150 jobs during construction and 23 permanent jobs.

3. North River Manufacturing Company, Beausoleil's biggest industrial plant, which employs 3,000 workers, this morning announced that its workers had voted 1,437 to 1,390 to unionize. It was the first time that a work force in Blue Ridge County had done so.

4. The Blue Ridge County Board of Supervisors voted 3–2 to build a new courthouse, and to raise property taxes countywide to finance the construction.

5. The Chamber of Commerce announced yesterday that its annual banquet four nights ago set an attendance record.

6. For the third year in a row, Valleydale City Schools met state requirements for student performance on the statewide Comprehensive Achievement Tests, the school board announced yesterday.

7. Following a nighttime roadblock to conduct sobriety checks, Valleydale Police announced the following arrests on charges of drunk driving: Preston Allen, Martha Blatchky, T.A. "Tater" Chipps and Sporrin Spruance.

8. Responding to complaints from county residents, the Blue Ridge County Board of Supervisors passed a noise ordinance aimed at limiting parties by Virginia Presbyterian University students.

4

Turning Information into News

In the previous chapter, we discussed how journalists determine what is news. In this chapter we will look at the processes they go through to find information and fashion it into meaningful stories. As explained in Chapter 1, reporters don't find news, they find information. Through hard and, we hope, conscientious work they turn it into news, a coherent account of what they decide is significant to their audiences. But how do reporters find the information that they turn into news?

Sometimes information comes to them. For example, people call the newsroom with tips, or asking for coverage of their group's meeting or planned demonstration. Others send in press releases announcing a new product or a candidate's campaign platform and schedule of appearances. Editors sometimes pass these to reporters for rewriting or as leads to pursue.

Most of the time, though, important information does not come looking for reporters; reporters have to go looking for it. They use several strategies to do that.

Finding Information

1. *Newspaper reporters are often assigned a beat,* a particular topic or area of interest in which the reporter has developed some expertise or is expected to. The beat system is perhaps the best-known method for finding information. Each day, reporters on beats go to certain places that in the past have been good sources of story ideas. For example, every newspaper and broadcast news operation has somebody check local police and fire stations several times a day by phone or in person for incident and arrest reports. Similarly, the reporter on the court beat hangs out at the courthouse, looking for interesting trials and other activity in the justice system. Increasingly, though, news organizations are structuring beats around *issues*—health care or education, for example—rather than *buildings* or *locations*—City Hall or Blue Ridge County. Often, several reporters will share responsibility for an issues beat that might cross the boundaries of several traditional beats.

Newspapers still rely on regular beat reporters more than radio and TV stations do, but that is changing. In broadcasting, small-market reporters

Journalists use several strategies to track down information that might become news. Looking over previous stories and keeping a tickler file are among them.

tend to be generalists rather than being assigned a full-time beat. In bigger broadcast markets with bigger news staffs, there is more room for beat reporters. Newspaper reporters like Tori Baxter who work in small bureaus combine beat reporting with general-assignment reporting. Tori checks City Hall, the police station, the sheriff's office, the courthouse and the local universities regularly for story ideas, but she also spends time simply pounding the pavement.

2. *Reporters develop regular sources, especially on their beats.* Once a reporter gets to know these sources, the sources can often be relied on to tip the reporter about events, issues or looming crises. Tori knows that much of what they tell her will not be interesting or significant to a large audience. It is up to her to decide which tips might lead to good stories. Like other good reporters, Tori spends hours every day simply chatting with one person after another, in person or by phone.

3. *Reporters read other publications for story ideas.* For example, if *The New York Times* does a story on the lack of affordable day care in New York City, Tori will decide to check the situation in the Blue Ridge County area for a possible story.

4. *Sometimes a competing medium in the same market will "break" a story, that is, get it first.* If she's been scooped on a story, Tori, acting on her own initiative or after prompting from her editors, will have to "follow" the previously published or broadcast story, seeking a fresh angle or something that wasn't reported in the first story.

5. *Good reporters keep a tickler file, a calendar reminding them to check for further developments in events or issues they have already covered, or to revisit the people involved in earlier stories.* For example, when a court reporter covers the preliminary hearing for someone charged with murder, she will put a note in her tickler file showing when the defendant's next hearing is scheduled.

Listening for the Audience

It is important to remember that much of the information reporters turn up doesn't become news; that is, it isn't shared with an audience in the form of a story. From the time they begin the process of deciding whether a bit of information is worth pursuing, reporters act as advocates for their audiences. They have to be expert listeners, and they have to become skilled at asking questions too, especially when sources are reluctant to part with information. Many times, the person who gives Tori the first tip is not the one on whom she depends for the bulk of her information. For most stories, whether she is writing for print, broadcast or the Web, Tori will talk to several people, sometimes more than a dozen, and check a number of documents before she is ready to write. (Since the advent of the Web with its so-called "instant publishing," as well as 24-hour news channels, some news organizations have been criticized for using a different standard for Web and broadcast news. They are said to rush to the Web with information that hasn't been subjected to the same process of verification that is the standard for print or conventional news broadcasts, with their slower production cycles.)

It's important to keep in mind that you can't write a good story without doing thorough reporting. If you don't know and understand what's going on, your audience won't either, no matter how stylishly you try to write.

Often a news story is about more than the event that generated it. By finding and carefully weighing information, good journalists can show their audiences the story's context.

A caution bears repeating here: Before you can begin even to gather information, *you must know your audience*. As noted in Chapter 3, mass media audiences are diverse. They come to news stories with widely different levels of knowledge and expertise about the event or issue. It's important to assume that most people will have little or no prior knowledge of it. They need to be shown, both by the way you gather information and by the way you share it with them, how the information will affect them. Also remember that, usually, audiences will choose to devote as little time as possible to catching up on the news. Leisurely readers of newspapers and watchers of TV news are increasingly rare. Online readers frequently are interested only in brief summaries.

Audiences for particular news operations in particular markets have differing needs. For example, Tori knows that any story about higher education is likely to generate a lot of interest in the Blue Ridge County area. Many of her readers work for one of the two universities. But 200 miles away, in Norfolk, at the mouth of the Chesapeake Bay, it is news about the military that attracts attention. Practically any information about military spending has a direct impact on the local economy because of the pervasive presence of the Navy. So all your decisions about turning information into news should start with an awareness of your audience.

The Process of Making News

As they turn information into news, reporters follow a six-step process: (1) discovery; (2) information gathering; (3) judging impact; (4) focusing on critical elements; (5) organizing; and (6) using words effectively. (See Box 4.1.) Some journalists identify the sixth step as *writing*, but it's important to remember that all six steps comprise the *process* of writing, and that the sixth step also encompasses *rewriting*. Tori Baxter goes through this process every day, and following the steps has become second nature. Almost always, the steps overlap to some degree. For example, Tori begins to judge impact (step 3) from the moment she gets a tip or a snippet of information (step 1). Similarly, information gathering (step 2) can go on even as she writes her story (steps 5 and 6), until the moment she has to ship her story electronically to Jeffersonville to make deadline, and sometimes after that. And like many reporters, Tori starts thinking early on about the words she will use. From the moment of discovery, she starts turning over potential sentences in her head.

Box 4.1

MAKING NEWS: A SIX-STEP PROCESS

1. *Discovery.* A reporter turns up something interesting, or someone passes along a tip.

2. *Information gathering.* The reporter tries to verify the tip, and to find out more.

3. *Judging impact.* The reporter carefully weighs whether the information will carry any impact for her audience.

4. *Focusing on critical elements.* She chooses the elements that will show her audience the impact.

5. *Organizing.* The reporter uses strategies to help her arrange the information in a coherent way that reflects its impact.

6. *Using words effectively.* By choosing and organizing words with great care, the reporter shapes a story that shows her audience why what she has learned is important. The story is often the product of several rewrites.

In this textbook we will focus primarily on the last four steps of the process. If you go on to take advanced reporting courses, you will get plenty of practice discovering and gathering information, possibly even covering a regular beat. As explained in Chapter 1, most of the newswriting assignments you are asked to complete here will be based on information that will be supplied to you.

Impact, Elements, Words

We can simplify those last four steps into a three-word mantra: *impact, elements, words.* (See Box 4.2.) Learn to recite it: *impact, elements, words.* Make it hang around in your head, creating an audible buzz each time you begin to write: *impact, elements, words.* It should define and focus the writing process for you. *Impact* should help us decide what the story is about and why anybody should care about it. The *elements*—who, what, when, where, why, how—show us what to focus on to convey that impact to our audience.

IMPACT, ELEMENTS, WORDS

As you judge the news value of information and then turn that information into news, remember to follow these steps, keyed to three words:

1. *Impact.* What's this story about? Why should anybody care? How will it affect the lives of my audience?
2. *Elements.* Asking who, what, when, where, why and how should show you how to convey that impact to your audience.
3. *Words.* Used properly, these tools will fashion information into something understandable and meaningful.

Words are the tools we choose, in writing and rewriting, to fashion the information into something not only understandable and usable but graceful.

Writing is mostly a craft, and a craft can be taught. Occasionally, newswriting rises to the level of art, but practically nobody can create enduring art without learning the craft first. The more you practice writing, the better you get. Forget the image of the 19th-century poet waiting, one wrist to his forehead, for his muse to anoint him with the fleeting genius to create art. That's crap. For one thing, muses don't recognize deadlines. Journalists have to.

Whether you are working in print, broadcast or online media, writing is a simple process, but not an easy one. Veteran reporters are continually driven crazy by trying to decide how a story will affect their audiences most profoundly, by which elements to focus on based on that impact, by what to put in and what to leave out, by the choice of words that will work. Each step along the way is fraught with the potential for failure. As Mark Twain said, the difference between the right word and the almost-right word is the difference between lightning and a lightning bug. But as tough as the process can be, if we don't approach doing news systematically, we are left with chaos—capricious decisions, fuzzy focus, unclear language, baffled audiences. The stakes are too high to approach news haphazardly.

Try to keep the process as simple as you can initially. Complexity should build logically. Let's look at each part of the process in turn.

Broadcast journalists strive to combine words and video to tell a story effectively.

Impact

In judging impact, limit yourself to three choices: *rational, emotional* or a *combination* of the two. You will recall that we looked at impact in Chapter 1 as we discussed the responsibilities that journalists have to their audiences. Remember that, in showing people how events and issues will affect them, you will be reporting about more than what affects them in measurable ways alone. Many good stories reach audiences because they engage audiences in more than a strictly rational way. The impact of a story, then, can be seen as rational, as emotional or as a combination of the two.

As also discussed in Chapter 1, journalism textbooks historically have urged students to consider a sackful of factors in deciding what's news. The list includes proximity, prominence, timeliness, consequence, magnitude, conflict, human interest, unusualness and so forth. Again, this list raises the question: Why do we say that those elements make a story worth telling? Why, for example, is the fact that someone is prominent make information about him newsworthy? If we ask the question for our audience's benefit, it comes out like this: "What's this story about?" or "Why should anybody care? Why should we ask people to spend their time on this story?" Our answer should be "because it affects them." It's our job to show them how and why it affects them.

If Valleydale City Council passed a budget last night that includes a tax increase, we know our story should focus on the rational impact: How much more will homeowners pay? If we find out that Virginia Presbyterian University student Meagan LeBlanc dived into a burning home to save her neighbor's 2-year-old daughter, the impact will be mostly emotional: How might anyone in our audience react in the same emergency? Who is this brave young woman? How would any other parents feel if their child was trapped? Even though few in our audience will know the child, her mother, or the rescuer, the event affects people emotionally. It makes them aware of their shared humanity.

If a Valleydale City Council member is charged with drunk driving (Exercise 3B), we can argue that the impact is both *rational* and *emotional*. Our audiences need and deserve to know that one of their elected officials stands accused of a serious violation of the law, one that could put other people at substantial risk. There is substantial rational impact in that information. But to the extent that the incident makes members of our audience think about foolish or ill-considered decisions that they have made in their own lives that might have caused harm to others, and whether they were made to suffer the consequences, there is significant emotional impact as well.

Elements

In finding the right elements, keep thinking of the five Ws and an H. Which one, or two, or three in combination, will show the impact that you've decided is most significant? Trying to give equal weight to all six elements at the beginning of your story—your *lede,* discussed further in Chapter 5—makes for a long, hard-to-follow sentence or sentences. Worse, you make your audiences try to do for themselves what you should be doing for them—making things clear.

So here is how I recommend you think through the first two steps of the process. We'll take the councilman charged with drunk driving as an example: *Impact*—rational and emotional. *Elements* (that show the impact)—who, what.

Making those two choices correctly leads you to the third.

Words

In choosing the right words, think about the ones that show your audience most directly what the story is about, that reflect the careful decisions you made about impact and the elements that show it. Stick with words that will be familiar to your audience. They can be informal, but avoid slang. Usually, you'll rely on nouns and verbs more than on adjectives and adverbs. Nouns and verbs *show,* adjectives and adverbs tell. You will use simple, declarative, subject-verb-object sentence structure most of the time. Show, don't tell. In our example, then: *impact*—rational, emotional; *elements*—who, what; *words*—Valleydale City Council Member T. A. "Tater" Chipps was charged with drunk driving.

It can be argued that this process is effective no matter what kind of writing you are doing. All writers seek to create understanding. Of course, fiction audiences have different expectations than audiences for news, and researchers read articles in scholarly journals with different expectations than people reading poetry. But all audiences have needs, and focusing on this process keeps you focused on your audience and its needs.

Characteristics of Audiences and Stories

Knowing your audience will have a profound effect on all three parts of your *impact, elements, words* process. So it's important here to review some characteristics of mass audiences that make newswriting different from fiction or scholarly writing.

First, you are writing for members of an audience who will be coming to your story with little or no expertise in what it deals with. What they understand will come from your story. Second, they may have little initial interest in your story, so you must show them right away why it might be important to them. Third, they are trying to assimilate a substantial amount of new information in a short time.

News stories, then, should reflect those audience characteristics. As a result, they will share some features that other kinds of writing might not emphasize: The story's importance is made clear early, often in the first sentence, almost always in the first paragraph. Because audiences have to know they can rely on the information they are getting, factual accuracy is stressed, and reporters verify their facts (remember to use your City Directory). Sources are identified, and statements are carefully attributed to particular sources. Most sentences and paragraphs are short, and reporters write in the active voice. They emphasize nouns and verbs rather than adjectives and adverbs. Finally, the reporter makes sure to provide his or her audience with adequate context and background. (See Box 4.3.)

Box 4.3

CHARACTERISTICS OF NEWS STORIES

1. The story's importance is made clear right away.

2. Factual accuracy is stressed, so that audiences know they can rely on the information.

3. Sources are identified, and statements and information are carefully attributed.

4. Most sentences and paragraphs are short. Reporters usually write in the active voice. They rely on nouns and verbs more than adjectives and adverbs.

5. Adequate context and background are included.

Ethics

Journalism shares a fundamental characteristic with all professions: Its practitioners are motivated by their obligations to those they serve. In the case of journalists, the primary obligation is to promote democratic self-determination by giving audiences the information they need to make decisions about their lives. Review the characteristics of news stories above, and think about how they reflect audiences' needs and journalists' obligations to meet those needs. Think especially about audiences' needs for accurate, reliable information presented so they can understand it clearly. Remember the discussion in Chapter 1 of objectivity and framing. Finally, think about the decisions journalists make about what information is not appropriate to share with audiences. Sometimes those decisions are centered on the audience's needs and interests, but they can also reflect the journalist's respect for an individual's privacy and the goal of minimizing harm.

Strategies

Remember that reporters find out a lot of information that they never craft into news stories. When you practice your three-word mantra—*impact, elements, words*—keep in mind that a lot of information doesn't get past the first filter—*impact*. If Tori can't see why her audience ought to care about a piece of information or set of facts, chances are audiences won't see it in a news story.

Box 4.4

STRATEGIES FOR TURNING INFORMATION INTO NEWS

1. Remember: *impact, elements, words.* Focus on each step in the process.

2. Keep in mind that a lot of information doesn't get past the first filter—*impact.* Can you show your audience why they ought to care about a story?

3. If you find sufficient impact for your audience, determine which *elements*—who, what, when, where, why, how—most effectively show that impact.

4. Use *words* to translate the information into a clear, coherent news story. Keep trying. Plan on doing a lot of rewriting.

If information passes the impact test, move to your next step, *elements*—the who, what, when, where, why, how questions. Which of those elements most effectively show the audience the impact? Seldom should all six be emphasized equally in a story. But it is equally infrequent that only one element will carry all the freight.

Only after you are confident that you have made solid decisions about impact and elements should you turn your attention to *words.* How can we as reporters translate the solid decisions we have made on their behalf into a clear, coherent news story? (See Box 4.4.)

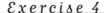

Exercise 4

What's This Story About?

Study the four scenarios that follow. Apply your mantra—*impact, elements, words*—to them. Discuss them in class before you attempt a written assignment based on the information in them. Take notes on them if you like, to bring to the class discussion, and feel free to ask questions in class.

Police Report

You find out from checking incident reports at the police department that there was a break-in at Valleydale Presbyterian Church's fellowship hall last night.

About 500 people are members of the church. Burglary was discovered at 6:30 this morning by the church's janitor, Norbert Patsy. Entry apparently gained through a window at the youth minister's office on the first floor of the two-story building. Access gained by shattering the window. The Rev. Edwin F. Younts reports that all that appeared to be taken were several sex-education videos that the youth minister had locked in his desk drawer, and the video recorder and TV set in his office. He estimates the value of the items at $600. Videos were church-approved for use with young-adult Sunday school classes. A passerby saw one person walking away from the church carrying something heavy about 3 A.M., but assumed it was a security guard doing his job. (*Source: Chief Honeycutt*)

Resignation

Luverne Trump has been Valleydale's finance director for 11 years. She was one of the first African American municipal finance directors in the South. Her responsibilities include overseeing city spending and preliminary review of the proposed city budget. She has a bachelor's degree in accounting and an MBA, both from the University of Virginia. She is single. Today in the city manager's office you find a copy of a letter she submitted to him late yesterday.

Dear Mr. Prentice:

I hereby regretfully tender my resignation as your Finance Director. I feel it is time to pursue other opportunities, although I have not yet identified them. My reasons for resigning are personal.

This, therefore, will constitute my notice of resignation, effective immediately.

I wish to take this opportunity to thank several of the members of Valleydale City Council for their support. As you know, during my tenure the city budget—and the services we provide residents—has grown enormously. Inevitably, with such growth there are tensions. I have dealt with those tensions to the best of my ability. I will always look with pride at my time with Valleydale city government.

Sincerely,

Luverne Trump, Finance Director

Trump will not discuss her letter with you, or give specific reasons for resigning. City Manager Prentice provides a statement:

"We accept Ms. Trump's resignation with regret. We wish her well. I am sure that recent unfounded accusations that touch on the Finance Department, but not on Ms. Trump, precipitated her decision, which is upsetting."

Prentice will ask City Council at its next meeting to appoint an interim finance director pending a nationwide search for Trump's replacement.

Lost Child

Police incident reports and news releases are often wordy and full of jargon. It's your job to focus on the essence and translate the jargon into words your audience will find understandable and compelling. This one is from County Sheriff Swofford.

Yesterday about 4 P.M. Blue Ridge County Deputy Sheriff Rubelia Pennebaker was patrolling Eden Pass when she observed a group of civilians engaging in frantic arm-waving activity at the Eden Pass Wayside. Upon arrival, a similar group of people was observed, one of whom was trying to console an agitated WF identified as Dorothy Foster of Cupp's Creek. Dorothy Foster advised DS Pennebaker that her child, Pat, WF age 3, had wandered away from a family picnic approximately 45 minutes earlier and could not be located. Numerous civilian volunteers were at this point engaged in a search for the child. DS Pennebaker radioed dispatch for backup. At which point help was requested from Madison County Search Canine Unit (SCU). Two bloodhound-type dogs arrived approximately 6 P.M. and began a search for the child, accompanied by approximately 30 sheriff's deputies and civilian volunteers. At approximately 4 A.M. in the morning this date, SCU canine "Old Blue" located child asleep at the base of a large tree, approximately three miles from picnic sight. Child was taken by ambulance to Stuart Hospital in Valleydale, where she was examined and released. Child is the youngest of five children belonging to Foster and her husband, Jeff.

Goodbye, Luverne

Some journalists say that nothing happens for the first time. News stories are often updates of events or issues that we have written about previously. But we can't always assume that our audiences saw the earlier story, so we have to be sure to place the new story in its appropriate context.

After a two-hour executive session of Valleydale City Council last night (closed to the public and the media), Valleydale City Manager Don Prentice named Deputy Finance Director Alice Turpin the Acting Finance Director. Prentice made the appointment as a result of the resignation of Luverne Trump a few days ago. The council did not comment publicly on Trump's resignation. It did issue the following statement:

"We wish Ms. Trump well, and we are pleased that Ms. Turpin has been appointed Acting Finance Director with the understanding that she will become one applicant to fill the permanent position. We are confident in Ms. Turpin's ability to lead the Finance Department through this difficult time."

chapter five

Ledes

Lede is a corrupted spelling of *lead,* as in to lead someone into a story. News people spell it that way because, in the old days, newspapers used lead (the metal) to print from. Putting extra lead (the metal) into a story— or *leading the story*—meant to stretch out the story so it would fill its allotted space. You can see how easy it was to confuse the two words, so they started spelling one *lede.* That's the convention I'll use. By the way, some newspeople say the term is archaic, but a recent Google search of keywords *lede* and *newswriting* yielded about 32,800 references, including ones from *The New York Times* and the *Columbia Journalism Review.* A few broadcast reporters and some online journalists have kept the convention.

In Chapters 3 and 4 we looked at how journalists define news, decide what is news, and use impact and elements to judge what information should be shared with audiences in news stories. In this chapter we will focus on determining what information an audience should get *first*—the *lede* of the story—and on how we can use words carefully to convey that information most effectively.

What Is a Lede?

Operationally, the lede is the first sentence of a news story. Sometimes—especially on the Web—a lede can run to two or maybe three sentences. Functionally, a lede has to do much more than just sit there at the beginning of the story. As discussed in Chapters 3 and 4, people bring expectations to news stories—chiefly, that they will find out sooner rather than later whether the story has any meaning for them. The lede must show them that, or at least create a promise that the key information will be delivered very soon.

There was a time when most news stories—particularly newspaper stories—were written with what were called *summary* ledes. That is, they summarized practically all that was going on in the story, giving equal or nearly equal weight to all six elements—the who, what, when, where, why and how of every story. Usually, that meant that they ran on a bit, sometimes a lot. It also meant that readers were left with a lot of work to do—sorting out which elements they needed to focus on and which could be left by the wayside. That's a tricky business for a couple of reasons.

First, it's the journalists who know the story. It's unfair to ask people in your audience to sort out the important stuff when they don't yet know anything about what they're reading or hearing. Second, by the time a reader, listener or viewer gets to the end of a 45-word lede, it's almost impossible to remember what was at the beginning.

By the 1960s, newspaper audiences had started relaying that message very clearly. They did it by putting their newspapers down and turning on their TV sets. For a broadcast journalist, trying to cram all the elements into the lede is even more foolish, because broadcast stories are recited to the audience, and once the words are spoken, the audience can't recapture them. Also, for the anchor or newsreader, getting through a lede of more than about 20 words gracefully is nearly impossible. (See Box 5.1.)

Today's audiences don't spend as much time with their news media as audiences used to. The day when people blocked out two hours each night to go through their newspaper is history. Even some 30-minute newscasts are losing audiences. Many people no longer spend more than a few minutes sitting through the evening news or skimming the home page of a news Web site

Box 5.1

CHARACTERISTICS OF LEDES

1. Good ledes are concise. Often they are confined to one sentence of 20 words or fewer. That's especially true in broadcast writing.

2. Good ledes focus on why people will or ought to care about a story. Journalists often talk about the *impact* of the lede—rational, emotional or a combination of the two.

3. Good ledes rely on answering the key two or three *who, what, when, where, why* and *how* questions rather than trying to deal with all six equally.

4. Good ledes rely on nouns and verbs and simple sentence structure to show the impact of the story.

5. Good ledes help audiences see how the story might affect them and decide whether to read the rest of the story.

6. Good ledes are the product of thought, hard work and several rewrites.

7. Good ledes help the writer organize the rest of the story, and the audience understand it.

8. Good ledes should sound right read aloud, whether they are written for print, online or broadcast media.

9. Good ledes serve the facts. They avoid assumptions and speculation.

before they start Web or channel surfing. So the job of sorting out for them what they really need to know is the journalist's, and it ought to be.

Sixty Percent of the Work

Asking a lede to carry that much baggage is a hefty request. That's why newspeople sweat blood over ledes, and why many of them say that when they've got the lede right they've done 60 percent of their work. Getting the lede right means you have done thorough reporting, you've judged the impact of your information, you've identified the elements that will convey that impact, you have thought a lot about organization, and you have chosen words that will convey the significance concisely. It is also a good indication that the rest of the story will be as well thought out. If you've got a handle on what you need to tell people first, then it follows that that sorting process will go a long way toward rank-ordering the rest of your information. It will also show you what doesn't need to be in the story. So getting the lede right doesn't just take care of your focus at the top of the story. It gives you a pretty good idea that the rest of the story will be right, too.

Try, Try Again

Getting the lede right takes practice and a lot of rewriting. Never settle for your first version. Try again and again to make it better. Almost always, you will. If you think you haven't gotten it right on the first try, good for you. Only complacent fools think the first version of their lede is good enough. If you're having to rewrite your lede several times, it means you care as much about your story as you ought to.

Impact, Elements, Words

What do you think about when you're trying to decide on a lede? Several things. Your lede is the place to put your *impact, elements, words* mantra into practice:

1. As emphasized in Chapter 4, *focus on the impact:* rational, emotional or a combination of the two.

2. When you've made that decision, *look for the two or three elements that will best show the impact.* In most news stories, the who and the what will be essential. The other elements tend to change with the circumstances. Sometimes it is appropriate to focus on how, or where. Less often, the significant element is when. As you might imagine, the toughest question we have to answer is often why. In fact, many times we have to rely on follow-up stories to determine and explain the why behind the news we wrote today.

3. *Nail the words.* Even if you get the impact and elements right, you can still screw up a lede if you get the words wrong. Impact and elements are necessary, but not sufficient. Concentrate on using nouns and verbs as your principal words. Nouns and verbs *show* your audience the impact. Adjectives and adverbs tend to *tell* the impact. Show, don't tell. But let the words serve the facts. Never go beyond the facts to make the words carry more impact.

Without any of those three steps in the process, you wind up with ledes that have the wrong focus, or are entirely unfocused, or are cluttered, unclear and wordy. You can be the most stylish writer in the world, but if you haven't made the right call about impact and elements, your story will be all sizzle and no steak. Similarly, without the right words, your story is the steak that nobody will want to eat. Again, this is a long way of telling you to think first, then write. What we've been doing is practicing a *systematic* way to think.

Writing a Lede

Now let's try to write a lede from one of the sets of facts you were given in Exercise 4 ("Police Report"). In subsequent chapters, when we focus in turn on ledes for print, broadcast and online news, we will look at how the needs and strengths of each medium shape ledes. For now, by trying to organize, structure and find good words for ledes we can develop the discipline journalists need to serve any mass audience.

By way of illustration, let's consider first what might happen if we tried to write a lede without going through our *impact, elements, words* process. (See Box 5.2.)

Box 5.2

REWRITING LEDES

First try: With crime becoming a major problem in our community, it was not surprising that a shocked janitor at Valleydale Presbyterian Church discovered at 6 A.M. this morning that valuables had been brazenly burglarized from the office of the youth minister.

Second try: The janitor of Valleydale Presbyterian Church discovered at 6 A.M. that valuables had been burglarized from the office of the youth minister.

Third try: Valleydale Presbyterian Church was burglarized sometime during the night, with the thief escaping with videos, a VCR and a television set worth $600.

Fourth try: A thief broke into Valleydale Presbyterian Church last night, taking videos, a VCR and a television set worth $600.

Final version: A thief shattered a window, forced open a drawer and stole sex-education videos from Valleydale Presbyterian Church last night.

If you have had some experience writing essays your first notions are probably to look for a theme statement, to work from the general to the specific, and to pay some attention to narrative flow. Something like this:

With crime becoming a major problem in our community, it was not surprising that a shocked janitor at Valleydale Presbyterian Church discovered at 6 A.M. this morning that valuables had reportedly been brazenly burglarized from the office of the youth minister.

Well . . . Remember when we said that good ledes are succinct and focused, so the audience doesn't have to spend a lot of time understanding them? About the first thing we notice is that this lede is way too long—40 words instead of the 20 we should be shooting for. Worse, many of those words are unnecessary, work against each other or reflect assumptions or opinion rather than fact. For example, do we know the introductory clause is true? Does our audience? Is crime becoming a big problem locally?

The lede also tells us that it is no surprise that the church was burglarized, then three words later reports that the janitor was "shocked" to discover the burglary. That's not only contradictory; it assumes that we know how the janitor felt.

Some of the words are redundant: "6 A.M. this morning" implies that there can be a 6 A.M. in the afternoon or the evening. Nope. Also, the janitor has both discovered the burglary and found that items were "reportedly" burglarized. If the janitor discovered the burglary, why can't he say definitively that the stuff was missing? *Brazenly* isn't redundant, but as an adverb it is a "tell me" word rather than a "show me" word.

Okay. Let's start over, using our *impact, elements, words* mantra this time. First, impact: Remember that we can look for rational impact, emotional impact or some combination of the two. Will the information we have affect most of our audience in a rational or in an emotional way? For most of us, the theft of $600 worth of stuff from a church office will cause no financial harm, even if we are members of the church. And even if we knew who the thief or thieves were, most of us would not be acquainted with him, her or them. So for practically everyone in our audience, the rational impact of this information is going to be zilch.

When it comes to emotional impact, though, for many of us it's a different story. Granted, the emotional impact is not going to be on the order of seeing cancer survivor Lance Armstrong win his seventh Tour de France, but we owe our audience the duty of showing whatever impact there is. The fact that somebody broke into a church, of all places, will probably anger many people. Then again, there are those among us who might find something amusing or ironic in the story. When we think about impact first, we realize that for most of us, the impact of this story will be emotional.

Our next step is to identify the elements that convey that emotional impact. Remember that we have six choices—who, what, when, where, why, and how—but that we want our lede to focus only on those elements that show our audience the emotional impact most clearly. Certainly, *what* happened—a burglary—carries much of the impact. What else? How about *where*? It wasn't just a burglary, it was the burglary of a church. The *who* is important in a lot of stories, but is it in this one? The only person we have identified is the janitor who discovered the burglary, and the janitor is not really central to the impact. The principal *who*—the thief—is unidentified. So for this lede, the *who* is not something to focus on.

Our audience will need to know the *when* at some point, of course, but again, *when* the burglary happened carries less emotional impact than *what* happened and *where*. As in many stories, the *why* is pretty much a puzzle at this point, so there isn't a lot of benefit in dwelling on it. But how about the *how*? We know something about how the thief got in, and it involved force. That carries some emotional impact; not only was the target a church, but whoever did it thought nothing of forcing his way in.

So far we have identified the *what*, the *where* and the *how* as our principal elements. I think we're doing pretty well. But keep in mind, there may be more than one of each who, what, when, where, why, and how to pay attention to. I suggested that for some in our audience the emotional impact might strike in the form of humor or irony. Is there an element that shows that? Sure—*what* was taken—sex-education videos, from a church, no less.

Right. Let's look at where we are in our three-step process: Impact—emotional. Elements: *What* (two whats, actually), *where* and *how*. Doing the first two steps right is necessary to write a successful lede, but not sufficient. Time for step three: Words.

Let's try another lede, this time wrestling with words that will show the two *whats*, the *where*, and the *how* that convey the emotional impact to our audience.

> *The janitor of Valleydale Presbyterian Church discovered at 6 A.M. that valuables had been burglarized from the office of the youth minister.*

Closer. By focusing on the emotional impact we've eliminated the long theme-statement introductory clause, the unsupported assumptions and a lot of unnecessary words. We've gotten to the *what* element—the burglary—somewhat sooner. But there are still problems. First, the structure of this lede still focuses on the who—the janitor—and when the theft was discovered. We've determined that neither of those elements carries much of the freight in this lede. Worse, as a result of this structure other critical elements, the two *whats*—the burglary and what was taken—are buried deep in the sentence. And our focus on one of the *whats*—the stuff that was taken—is fuzzy; we identify it only as "valuables." We have another critical element, *where*, identified, but we probably waste words by being too specific at this point. The emotional impact is served simply by knowing it was the church without showing at this point that it was the youth minister's office.

Finally, there is no attention at all paid to the *how*, the third crucial element we identified. So let's take another crack at it.

Valleydale Presbyterian Church was burglarized sometime during the night, with the thief escaping with videos, a VCR and a television set worth $600.

Better, even though it's a little longer than the previous version. By now we are focusing on a couple of the critical elements: the *what*—the burglary and what was taken—and the *where*—the church. Still no attention paid to the *how*, though. We need to fix that. And you might notice that there is something still a tad fuzzy about what was taken. That fuzziness means we lose some of the emotional impact.

Right. Another try:

A thief broke into Valleydale Presbyterian Church last night, taking videos, a VCR and a television set worth $600.

The good news is that the lede is a lot tighter, we are beginning to focus on the crucial elements, and our words are starting to show the impact. For example, instead of just referring to a burglary or the church being *burglarized*—an awkward word anyway—we are now showing some action: "A thief broke into Valleydale Presbyterian Church . . ." That alone will go a long way toward conveying the emotional impact to our audience.

But we're not quite there. How the thief broke in can be sharpened even more, and in attempting to show what was taken, we have let our focus wander. It's not the television set, the VCR or the $600 value of the items that will carry the emotional impact here. It's the nature of those tapes, isn't it?

A thief shattered a window, forced open a drawer and stole sex-education videos from Valleydale Presbyterian Church last night.

Now our words show the emotional impact. They focus graphically on *what* happened and *what* was taken, *where,* and *how.* Because we have relied on verbs and nouns and a simple sentence structure, our audience can feel the emotional impact of this story. We have also stayed with what we know, avoiding characterizations or judgments that are based on assumptions or speculation. By the way, the lede is exactly 20 words.

It's not a perfect lede. We refer to "a thief" when there could have been more than one perpetrator involved. We do know that a witness saw one person walking away from the church in the middle of the night. I suppose we could substitute "somebody" for "a thief" to accommodate the uncertainty, but the word choice sounds a little lame. We begin the lede with "A thief" even though we decided that the *who* does not carry the emotional impact of this story. At least now the focus is on the thief and not the janitor, and introducing a person into the lede, even an unidentified one, helps us show action graphically rather than passively as "burglarized." So maybe you can continue to fiddle with this lede and improve on it even more. That's the point. What we have is the product of several tries, each better than the one before it. Get used to doing that with your ledes, and your stories.

We should realize that this is not the most earthshaking story that will appear on today's Web page, tonight's newscast, or in tomorrow's *Jeffersonville Herald.* It would be structured somewhat differently for broadcast, as will be shown in a subsequent chapter. In fact, it might not even make it onto the newscast, and if it's in the regional edition of the paper, it will be short. Doing news is like that: Sometimes you put in a lot of work, trample some shrubs and annoy a few people for what looks like a pretty skimpy payoff. Then again, sometimes audiences will reach out and hold onto something more tightly than you thought they would.

If you still don't think there is much impact in some clown stealing sex-ed videos from a church, bear with me. This same *impact, elements, words* process will help you later, when things in Valleydale start to get pretty hairy. For now, I wanted to kick us off with a simple set of facts. As with any story, whatever impact these facts will have on the audience should be apparent from the lede. Again, as you work through the exercises in this textbook, and the events and issues become more complex and more significant, remember that you should be able to use this process no matter how important or complex the story.

Ethics

We owe it to our audiences and to the subjects of our stories not to go beyond the facts in trying to show the importance of the story. Make your words serve the facts; never twist the facts to accommodate snappier writing. Let facts in context carry your lede and your story; keep your opinions and assumptions to yourself.

Some textbooks and writing teachers argue that a well-written lede should entice everyone to read, watch or listen to the story. In a world of multiple media outlets competing for audiences' limited time, though, that is probably an unrealistic expectation.

A more realistic goal might be for every lede to show everyone in the audience what his or her stake in the story will be. Will the story affect its readers or viewers rationally or emotionally? Will most in the audience find the story essential to their lives? Or is this story discretionary—that is, certainly worth a reader's or viewer's time, but not a matter of life, death, wise parenting or financial solvency? "Selling" a story by misleading an audience is a disservice. It can make journalists seem less trustworthy to their audiences, and audiences less likely to read or watch stories that really are essential to them.

Strategies

In the next several exercises, you will work on finding and writing ledes. In Chapter 6 we will begin working on full stories. Remember the following strategies for writing ledes (see also Box 5.3).

First, even if you use your *impact, elements, words* process conscientiously, it's easy to get lazy writing ledes because you know you will be writing the rest of the story. You will have a tendency to think that whatever crucial information you don't focus on in the lede will be available to your audience later. But if you make the wrong call in your lede, chances are your audience won't get any farther than that. That's why, for the exercises in this chapter, the focus is the lede alone.

Second, for now, keep your ledes to one sentence, and to no more than 20 words, including short words and articles like *a* and *an*. This is challenging, I know, it takes work, but as we've demonstrated in this chapter, you can do it.

Third, focus on nouns and verbs rather than on adjectives and adverbs.

Fourth, always, make the words serve the facts.

Fifth, whether you are writing for the Web, for broadcast or for print, *always read your lede—and the rest of your story—aloud*. No matter what medium you are writing for, stories make a noise in people's heads. If it doesn't sound right, they will not embrace the story, and chances are they won't understand it.

Box 5.3

STRATEGIES FOR LEDES

1. Use your *impact, elements, words* process to organize, structure and choose words for your lede.

2. Keep your ledes to one sentence of 20 words or fewer.

3. Let nouns and verbs do the work of showing your audience the impact. Nouns and verbs show; adjectives and adverbs tell.

4. Never go beyond the facts to grab your audience. Instead, make the words serve the facts.

5. Read your lede aloud. If it doesn't sound right, it isn't. Read it as if it were the only part of the story your audience will see or hear. Is the impact of the story clear?

6. Never settle for your first try. Good ledes are the product of hard work and several rewrites.

Sixth, writing is rewriting. If writing suddenly seems like hard work to you, it's because you're doing it right. Don't settle for your first try.

Exercise 5

Ledes

Go back to Exercise 4 and write a lede for the three sets of facts following the Police Report, which was used as the example in this chapter.

chapter six

Writing for Print

Writers who think their work begins when their fingers first touch the keyboard are bad writers. So are writers who think that a first draft is good enough. Writing is a process that begins with thinking and ends with tinkering. It's also a craft, and the more you practice a craft, the better you get at it. In Chapters 4 and 5 we focused on ledes. In this chapter you will learn more about and then practice the craft of writing complete stories. As you might expect, we will start out modestly, with pretty brief stories. Even with brief stories, though, you will find writing well a challenge.

You can't become or stay a good writer if you don't write every day. People who try to tell you that writing is fun don't know what they're talking about. Writing well is damned hard work, even for gifted writers, and there aren't many of those. The 20th-century author Gertrude Stein said she didn't like writing, but she liked having written. Writing is a pain; *having written*, when you've done it well, is like being in love.

Writing is a process that begins with thinking and ends with tinkering. Doing it well requires dedication, hard work and a willingness to go through many rewrites.

In the pages that follow we will identify and examine some components of news stories in addition to ledes, focusing for now on print media: the *nut graf,* the logically organized *narrative,* as well as *transitions, quotes* and the *kicker.* Learning them will help you organize and shape stories that your audiences find readily understandable.

The Go/No-Go Decision

Not everyone is going to read, watch or listen to every story you write. But just about everybody should read, watch or listen to every lede that you write. Part of our job as journalists is to help people decide whether they ought to stay with a story. Whichever medium you are working in, your lede often functions like the on/off switch for a lamp, allowing an audience to make a decision about whether to be illuminated or not. (Sorry. If you don't like that simile, think about audiences using ledes to make a go/no-go decision on a story.) As we have said already, many news Web sites are set up on that assumption. With a 30-second RDR for television, we won't take our audience much beyond the go/no-go decision. For print stories, the tight, focused lede is especially important to show our audiences what the story is about, because print stories run longer than broadcast copy and are not "chunked"—broken into separate pages or links—the way many Web stories are.

Essential and Discretionary Stories

Naturally, in some stories we write, we want to keep everyone involved, because we think there is something in the story for everyone. With other stories, we know we are serving only part of the audience. For all stories, our goal is to help our audience make that go/no-go decision properly. Your lede should do that. If it does, no one who reads the lede and decides not to read or listen further will be deprived of information that would have affected his or her life significantly. Similarly, if someone reads your lede and decides to stay with the story, you want him or her to think that the story was worth the time. The best way to serve your audience is not to delay the important stuff. Get it in the lede.

What Happened Next? The Logic of Narratives

Whether you are writing for print, broadcast or the Web, the second paragraph of your story should expand on information in your lede. In fact, each sentence and each paragraph of your story should be linked to the one before it and the one after it. One way to make sure you are doing that is to ask yourself what question or questions a paragraph raises, and then answer those questions in the next paragraph. To some extent, all good *narrative* does that, whether you're writing a news story or a novel, even if the only questioned answered is "What happened next?" Keep in mind that news stories are just that—stories. As such, they rely on solid, compelling narrative. With broadcast stories, you will often have the additional tools of sound bites or video to illustrate the story, but your organizing principles should remain the same. Look for stuff that moves the story along.

Building Blocks

You are probably less familiar with the other story components identified at the opening of this chapter: the *nut graf, transitions, quotes* and the *kicker.*

Box 6.1

BUILDING BLOCKS FOR STORIES

1. The *lede.* The top of the story, usually the first sentence. The lede focuses on the story's importance for the audience.

2. The *nut graf.* A summary, shortly after the lede, giving background and context for the story.

3. The *narrative.* The logical organization of the story. Fiction often proceeds chronologically; news stories usually are organized by the importance of the information.

4. *Transitions.* "Road maps" that show the reader where the story is going next.

5. *Quotes.* Verbatim representations of what people involved in the story say. Quotes ensure that stories are about people involved in events and issues, not just about the events and issues.

6. The *kicker.* The end of the story. The kicker is frequently structured to remind audiences that, while the news story has an ending, the people written about must continue to deal with the event or issue.

(See Box 6.1.) Rather than try to define them separately, let's learn what they are by identifying the work that they do. To do that, we will look at a sample story. (See Box 6.2.) In Chapter 1, Tori Baxter was getting ready to write about two Valleydale City Council members attempting to force the resignation of City Manager Ron Allen "Don" Prentice. A workable, impact-oriented lede would probably have read something like this:

> *City Manager Don Prentice's job remains secure for now.*
>   *Impact:* rational. *Elements:* who, what. *Words:* City Manager Don Prentice; job remains secure; for now.

As short as it is, that sentence sends a message to readers and viewers in Valleydale that this is a story that could have a significant effect on their lives. For one thing, the fact that there will be no change for now affects them. The hint in Tori's lede that the situation has existed for a while, and could change, also carries impact for her audience. For audiences outside Valleydale, the lede says that the story carries little rational impact for them. They can continue with the story, but for them it is discretionary, based on how much emotional impact they're looking to derive from a juicy political scrap.

Box 6.2

TORI'S STORY

City Manager Don Prentice's job remains secure for now. *(Lede)*

Last night Prentice survived the latest attempt by two City Council members to force him out. City Council refused to discuss Prentice's performance. And Council members Eaton Wise and Rondah Bullard could not persuade their colleagues to consider a resolution asking Prentice to quit. Mayor Delmer Hostetter called the resolution ill-advised. *(Narrative)*

Wise and Bullard had approached the Finance Committee last week with the same resolution, but the three-member committee also declined to vote on it. Wise and Bullard say the city budget contains irregularities that Prentice won't explain. *(Narrative)*

It was the second time in six months *(Transition)* that Wise and Bullard had sought to have council dismiss the city manager. Wise and Bullard say Prentice is unresponsive to their requests for explanations of what they call the financial irregularities. They have never detailed those publicly. *(Nut graf)*

Wise last night asked the council to go into closed session to discuss Prentice's performance. *(Transition)*

"We don't need to air our dirty laundry in front of the news media," Wise said. "Just look at them out there, champing at the bit. I want to be fair to Mr. Prentice." *(Quote)*

Mayor Hostetter refused to ask council to vote on the request. Council Member T. A. "Tater" Chipps accused Wise of hypocrisy. *(Transition)*

"First, you announce publicly that you want the man's resignation because he's cooking the city books," Chipps said. "Then you say you're trying to protect him." *(Quote)*

Prentice said after the meeting he wasn't surprised by the actions of Wise and Bullard. *(Transition)*

"Call it a vendetta," he said. "They just don't understand municipal finance." He would not elaborate. *(Quote/kicker)*

By the way, when most of the impact of a story is *rational,* and the *who* is one of the key elements that show that impact, using the person's name in the lede is probably a good idea. For stories with *emotional* impact, though, often the *who* conveys that impact more effectively if we look for words that give audiences what I call a *descriptive identification.* For example, one of the scenarios in Exercise 4 concerned a lost child who was rescued by a bloodhound. Had we identified the rescuee in the lede simply as Pat Foster of Eden, we would have lost much of the emotional impact, because practically no one in our audience would have recognized Pat Foster as a child. But by identifying her as "a 3-year-old girl"—a descriptive identification—we bring the emotional impact of the story home to everyone.

So much for what the lede does. Now think about the questions it raises: With respect to the story about Valleydale's city manager, why is Prentice's job security in doubt in the first place? What happened that's protecting him for now? How did that come about? Who was involved? Who are the key players? Notice that the questions the lede raises fall into our focus on the key elements of who and what, but now are expanded to why and how as well. As with the lede, it's probably not a good idea to address all six elements in each succeeding paragraph. Tori focuses her next few paragraphs again on the key elements, and will take care of the less important elements in subsequent paragraphs. In the body of longer stories, she might spend most of a paragraph expanding on a single element.

Let's look at how she builds a few more sentences.

Last night Prentice survived the latest attempt by two City Council members to force him out. City Council refused to discuss Prentice's performance. And Council members Eaton Wise and Rondah Bullard could not persuade their colleagues to consider a resolution asking Prentice to quit. Mayor Delmer Hostetter called the resolution ill-advised.

Wise and Bullard had approached the Finance Committee last week with the same resolution, but the three-member committee also declined to vote on it. Wise and Bullard say the city budget contains irregularities that Prentice won't explain.

So now Tori's audience knows how Prentice's job was saved, who was responsible and how the attempt to fire him came about. By adding a few key sentences she has supported her lede and given her audience a lot more information. And while we are focusing on print stories in this chapter, the sentences above would work pretty well as a 30-second RDR for broadcast. (Try reading them aloud, and time yourself.)

But for her print story Tori has still got to address some important questions: Who, specifically, wants Prentice out? Why? Often she will provide answers to those questions by focusing on the *background* of the story: What happened before last night that got us to this point? Journalists sometimes call that paragraph the *nut graf*—that is, the paragraph (or *graf*) that contains the story's context in a nutshell. Usually, they try to get it into the story by

the third or fourth paragraph, to enable people who may not have been following the story all along to get quickly up to speed:

> *It was the second time in six months that Wise and Bullard had sought to
> have council dismiss the city manager. Wise and Bullard say Prentice is un-
> responsive to their requests for explanations of what they call the financial
> irregularities. They have never detailed those publicly.*

Now we know the principal players in this drama, and the reasons they cite
for wanting the city manager gone. But notice what we still don't know: Is
there any substance to these accusations? As Tori told Faith Palmer in Chapter
1, she hasn't seen any substantiation yet, and she suspects there is a hidden
agenda. So far, she has not been able to discover it. We also have not heard
directly from any of the players involved. What is Prentice's reaction to the firing attempt and to the accusations? Did council members say anything to the
Finance Committee members last night? Did Wise and Bullard support their
recommendation with any comments in the meeting or afterward?

You can see that subsequent paragraphs would probably contain quotes
from the players, plus more detail about what went on last night and the
events leading to the meeting. If that information had not come out at the
meeting, Tori would have known to press the players for explanations afterward. Notice that she has mentioned fairly early in the story that no one has
yet offered details substantiating the accusations made against Prentice.

You can also see how each paragraph in this example is *related to the one
before it and the one after it,* and how each succeeding paragraph addresses
questions raised by the paragraph before it. As Tori gets further into the story,
and even beginning with the nut graf, she uses devices called *transitions* to link
information and help place it in context for the audience. At the beginning of
the nut graf, for instance, she writes: "It was the second time in six months,"
to take her readers from last night's events into the historical context of those
events. Similarly, when Tori gets to *quotes* from the participants, develops her
narrative more fully, and sets up her *kicker,* she will use transitions to introduce each speaker and make clear to her readers that she is again writing about
what happened last night:

> *Wise last night asked the council to go into closed session to discuss Pren-
> tice's performance.*
>   *"We don't need to air our dirty laundry in front of the news media," Wise
> said. "Just look at them out there, champing at the bit. I want to be fair to
> Mr. Prentice."*

> *Mayor Hostetter refused to ask council to vote on the request. Council Member T. A. "Tater" Chipps accused Wise of hypocrisy.*
>
> *"First, you announce publicly that you want the man's resignation because he's cooking the city books," Chipps said. "Then you say you're trying to protect him."*

Transitions often are described as road maps because they show the reader where the story is going next.

Because of the importance of *quotes*—they put people in each story—we will treat them in a separate chapter. For now, notice how they are used here not to provide background or key facts for the story, but to convey the participants' emotions and reactions to what is going on.

The *kicker* is what many journalists call the end of the story. Some stories tend just to peter out. In others, the writer tries to give the story a definite sense of completion. Often, he or she does that by keeping in mind the people involved: While we may be finished describing the event or issue, the lives of the people in the story will go on, and they will continue to have to live with the consequences of the event or issue. Tori knows that the best way to get a sense of that is usually through a quote or paraphrased quote in which the participants show us how they will try to cope with what has happened. So she ends this story by reminding her audience that (1) this story is not simply about something happening, it's about something happening to people; and (2) her account of this event or issue is finished, but the people involved in it will continue to be involved:

> *Prentice said after the meeting he wasn't surprised by the actions of Wise and Bullard.*
>
> *"Call it a vendetta," he said. "They just don't understand municipal finance." He would not elaborate.*

Remembering the Mantra: *Impact, Elements, Words*

You can see how Tori thought about impact and elements to choose for her audience the information she decided they really needed to know. But if she had stopped there, nobody would have benefited. Notice how hard she worked on the third step: choosing the words that would *show* her readers and viewers what was important and why. Like Tori, you will learn to use words to craft raw material into a useful—maybe even a graceful—finished product.

Because there are only 26 letters in our alphabet, you would think it wouldn't be hard to choose the right words, and only as many as you need. But if you're good at math you have some idea of how many possible combinations we have for those letters, and even if just a tiny fraction of that number constitute recognizable words, that's enough choices to drive anybody crazy.

Fortunately, we know how to reject most of the choices out of hand. We wouldn't consider using *pizza*, for example, when we mean *gun*. It's when we get to the fine-tuning that it gets hard. Was it really a pizza, or a stromboli? Did the assailant use a gun, or a rifle? Do we need to introduce a relative clause with *that* or *which*? And what about the sequence of the words? Should we be in passive voice, where the receiver of the action gets the emphasis, or in active, where the doer is emphasized? If I move the location of *only* in the sentence, how will it change the meaning of the sentence?

When a story is poorly written, it's usually for one or more of three reasons: The focus is wrong, the organization is wrong, or the words are wrong. We have seen how to use impact and elements to make sure our *focus* and *organization* are right. In Chapter 2 we talked about eliminating jargon, clichés and wordiness to help make sure the *words* are right. But finding the right words is not just about cutting out jargon, clichés and detritus.

Ethics

We need to be careful about the words we choose, and the combinations in which we use them. Careful use of words will make us more stylish writers. More importantly, precision is essential if our audiences are to understand our stories the way we meant them to be understood. We owe our audiences accuracy and clarity, and we owe the subjects of our stories fairness. Taking your audience's understanding for granted is a sure way to mislead. And because audiences for news are large and diverse, most of the time we have to be careful to stick with words and constructions practically everybody recognizes. Contrary to the snide old observation that newspaper or broadcast stories are written to be understood by someone with an eighth-grade education, stories should be written for a person who is trying to understand a lot of unfamiliar information in a short time. As writing coach Don Fry says, audiences aren't stupid, they just don't know much. So we need to be accurate, and we need to be clear. We should avoid jargon, technical language and slang.

As a journalist, your primary obligation is to serve your audience. Often, as in one of the exercises below, you will make decisions on behalf of your audience that change the focus of a story from what your sources of information believe it should be. In the example above, Council members Wise and Bullard probably want us to report categorically that City Manager Prentice is messing with the city budget and should be fired. As journalists serving our audience, though, our obligation is, first, to show the accusations in their appropriate context—including the absence of evidence at this point—and second, to keep digging until we can get at the truth of what is going on. That changes the focus from what Wise and Bullard might like it to be.

News releases are a good example of a source of information with a particular focus. The writer of the news release is interested in publicizing an event or in promoting his or her organization. You might find a more appropriate focus once you have judged the information in terms of impact on your audience. On such occasions it is not only permissible to change the focus; you should look on it as your obligation to your audience to do so.

Strategies

Keep these tips in mind, several of them identified by Ken Metzler in *Newswriting Exercises* (see Box 6.3):

Use the first two parts of your process—*impact* and *elements*—to make sure your focus and organization are right.

Use *words* carefully to make sure your work on focus and organization is not wasted.

Write your lede so that your audience can make the right go/no-go decision for the rest of the story.

Link each sentence and each paragraph to the one before it and the one after it. Use transitions where you need them.

Use the nut graf, narrative, transitions, quotes and the kicker to move your story along clearly and compellingly.

Use short sentences, short words, short paragraphs. Keep your average sentence length to fewer than 20 words, 15 for broadcast copy. Avoid

Box 6.3

STRATEGIES FOR WRITING WELL

1. Use *impact* and *elements* to help you check your *focus* and *organization.*

2. Choose your *words* carefully. They will show your audience what your story is about.

3. A good *lede* should help your audience decide whether to read, watch or listen to the rest of the story.

4. Use *transitions* to link sentences and paragraphs. Create road maps for your audience.

5. Your *narrative,* including your *nut graf, transitions, quotes* and *kicker,* should move your story along with clarity.

6. *Keep sentences, words and paragraphs short.* Focus on nouns and verbs. Stay with one thought per sentence, one idea per paragraph.

7. Show your audiences where information came from by *attributing* carefully and often.

8. *Identify* your sources. Unnamed sources arouse suspicion in audiences, with good reason.

9. *Stick to the facts,* and place them in their appropriate context. Use your City Directory to check accuracy.

10. *Read your story aloud.* Even if it is written for a newspaper or the Web, it should *sound* right.

long introductory clauses. Stay in the active voice, usually, and use simple declarative structure most of the time. Focus on nouns and verbs. Limit your paragraphs to no more than five lines. Stay with one thought per sentence, one idea per paragraph.

Attribute. It's important for audiences to know where information is coming from, so that they can judge how much faith to put in it. Acknowledge the source of your information frequently, although not necessarily in every sentence. When your source changes, let your audience know that. But be careful not to overattribute. An editor from the Associated Press says he once worked at a newspaper that made him attribute to local police the fact that fall was coming ("Fall is just around the corner, police say.").

Identify. Avoid using unnamed sources. People put less faith in them, for good reason. Identify everyone in your story. Stories are not about things happening, they are about things happening to people or about the people involved in issues. When we take identifiable people out of the story, we let things happen in a vacuum. As a result, audiences are less able to see the story concretely, and the impact of the information in it is diminished. Not identifying the people in our stories also tends to turn them into statistics. We should write about human beings, not statistics. Remember also that sometimes, particularly with stories for which most of the impact is emotional, a *descriptive identification* in the lede will show that impact more effectively than simply naming the person. Of course, the name should be provided later in the story. Occasionally, you will choose, or be persuaded, not to include a name in a story. For example, when witnesses might be placed in danger by being identified, news media grant them anonymity. Sometimes we decide not to name someone because it would embarrass him or her unnecessarily. If you decide not to name someone in a story, always tell your audience why you made that decision, because it is the exception to the rule.

Be accurate. Fiction writers must be true to the characters they create and the situations they put them in, but they get to make up the characters, the situations and their dialogue. Reporters don't. Stick to the facts, in context. Double-check spellings, addresses, times, places, quotes. Wear out your City Directory.

Read it aloud, whether you're writing for print, broadcast or the Web. If you can't get through a sentence in one breath, it's probably too long. Stories make a noise in people's heads. The noise should not be discordant. If it doesn't *sound* right, it isn't right.

In the exercises that follow you will not have as much on your plate as Tori Baxter did after the City Council meeting. You can convey the impact and the crucial elements in these exercises in about three or four short sentences. Most of these stories will need little background. Remember your process: *impact, elements, words.* Remember to approach your lede so that your audience can make a go/no-go decision for the rest of the brief story based on it. And remember to link each sentence and each paragraph to the one before it and the one after it.

Exercise 6

Brief Stories

Loitering Program

"Jesus Does Not Hang Out in Shopping Malls," will be presented this coming Sunday night at 7 P.M. at the Grace Presbyterian Church, which is located at 506 N. Main St. in Valleydale.

Mr. Elton Sowell, proprietor of Lloyd's Bristo in Valleydale and President of the Valleydale Downtown Development Association, will discuss loitering from a merchant's prospective. Recent changes in the state's loitering laws will be discussed by Lt. John Pollard of the Valleydale Police Force.

Also, young people from the Jeffersonville Chapter of Loiterers Anonymous, an organization that uses contact with Jesus Christ to rehabilitate young people addicted to hanging out in shopping malls, will speak. They will share their experiences.

The Reverend Fred Fender, pastor of the Church, says that the public is invited and refreshments will be served.

Baby Gator

A drowned baby alligator was found in a sewage pipe yesterday evening. Its body was "rolled up in a little ball," according to one Valleydale city worker, and had blocked the line. As a result, about 300 homes in the Rebel Heights and Country Club sections of town had sewage backed up in their homes for about four hours. Fred "Rick" Jones, city sanitation supervisor, believes someone brought the baby reptile home from a vacation to Florida and tried to flush it down the toilet after it either died or they got worried because it was getting too big. In large cities such as New York the reptiles have been known to survive such treatment and live and grow in the sewer systems. The city has no plans to try to locate the perpetrator, but Jones warns citizens about the consequences of such actions. Besides the inconvenience to neighbors, it is a violation of Municipal Ordinance 91-5, punishable by a fine of up to $500, to flush live animals down toilets in the city limits. Goldfish not exceeding three inches in length are excepted.

Climbing Accident

Yesterday about 3 P.M. three young men were climbing the face of a cliff at Eden Pass. They were identified as Billy Joe Tolliver, 22, of Bluefield; his uncle, Sporrin Spruance, 35, of Rock Falls; and Tolliver's younger brother, Joey, 10. They were anchoring themselves to the rock face as they climbed. It is about 200 feet to the top. As they neared the top, several of their anchors pulled out.

The cliff face is called "The Old Man of Eden" because from a distance it looks like a human face. It is a favorite spot of local high-angle rock climbers, even though a county ordinance makes it an offense that carries a fine of up to $500. In the past 50 years over a dozen people have been killed climbing it.

The two older climbers grabbed hold of creases in the rock face as they fell, saving themselves, but 10-year-old Joey fell another 40 feet before catching a limb and hanging on, 50 feet above the rocky bank of the river. He screamed frantically, but not one of about two dozen people on the ground tried to climb to his aid. His brother and uncle were unable to descend to him. After five minutes the branch broke and Joey fell to the rocks below. Child pronounced dead on arrival at Jed Stewart Hospital in Valleydale.

chapter seven

Story Forms and Organizing Stories

In Chapter 6 you worked on complete but brief stories. In this chapter, we'll take the plunge into writing a longer story for Tori Baxter's newspaper, the *Jeffersonville Herald*. It will include substantially more information than you have used for the brief newspaper stories you wrote at the end of Chapter 6. But the process will be about the same, and your experience with weighing and selecting information has already helped you organize significant amounts of it by relative importance. That should give you a substantial head start when you write a full-length newspaper story. In Chapters 8 and 9, respectively, we will look at writing for broadcast and the Web.

First, an inviolable rule: Whether, as a journalist, you work from your own notes, from clippings or file tape or from documents, and whether you're writing for print, broadcast or the Web, *compose your story in the computer from the first draft.* There simply isn't time on deadline to do a handwritten draft. Once you get used to it, you'll find that composing in the computer is much easier than writing an article out longhand, because it's so much easier to make changes to your work.

The Choices: Story Forms

At some point when your reporting is nearly done, you will have to face a blank computer screen, a truly scary confrontation. When you were a little kid you probably clung to a security blanket or your teddy bear when you had to face the world. Many a journalist will face a blank computer screen by doing pretty much the same thing: Her teddy bear is her knowledge of several *story forms* that journalists may choose from: the inverted pyramid, the hourglass, the anecdotal or *Wall Street Journal* form, the classic chronological narrative. You will learn even more forms for broadcast and the Web. Of course, you can invent your own form, which might even work, but most of us don't have the guts to do that when that blank screen is staring back at us.

In the paragraphs that follow, I have included examples of what the ledes for three story forms might look like. For longer versions of the same story forms, see the accompanying boxes.

The *inverted pyramid* puts heavy emphasis on the lede and the first few paragraphs, cramming every bit of important information into the top of the story. It is called the inverted pyramid because it is so top heavy:

> BAGHDAD—A U.S. Army solider was killed today and two were injured when the armored vehicle they were riding in was struck by a rocket-propelled grenade fired by Iraqi insurgents just north of the city, the U.S. Central Command reported.

As you can see in Box 7.1, the inverted pyramid story eventually tapers to a much less significant point at the bottom. The inverted pyramid form does not rely much on quotes. It focuses on things happening, not on the people involved. Its advantage is that it is a fast and efficient way to organize your writing when you're facing a tight deadline and your information is confined to distinct facts. Its bare-bones reliance on facts also leaves room for a good bit more development in later versions of the story, or in follow-up stories.

But for the reader, the inverted pyramid has a number of disadvantages. For one, as in the example above, the lede frequently focuses on all six elements—who, what, when, where, why and how—nearly equally. As shown in Chapter 5, that can make for fuzzy focus and long sentences that are hard

Box 7.1

THE INVERTED PYRAMID STORY

BAGHDAD—A U.S. Army solider was killed today and two were injured when the armored vehicle they were riding in was struck by a rocket-propelled grenade fired by Iraqi insurgents just north of the city, the U.S. Central Command reported.

The Pentagon identified the dead soldier as Specialist First Class Homer Dempsey of Loafer's Glory, N.C. He was the 257th U.S. soldier killed in Iraq since the U.S.-led invasion in April, the 150th to die since President Bush declared an end to major combat in June. The ranks and identities of the two injured soldiers were not disclosed. Both were expected to recover.

A Central Command spokeswoman said the three were patrolling an area north of the city that has been unsettled for weeks.

for a reader to understand. For another, by making it difficult to get people into a story, the inverted pyramid tends to make for dry reading devoid of the human element. And the way it leaves the least important information for last gives the reader little sense of narrative or of completion when the story ends. Studies have shown that only longtime readers of newspapers readily understand inverted pyramid stories, probably because they have had years of experience deciphering them.

Like the inverted pyramid, the *hourglass* story takes its name from its shape. It too is top heavy, beginning with a heavy emphasis on facts high in the story so audiences can see how the story will affect them. It then "narrows" to what is usually a brief chronological narrative of an event or how an issue developed.

> BAGHDAD—A U.S. Army solider died today when Iraqi insurgents attacked his armored vehicle just north of the city.
>
> A Central Command spokeswoman identified the victim as Specialist First Class Homer Dempsey, 20, of Loafer's Glory, N.C. She said two other soldiers were injured in the attack but are expected to recover. She did not release their names but confirmed they were members of Dempsey's unit.
>
> The spokeswoman gave this account of the incident: . . .

The hourglass story then "widens" again by focusing on how the event or issue has affected the participants, relying more on quotes than the inverted pyramid story does. (See Box 7.2.) The human-interest elements of the story are often in the lower "bulge."

Box 7.2

THE HOURGLASS STORY

BAGHDAD—A U.S. Army solider died today when Iraqi insurgents attacked his armored vehicle just north of the city.

A Central Command spokeswoman identified the victim as Specialist First Class Homer Dempsey, 20, of Loafer's Glory, N.C. She said two other soldiers were injured in the attack but are expected to recover. She did not release their names but confirmed they were members of Dempsey's unit.

The spokeswoman gave this account of the incident:

About 7 P.M. Tuesday, the Bradley Fighting Vehicle in which Dempsey was riding entered an area that has been unsettled for several weeks. Dempsey's unit had been patrolling for looters for several days, she said.

As the vehicle approached a former power substation, a single rocket-propelled grenade struck the front of it. Occupants of the Bradley vehicle said the missile appeared to have been fired from behind an abandoned car, the spokeswoman said.

The two injured soldiers were evacuated by helicopter to a field hospital, she said, but Dempsey was killed outright.

At the former police station that serves as Charlie Company headquarters, Dempsey's comrades remembered him as a quiet kid.

"He wasn't the gung-ho type," said Cpl. Brian Essex, of Stamford, Conn. "But he took his job seriously. Quiet courage, I think they call it."

Dempsey's squad leader, Staff Sgt. Billy Kimball of Moultrie, La., was still shaken 12 hours after the attack.

"They did everything right," he said of the patrol. "No grandstanding, no foolhardiness. Dempsey was a professional, even though he was just a kid.

"There are just no damned guarantees over here."

The *anecdotal* form is often used when a journalist is trying to explain a large or complex issue in human terms. Often, he or she will begin the story with an example, or anecdote, hence its name. The anecdote is intended to illustrate how one person or family has been affected by an event or issue—a change in the law or public policy, for example, or a natural disaster.

BAGHDAD—The death of Specialist First Class Homer Dempsey sent a shock wave through his buddies in Charlie Company.

When a rocket-propelled grenade, the weapon of choice of many Iraqi insurgents, took out the Bradley Fighting Vehicle the 20-year-old Dempsey was riding in last week, the boredom of weeks of patrol was shattered by the sudden realization of what's at stake in the U.S.-led occupation.

"Homer was a terrific kid," said his squad leader, Staff Sgt. Billy Kimball of Moultrie, La. "He understood that we need to win these people's hearts and minds."

Kimball paused.

"Their hearts, their minds. Our blood. I'm beginning to wonder how much it will take."

Then the writer will broaden the focus of the story with a well-crafted nut graf. (See Box 7.3.)

In this example, the story is about more than the event of Dempsey's death. The death is the anecdote that introduces more complex elements—the

Box 7.3

THE ANECDOTAL STORY

BAGHDAD—The death of Specialist First Class Homer Dempsey sent a shock wave through his buddies in Charlie Company.

When a rocket-propelled grenade, the weapon of choice of many Iraqi insurgents, took out the Bradley Fighting Vehicle the 20-year-old Dempsey was riding in last week, the boredom of weeks of patrol was shattered by the sudden realization of what's at stake in the U.S.-led occupation.

"Homer was a terrific kid," said his squad leader, Staff Sgt. Billy Kimball of Moultrie, La. "He understood that we need to win these people's hearts and minds."

Kimball paused.

"Their hearts, their minds. Our blood. I'm beginning to wonder how much it will take."

The men of Charlie Company are learning the lesson that thousands of their comrades throughout Iraq have learned in hundreds of ways since the U.S.-led invasion began in April. Critics of the occupation say that administration and Pentagon officials should have known that acceptance by Iraqis of an American-led presence would not be universal.

That thinking by planners meant the occupation force is dangerously small, those critics say, and U.S. soldiers don't have the resources to protect each other and keep order.

difficulty of the soldiers' task in Iraq, the debate over whether troop strength is adequate for the mission, the adequacy of their equipment. The anecdotal story form is sometimes called the *Wall Street Journal* form because that newspaper developed it in a special way. While the *Wall Street Journal* form begins with an anecdote, it is often reserved for long, complex stories, and because of that it has some structural features that other anecdotal stories might lack.

Using Your Knife and Fork: Form Follows Function

The first thing to remember about any of these story forms—or any one that you devise yourself—is that *the form serves the story.* As one of my journalism professors, the University of Florida's Rob Pierce, used to say in a different context, "Use your knife when you need your knife and your fork when you need your fork." The goal is for your audience to understand what you are saying in the way you meant it to be understood. Use the story form that will best do that. Some journalists, especially when they are on tight deadlines, will still try to cram every story into the inverted pyramid form. As mentioned, that may be all right for people who have been reading newspapers for years. For everybody else, though, it's tough sledding.

The caveat to other story forms is that they require more reporting than do inverted pyramid stories. You will need more information and numerous quotes from the people affected by events and issues, so you will have to spend more time with them and interview them in more depth. You will also need more time to write. Again, instead of choosing a story form and trying to cram your story into it, let your story dictate the form you choose. (Of course, if you're on a tight deadline, your choices might be quite limited.)

All story forms have some parts in common. You won't use all those parts in every story. We have discussed most of those parts in previous chapters. Keep them in mind as you think about organizing your story: the *lede*, the *nut graf*, the *body* or *narrative, transitions, quotes* and the *kicker*.

Ethics

Having a number of story forms in our tool kit allows us to focus on some ethical issues as we do our work as journalists. For one thing, we should be able to recognize that many stories involve more than two sides. We need to be able to find ways to represent the multifaceted nature of many events and issues. Stories that focus only on two sides, represented by marginalized, strident advocates from each end of the spectrum, do a disservice to your audiences, because many people find themselves deeply ambivalent about difficult issues and seek compromise solutions they can live with. Knowing of different story forms also allows us to choose many ways to frame stories instead of framing every story primarily as conflict.

Most importantly, perhaps, using the appropriate story form allows us to write about people, not statistics. It allows our audiences—and us—to care about the people we write about, and to remember that things don't happen in a vacuum. But we should be careful about how we use the forms, and the anecdotal form in particular. When you portray someone briefly in an anecdote to lead your audience into a complex issue, remember to return to that person or those people later. We should show our audiences what happened to the people in our anecdote, how they must adjust their lives to an event or issue. As the moral philosopher Immanuel Kant said, treat people as ends in themselves, never merely as means to an end.

Finally, keep in mind that a number of recent journalistic scandals involving plagiarism or fabrication probably resulted from the reporter trying to fill a story form with what he or she didn't have—a compelling anecdote, dramatic quotes, or the human face on a story. Do your own reporting, do it carefully, and do a lot of it.

Strategies

Before you try to decide which story form to use, always familiarize yourself thoroughly with the facts, quotes and details from your reporting. Then do the first two steps of your *impact, elements, words* process. Then think about the strengths and weaknesses of each story form. That should help you match your story form to your story. Remember that story forms are not straitjackets; they should enable rather than hinder you in writing a story your audience will understand. You might even find yourself combining elements of several forms.

Often, as in the exercises that follow, you will receive information in the form of a news release or statement that is organized according to the agenda of the person or group issuing the release. As discussed in Chapter 6, your agenda should be your audience's. Evaluate the information you have based on the impact of the story for your audience. Sometimes the emphasis you

Box 7.4

STRATEGIES FOR USING STORY FORMS

1. Before you write, familiarize yourself with your reporting—facts, quotes and details.

2. As always, look for the impact, then find the elements that show that impact.

3. Match the story form you choose to your reporting. Consider the strengths and weaknesses of each form.

4. Make your story form work for you. It should enable rather than hinder you in writing a story your audience will understand.

5. When you are working from a news release, remember to keep your audience in mind. That might mean using a different focus than is in the news release. You might need to do additional reporting as a result.

decide on, the impact and elements you choose, will take you in a different direction from the one the information source highlights. When that is the case, it's not only okay to change the focus from that in the news release, it's your obligation to your audience to do so. Often, pursuing that focus will involve additional reporting, as in this exercise. That's your job, too. Depending on the exercise your instructor chooses, you will be taking notes in class on an interview with Dr. Pritchard or Ms. Trump, or both. (See Box 7.4.)

Exercise 7

Building a Story Using Story Forms

For Immediate Release

There will be a one-day conference, "Domestic Violence among Older Women: Black and Blue and Gray," Tuesday, Nov. 17, in the West Meeting Room of the Inn at Howler's Bluff, Rt. 22.

The conference is jointly sponsored by The Hope Project and the Department of Sociology at Virginia Presbyterian University. It will last from 9:30 A.M. until 3 P.M. and the $15 registration fee includes a box lunch.

The conference will focus on the problem of spouse and partner abuse among older women, those who have attained the age of 55 at least. A variety of interesting and informative speakers have been scheduled.

The conference will open with a welcoming address from Glynnis Santabrie, education coordinator for The Hope Project. She will introduce Murray Klemperer of the State Division of Health and Human Services in Richmond, who will discuss the statewide funding situation for older battered women.

Then Ella Kramer, associate professor of sociology at VPU and acting department head, will introduce the keynote speaker, The Hope Project's Executive Director Anne-Marie Pritchard, Ph.D., who will lecture on the sociology of spouse abuse among older couples, focusing on differences from younger couples. Her talk, "Do Not Go Violent Into That Good Night," will include tips for older women to determine whether they are in an abusive relationship and how to get out of it.

The Hope Project is the Blue Ridge County area's advocacy agency for victims of domestic, dating and sexual violence. It was chartered in 1984.

Interested persons may preregister by calling the Department of Sociology at VPU, phone 555-8888, or The Hope Project at 555-8000. Registrations will also be accepted at the door. The $15 registration fee includes lunch.

For Immediate Release

The Virginia Municipal Finance Managers Association has announced the election of Luverne Trump as its president.

The organization represents finance directors from cities and counties across Virginia. At its meeting Sept. 30, the 200-member association unanimously picked Ms. Trump, Finance Manager of Mountain City, to lead it for the next year. Her term will begin Jan. 1. Until recently, Trump had been finance director in Valleydale, a post she held for 11 years. Mountain City, population 35,000, recently suffered a budget crisis precipitated by the loss of tax revenue when the city's biggest employer shut down it's plant. Trump faces the challenge of helping the city absorb that loss.

Ms. Trump was one of the first African American women in the South to serve as a municipal finance director. She is the first African American president of the VMFMA. Previously, Trump, 44, served as treasurer of the organization. A native of Beausoleil, she has a bachelor's degree in accounting and an MBA, both from the University of Virginia.

For more information about the VMFMA, contact publicity chair Hiram Flurtz at 703-555-1010.

8

Writing for Broadcast

In addition to its newspapers, the *Jeffersonville Herald*'s parent company owns numerous radio and TV stations. One TV station, Channel 5, serves the Jeffersonville area. Unlike the newspaper, though, the TV station can't vary its news coverage for different zones, so its viewers in Steubenburg will see the same newscast as viewers in Valleydale. That means that the station seldom sends a reporter and videographer to Blue Ridge County to cover a story, because few stories from Blue Ridge County will be of enough interest to all the station's viewers to merit a one-and-a-half-minute video "package." An exception is a story like Southern Military Academy's first coeducational class, which got a lot of coverage.

In this chapter you will begin to work on brief stories written for broadcast. It is beyond the scope of this textbook to offer you full-fledged training as electronic (broadcast) journalists. In subsequent courses you may well learn to gather and edit sound and video to produce stories for radio and television, and to "write to tape"—that is, build a story script around the story's

Fire Marshall/Brent Courtney Version:1 (Read Only)
(duration: 02'31)

Page 1 of 29

Printed By: de Maria Bob

8/22/2005 9:53:20 AM

((AOC))

((Ligia))
The owners of historic buildings in downtown Lexington can breathe a sign of relief. The city has hired a new fire marshall and formally adopted the state fire code. Lisa Baratta reports.

((TAKE PKG))

2/3FireMarshall

00;02;22

((...problems for sorrounding businesses.)

(TAKE CG))
Lisa Baratta The Rockbridge Report

((...to include the duties of fire marshall.))

((TAKE CG))
Steve Paulk
Fire Marshall—Building Inspector

((...restaurant and an inn under the same roof.))

((TAKE CG))
Shane Gonsalves, Executive Chef
The Sheridan Livery Inn

((Out. . ."Flammable stuff in a kitchen."))

((END TAPE Out: For the Rockbridge Report, I'm Lisa Baratta.))

Figure 8.1. Scripts for television news stories include the words the anchors read, highlighted instructions for studio camera crews, the producer and director, and cues from the story package itself.

visual images. For now, we will focus on stories presented by newsreaders and not accompanied by video or other images. Called "readers," or RDRs, these almost never run longer than 30 seconds. By looking first at RDRs, you should gain an understanding of how and why broadcast writing differs from writing for print media.

The 30-Second RDR

When Tori writes a broadcast story that concerns only Blue Ridge County, Valleydale and Beausoleil, she knows it must be very short, and will probably stand alone without video or accompanying sound. Writing effective broadcast copy means cutting to the chase as quickly as you do in a lede for a print story, but in an even more conversational style. And unlike a print story, while your broadcast copy will expand a bit on your lede, a 30-second RDR will comprise only about seven lines in your computer.

Whether you are writing a RDR or a script for a "package"—a story with video and on-air interviews—your words should show rather than tell, just as they should in print stories. You might think that with visual images to rely on, broadcast writers put less of a premium on words. Not so. Good broadcast writers make the words evoke images, too. Try reading this aloud, from a story by NBC correspondent Steve Dotson about a cave rescue:

> *Imagine slithering through a block of Swiss cheese a mile and a half long. Climbing up a thousand-foot maze, dragging a broken leg. That's what it was like for Emily Mobley. She clawed her way beneath the earth for four days, after an 80-pound boulder slipped and crushed her in a cave. . . .*

Or this, from the late CBS correspondent Charles Kuralt, about Little Big Horn:

> *This is about a place where the wind blows, the grass grows, and a river flows below a hill. There is nothing here but the wind and the grass and the river. But of all places in America, this is the saddest place I know.*

That's a great story, with or without video. You can't *wait* to learn why such a simple place can be so sad.

The Process

Remember the writing process we have been working on since the beginning. Think before you write. Find the impact and the elements, and then wrestle with the words. The first two steps of your process—*impact* and *elements*—will happen pretty much the same as they do for print stories. For example, writing for broadcast begins with thinking about your audience, and how information will affect that audience. Your lede, story focus, and details about a strike by bus drivers in New York City, for example, will be different for an audience in Jeffersonville than for one in New York, so you will probably make different decisions about impact and elements—again, the who, what, when, where, why and how—that show that impact. The Jeffersonville piece might quickly tell viewers that 6,000 New York bus drivers called in sick today, leaving hundreds of thousands of commuters stranded. One more sentence could explain why they're striking and what they want. But in New York, the commuter angle is the most important—who was stranded where, for example. Commuters are your New York audience, and they're directly affected by the strike.

It is in the way we put words together that RDRs differ most from print copy. To help you with the brevity and more conversational style of broadcast writing, try the following.

Use a key facts outline.   Whether you're working from notes, a wire story, or even a print piece you've written, get down to basics by listing facts and then going back and putting them into the best order for telling the story. In other words, use a strategy that helps you focus on answering our fundamental question: "What's this story about?" By getting started this way, you can easily spot key information to home in on. You can also target superfluous information to dump.

Write as you speak, only better.   Remember that radio and TV are conversational media. We begin by writing stories, but then we tell them orally. Tell your story to your audience as though you're telling it to your best friend or your mother. Let's say you saw a church burning in Valleydale. Would you say, "Mom, 150 years of history went up in smoke today"? Not unless your mother was a little strange. You'd say something like, "Mom, Valleydale Presbyterian Church is on fire. Its steeple is about to fall." Use conversational language, but avoid slang and bad taste, and don't insult the intelligence of your listeners or viewers.

Limit yourself to one thought per sentence.   You'll be able to develop clearer, more concise stories if you do. Keep not just your ledes but all your sentences to no more than 20 words. Strive for an average of about 15.

Good broadcast stories should resonate even without pictures.   Using the right words often means using senses besides vision to show your audience what is going on. Read again the examples above from Steve Dotson and Charles Kuralt.

Write for the ear.   Remember, a viewer or listener will hear the story rather than read it. Rely on the active voice, short sentences, short words, a conversational style. Avoid subordinate or relative clauses. Treat them instead as separate sentences.

> *Not*: "Two people were killed today when a light plane, which had just taken off from Jeffersonville Regional Airport, crashed into a mountainside."
>
> *Instead*: "Two people died in a plane crash near Jeffersonville this morning. The Cessna two-seater slammed into a mountain just after taking off from the regional airport."

Look for ways to put the story in the present tense.   Broadcast news strives for more immediacy than print news. But don't lie; if an event has ended by the time you broadcast, put its aftermath in the present tense, not the event itself. "President Bush meets with his cabinet" may be okay as a five-second tease to a newscast, but if the meeting has already happened, focus your story on the result: "Cabinet members are refusing to comment on what happened during a four-hour meeting with President Bush this morning."

Avoid quoting people in RDRs.   Remember that it is awkward or impossible for the newsreader to convey when someone is being quoted. If you must use quotes, look for ways to do so clearly but stylishly:

> *Not* the hackneyed: "The president said, and I quote . . ."
>
> *Instead*, try: "The president praised crew members for handling themselves, as he put it, 'with such class and dignity.'"
>
> *Or*: "The president added: 'We appreciate your mission, but most of all we appreciate your character.'"

WSLS News Channel 10's Juliet Bickford delivers the news from her anchor desk. Broadcast stories are written to be read aloud. They should rely on short, clear sentences.

Read it aloud.   Remember that an anchor has to read your story aloud, and an audience has to understand it the first time. Viewers or listeners can't go back and read it again. The best way to get a newsreader—or a viewer—to come after you with an ax is to write a sentence like this: "City Manager Ron Allen 'Don' Prentice, who has been tenaciously resisting efforts by two City Council members to secure his dismissal, today again refused to resign, saying he would fight to keep his job." Sharpen your focus: "City Manager Don Prentice vowed today to fight to keep his job. Two City Council members have tried repeatedly to force Prentice to quit. The latest effort came at last night's City Council meeting."

Now time yourself reading it aloud.   RDRs should run no longer than 30 seconds. Again, that's about seven lines, because the anchor will read at a pace of about four seconds per line.

__Ethics__

The focus of many discussions of ethics in broadcast journalism is on the intrusive nature of gathering information for electronic media. Even modern cameras are pretty noticeable, and the mechanics of shooting good video can mean that sources and subjects of stories feel as if they have been assaulted. I hope you have an opportunity to discuss the ethics of broadcast journalism more extensively in subsequent courses. But even if you are writing RDRs without having to worry about visual images, there are some ethical considerations to keep in mind.

First, the format itself creates some issues: Is 30 seconds enough time to give audiences a fair account of an event or issue? For some stories, it obviously is not. RDRs should be used for stories whose impact can be conveyed in three or four 15-word sentences. Where the event or issue is more complex, consider a longer package that includes video and sound bites.

The sometimes baffling technological requirements of broadcast news may require a special writing touch.

Second, in striving for a conversational tone, are we trivializing a story or ridiculing the people in it? There is a difference between a conversational tone and inappropriate lightheartedness, mocking, or sarcasm.

Third, do the characteristics of broadcast writing give audiences a false impression of events or the timing of action? The most obvious example is the focus on present tense in RDRs: "Beachgoers find their favorite seashore infested with sharks" is fine if the sharks are still there. If we are still using present tense to "freshen" a story that described the situation yesterday, we might be misleading our viewers and causing unnecessary concern.

Fourth, as in print writing, are we careful to make the words serve the facts? In making our writing as compelling as possible, there is a constant temptation to outrun what we know.

Strategies

Familiarize yourself with this summary of tips for writing effective broadcast RDRs (see Box 8.1):

1. As you do when you write for print, find the impact and the elements, and then wrestle with the words that will show the story to your audience.

2. Use a key facts outline.

3. Write as you speak, only better.

4. Limit your copy to one thought per sentence.

5. Make your story resonate even without pictures.

6. Write for the ear.

7. Look for ways to put the story in the present tense.

8. Avoid quotes, but if you must quote someone, keep in mind that the newsreader or anchor must convey when someone is being quoted.

9. Read your story aloud.

10. Time yourself reading it aloud.

Box 8.1

STRATEGIES FOR BROADCAST WRITING

1. Remember: *Impact, elements, words*.

2. Find and focus on your key facts. In a 30-second RDR, you won't have room for anything else.

3. Write just a little more formally than you speak. Try for a conversational tone.

4. Keep your sentences to about 15 words. Don't clutter them with multiple facts.

5. Even though you are writing for broadcast, don't assume that images will accompany your story. Brief RDRs often don't use them. Make your story resonate without pictures.

6. It is not enough for your story to make sense; it should *sound* good. Write for the ear.

7. Use the present tense, but only if you can do so without misleading your audience.

8. Avoid quotes. If you must quote someone, keep in mind that the newsreader has to be able to convey clearly when someone is being quoted.

9. As you work through successive drafts, read every one aloud.

10. Time yourself reading your final version aloud. If it runs longer than 30 seconds, tighten it. Don't simply read it faster.

Now use the exercise that follows to help you understand the differences between writing for print and for broadcast. Try writing the story for print first, then for broadcast. Are you writing for the same audience? Will you structure the story the same for both audiences? What will be in the print story that you will leave out of the broadcast story? How will you choose words differently for the two stories?

In my experience, students' first try at the broadcast story typically looks like the first several sentences of the print story. Is that good enough? What can you do to serve your broadcast audience better? (Hint: Think about getting your broadcast lede into the present tense.)

Exercise 8

A RDR

Write a RDR for today's 6 P.M. newscast from the following set of facts. Remember to edit and rearrange the information into a key facts outline first. Make sure your story runs no longer than 30 seconds on the air. That means you will have to weigh the information carefully, because you can't possibly include it all. Remember your audience and your medium, and remember to read your copy aloud as you work. Time yourself reading the story aloud. At the top of the story, write in the number of seconds it runs. Remember to use your City Directory to check local names.

Emergency situation today at Blue Ridge County High School.

15-degree (Fahrenheit) temperatures thought to be a factor.

Blue Ridge County High School and school board officials will not comment.

All students were walked to the parking lot of the North Service Authority one half-mile away, where buses took many home.

Buses could not go near the high school for fear of causing an explosion.

Propane gas leak detected at 10:40 A.M.

Leak appeared to come from one of two 5,000-gallon tanks behind the school.

No injuries reported, but one janitor is still unaccounted for. He has not been identified.

County fire-rescue squad's Hazardous Materials Response Team responded, but hampered because they could not drive their equipment near for fear of explosion.

Shut-off valves occasionally fail in very cold weather.

LP gas is heavier than air, so it doesn't dissipate quickly.

Area was still not reported secure as of 5 P.M.

Traffic on Route 15 near the high school was rerouted to Interstate 88, causing 3-mile jams in the north- and southbound lanes of the interstate until 3:30 P.M.

(Sources: Blue Ridge County Fire-Rescue Chief Sissy Baxter and a Virginia State Police spokeswoman.)

chapter nine

Writing for the Web

As you might have surmised from Chapters 6, 7, and 8, there is a fair amount of agreement among practicing journalists and journalism teachers about effective writing for broadcast and print media. There is less of a consensus about writing for the Web. Although the World Wide Web has been around for as long as you can remember, it's important to keep in mind how new this medium is both as a resource and—our focus here—a news-delivery system. Compared to broadcast and certainly print journalism, Web journalism is still in its infancy. We can expect it to demand a lot of care, and to show some growing pains. So norms on writing for the Web are still somewhat elusive, partly because we still don't know enough about how audiences use Web sites when they want to find and understand information. (See Box 9.1.) If you are annoyed by the ambiguity in what follows, that's understandable, but get used to it. Even though journalists are obligated to sort out the world by putting facts in context, the world is full of ambiguity.

Box 9.1

CHARACTERISTICS OF THE WEB

1. Web sites allow every newspaper and broadcast station to be both global in reach and local in focus.

2. Blogs and other feedback loops on the Web make it much easier for audiences to respond to stories.

3. Space on the Web is almost limitless. By creating links to other sites, news organizations can share far more information with audiences than ever before.

4. Many news Web sites have only recently become marginally profitable. As a result, news organizations often do not invest enough in them to take full advantage of the Web.

5. The Web's display characteristics and limitations create a challenge for writers and editors. Audiences are likely to encounter information first as freestanding one- or two-sentence "blurbs." Those blurbs must arouse enough interest that audiences will click one or more times to find the rest of the story. Writing Web blurbs well becomes critical.

Characteristics of the Web

What we do know is that the Web allows every newspaper and broadcast station to be both global in reach and intensely local in focus. At Washington and Lee University, where I teach, our converged news Web site, The Rockbridge Report (http://rockbridgereport.wlu.edu/), covers a tiny community, but it is seen all over the world. Our blog and other feedback loops contain messages from alumni in South Korea, Johannesburg and New York. Another feature of Web news sites that is not shared by newspapers and broadcast news is that, while they are still limited in their coverage by staff size and resources, you can throw out the window the old concepts of having to shoehorn stories into the space or time between ads or commercials. Because space on the Web is almost limitless, Tori Baxter knows that Web surfers in Valleydale, Steubenberg and Jeffersonville can all find plenty of local news about their widely scattered communities.

Unlimited space can be a mixed blessing, though. Some online journalists who work for newspaper Web sites simply import print stories wholesale, with little or no reworking. Often this practice is dictated by resources: Many

Melissa Worden and Patrick Beeson of *The Roanoke Times* look over the paper's Web site. The Web offers almost unlimited space for publishing news, as well as the possibility of converging print and broadcast stories.

newspapers still treat their Web sites as merely another mode of distribution, like a printing press and delivery truck; they do not maintain separate reporting and editing staffs for their Web sites. Until recently, most news Web sites operated at a loss, so there was a reluctance to spend huge amounts of money on them. While online advertising and other income streams are taking up some of the slack now, even leading to modest profitability, the revenues generated by news Web sites do not approach those of other news outlets.

To say that the Web has unlimited space is not to say that it has no limitations at all. Even Web sites that contain only material that has been "shoveled" over from print or broadcast are challenged by some of those limitations, including the Web's display characteristics. For example, unless your Web page is just a block of gray type (a sure way to send audiences fleeing), you won't be able to get much of a print story on one page. That means that you rely on your audience to keep clicking or linking to other pages, a cumbersome process even for those with the most powerful desktop setup.

In addition to being able to watch and listen to streamed video and audio on some Web sites, Web audiences can take advantage of interactive graphics that allow the user more control.

We know that, as a result, many Web users surf Web pages for summaries of breaking and developing stories. They do not want to wade through long stories when all they are seeking is an instant refresher course on the day's news. Their commitment to a story must be demonstrated not just by continuing to read or listen, but to finding and clicking on a link.

Ledes and Blurbs

Increasingly, effective Web operations rely on one- or two-sentence story summaries—called ledes, teases or blurbs—with a link to the full story for those who are interested. *Blurb* is the term I will use in this book. You can see how crucial it is for the blurb to convey the impact of the story clearly in one or two sentences. For effective examples of such summaries, see CNN.com or Washingtonpost.com. Many others can be found simply by surfing the Web.

As you work through your journalism major, you will probably have ever-expanding opportunities to write and rewrite stories for the Web. You might learn to stream video and audio as part of your story as well. You will gain experience "chunking" longer print stories into more manageable Web packages. And you will learn to develop appropriate links from your stories to other stories on the same Web site or to entirely different Web sites.

All those skills are beyond the scope of this course. For now, you will focus on writing effective, impact-oriented blurbs for the Web. In the exercises at the end of this chapter, remember that the one or two sentences that you write will be all the news about that story that many in your audience will see.

The Process

Recall the print story discussed in Chapter 6, about the conflict between two Valleydale council members and the city manager. This was Tori Baxter's lede:

City Manager Don Prentice's job remains secure for now.

In that chapter I discussed how that lede focused on the rational impact for a local audience, and on the relatively lower emotional impact for a regional audience. I showed how two elements—who and what—conveyed most of that impact. I demonstrated the impact of simple, direct words and a short sentence. I said that the lede would serve pretty well to begin a 30-second RDR as well. And I talked about the questions that the lede did not answer.

Now look at that lede with the second sentence of the story added:

City Manager Don Prentice's job remains secure for now. Last night Prentice survived the latest attempt by two City Council members to force him out.

Those two sentences would make an effective blurb for the Web. Why?

The short answer to the first question is that good Web writing depends first on the *impact, elements, words* process, just as print and broadcast writing do. We already know that those two sentences, in their print and broadcast versions, were the product of that process. A Web audience that is potentially bigger than either the print or broadcast audience will still react to the story either emotionally or rationally. The who and the what still convey that impact most effectively. In writing for the Web we still look for short, active-voice sentences that are carried by nouns and verbs.

But if just one sentence sufficed for the lede for both broadcast and print, why do we need a second sentence for the Web?

Mostly because of the work that a Web blurb does. If you look at examples of Web home or splash pages such as CNN.com, you will notice that full stories almost never run on those pages. Instead, the splash page contains the briefest summary, and the reader (or viewer or listener, if the story is streamed to the Web) must link to the full story. This presentation creates a filter that will lose the vast majority of the audience. While a print or broadcast lede must convey the impact in the first sentence, the reader, viewer or listener has immediate access to the rest of the story. The Web reader is, typically, a browser first. He or she will not see the rest of the story without making a positive, physical act of clicking on a link. So the consensus among Web writers is to make sure those folks will have enough information to make a good decision about whether to link to the story, and to go away from the blurb with what they need to know if they don't make the link. Remember, most of your audience will take what they need from the blurb alone.

If you study well-prepared splash pages, you will also notice that most of them stick to the 20-word sentence. You are far more likely to encounter Web blurbs comprising two 20-word sentences than to find a blurb of one long sentence. You already know the reason for that: Two short sentences are almost always easier to understand than one long one. They are also more likely to reflect a careful thought process on the part of the writer. Impact, elements, words.

Ethics

Writing for the Web presents at least three issues that can be addressed ethically. One or two may be beyond the scope of this book and your work in this course, but they bear thinking about just the same. The first issue has to do with where information you find on the Web comes from, and how we judge its reliability. The second concerns how we appropriately attribute and credit material we find on the Web. The third is about how much information you choose to share with your audience. Let's look at each in turn.

The author John Updike was moved several years ago to observe that much of what is on the Information Superhighway is road kill. Information from *The New York Times*, the federal government, and the Ku Klux Klan and other fringe groups is equally accessible on the Web. For journalists, the Web is a staggering resource. But that also underscores the importance of understanding how information ought to be used. For example, if you believe it important for your audience to know a fringe group's reaction to proposed legislation regarding immigrants, a visit to the Klan Web site could be illuminating—for you and your audience. But it would be another matter to depend on that same Web site for factual information about the proposed law. And it would be worse if you relied on the Klan for "facts" and then put them in front of an audience without telling that audience the source. Many Web surfers have a hard enough time judging the value and reliability of information they get from various Web sites. Others don't even try to make those distinctions. When the journalist colludes in that confusion by being equally careless, audiences are ill-served.

The second ethical question concerning the Web has to do with how we attribute the information we decide to use. Making bad decisions carries risks of harm to both your audience and the owner of the Web site. Just as with other stories and sources, your audience needs to know where on the Web information came from. But it's not enough to say simply, "according to Democrats.org, the official Web site of the Democratic Party." Again, if you are seeking to show your audience the Party's reaction to a Republican initiative, that's one thing. If you are relying on the site for facts about the initiative, that's something else, and simply attributing the "facts" won't resolve that problem. We'll discuss appropriate sourcing further in Chapter 11. When it comes to neglecting to provide attribution, it's not just your audience who suffers. You are harming the source of the information by taking what belongs to that source and passing it off as your own. Remember that that applies to graphic information as well—charts, graphs, photos and other images. Not only should you provide attribution for graphics, you should ask permission of the source to reproduce that kind of material. Because information on the Web is so accessible, people often assume it is in the public domain, that appropriating it without citing your source is okay. It isn't. It's plagiarism. As mentioned in Chapter 1, some things that are characterized as ethical issues don't really involve principles in conflict. With plagiarism the question is simply whether you will behave appropriately or yield to temptation.

A third ethical question concerning the Web has to do with how much of your reporting you should make available to your audience. Because space on the Web is virtually unlimited, and access to information is easy and free, or at least cheap, journalists are increasingly linking audiences to the source material they used for their story. Sometimes this includes transcripts or video of an entire interview. Traditionally in journalism, the story was expected to speak for itself. Audiences were not privy to most of the material reporters used in making the story, or that revealed the way reporters and editors decided what would be in the story and what would not. There were good reasons for that, reasons that lately are being reinforced every day. Journalists worried that sharing too much information would not only confuse audiences; it would give police, prosecutors and other government officials and agencies the idea that journalists were an investigative resource to be relied on rather than a monitor of the power of the investigators. With the jailing of *The New York Times* reporter Judith Miller in 2005 for refusing to reveal a source, the risks of revealing too much about the reporting process were underscored.

Still, the danger that audiences and government would begin to see journalists as part of the groups they should be monitoring must be weighed against the potential value of making available to audiences much more information than we ever could before. At some point, journalists must rely on faith that audiences will make wise use of the resources we are now able to provide them.

Strategies

1. As always, think clearly and carefully about impact, elements and words.
2. Keep your Web blurbs to one or two sentences.

Box 9.2

STRATEGIES FOR WRITING WEB BLURBS

1. *Impact, elements, words.*

2. The most effective Web blurbs comprise one or two short sentences. Try writing a lede as short as your print or broadcast ledes. Then add one or two more facts or a bit of context in a second brief sentence.

3. Rewrite until each of your sentences is 20 words or fewer. Two 20-word sentences are much easier to understand than one 40-word sentence.

4. Write your blurb as if you will not be writing the rest of the story. Thinking that you can add important facts later allows your focus to go fuzzy.

5. Remember that many in your audience will see only the two sentences of your blurb. Get the right stuff in.

6. Read both sentences aloud. As with print and broadcast, they have to *sound* right.

3. Keep your sentences to 20 words, no more. (Again, little words count, including *a*, *an*, and *the*.)

4. For now, don't worry about writing a third sentence. That could cause your focus in the first two to become fuzzy.

5. Remember that your Web blurb will stand alone on a separate page from the rest of the story.

6. As you have been doing with your print and broadcast stories, remember to read each blurb aloud. If it doesn't sound right, it isn't.

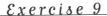

Exercise 9

Web Blurbs

Write Web blurbs for each set of facts. Keep your blurbs to one or two sentences of no more than 20 words each.

1. Valleydale Police Chief Buford Hunicutt spoke to the Valleydale Rotary Club yesterday. Hunicutt said he employs women officers "just to keep the Equal Opportunity folks in Washington happy. If it had been down to me we'd still be an all-male force. Women aren't as strong as men, and I think we're letting ourselves in for some trouble. It's bad news when perpetrators can start pushing officers around. I pray for the day when we see the end of this foolishness."

2. About 9 A.M. this morning a Blue Ridge High School junior was hurrying to soccer practice in her Chevrolet Blazer. It was raining and she skidded on wet leaves in the road on Route 15 near Wal-Mart. As a result the vehicle veered off the road. When she overcorrected it swerved across the center lane and into a tree on the other side of the road, with resultant death to the driver. She was alone in the vehicle. Police are withholding her name. Her family has not yet been notified because they are out of town. (*Source: Sheriff Swofford*)

3. Construction is about half completed on Beausoleil's new high school, to be called Erland Bromfield, just like the current, outdated one. The building is just three months behind schedule due to all the recent rain, said School Superintendent Holly Fairborn.

4. According to a report from the Beausoleil police, a 53-year-old Beausoleil man, T.D. "Pete" Rollins, 501 Spruce St., is reported dead, possibly of a work-related accident. He was riding a sanitation truck this morning when a sudden heavy thunderstorm began. The truck pulled over, and Rollins

crawled inside the compacter in the rear to get out of the rain. Driver of the truck apparently then activated the compacter to compact the most recent garbage, unaware that Rollins was inside. Cause of death was not officially determined, but police say they believe it was an accident, pending the outcome of an autopsy.

5. At approximately 3 A.M. tomorrow morning a crew will replace a sewer line damaged during a recent incident in which a baby alligator was stuck inside it. As a result, city sewer service will be cut off to the Rebel Heights and Country Club sections of Valleydale for about 20 minutes. About 300 homes will be effected. Residents should refrain from flushing toilets during this period, commencing at 3 A.M. in the morning. They also should not take showers or baths or run dishwashers, according to city Public Works Director George "Adam" Apple. The sewer line replacement is expected to cost about $20,000.

6. When County Sheriff J.E. "Jink" Swofford stepped outside his house this morning to go to work, he discovered a slight problem. Somebody had stolen his car during the night. His wife had to drive him to work in her car. Car was later found parked alongside Buffalo Creek near Culleytown. The radar gun had been stolen. Case turned over to detective division of the sheriff's office. No suspects named yet. *(Source: Sheriff Swofford)*

chapter ten

Using Quotes

As discussed in Chapters 1 and 2, news stories ought to be about people, or about people involved in events or issues. They should not be just about the event or issue. As journalists we need to find ways to get people into our stories. In this chapter we will look at one of the most effective ways of doing that—by using their quotes. Often, especially in print news media, we look to use a good quote right away to support our lede. You need to practice recognizing good quotes, whether you have recorded them to be used as bites for radio or TV or written them down to be included in a print story. (Remember, with the Web it is possible to combine a print story with audio or video bites.)

The Work That Quotes Do

In any medium, good quotes, used well, let your audience know the people in the story in several ways. (See Box 10.1.)

Quotes lend immediacy, so your audience has a sense of being there and gets the sense that you were there. Even a well-written narrative, by itself, can't do that.

Quotes impart emotion, the reactions of the people involved and affected, in their own words. Allowing the people in our stories to report their own emotions carries more weight than our attempts to describe those emotions.

Quotes help us show—rather than just tell—what's going on.

Quotes help convey the personalities of the people in our stories. As in personal relationships, audiences best get the sense that they know others when they feel that they are conversing with them.

Box 10.1

QUOTES WORK HARD FOR YOUR AUDIENCE

1. Quotes give your audience a sense of being there with those involved.

2. Quotes convey the emotional reactions of the people in your story.

3. Quotes show, rather than tell, that your story is about people.

4. Quotes allow audiences to see personalities.

Types of Quotations

Whichever medium we are writing for, we can use quotes in any of several ways in our stories. In *Newswriting Exercises* (1987), Ken Metzler identifies five of them. (See Box 10.2.)

    1. *Direct quotations* depict word-for-word what the speaker said. In print stories, they are set off by quotation marks:

"We will find Osama bin Laden even if we have to turn over every rock on earth," President Bush said.

Box 10.2

QUOTES AND OTHER ATTRIBUTED STATEMENTS

1. *Direct quotations* are always set off by quotation marks because they indicate word for word what the speaker said.

2. *Indirect quotations* do not use quotation marks, because the quote has been altered slightly. Sometimes called *close paraphrase*, indirect quotations still closely represent what the speaker said.

3. *Paraphrased quotations* use the reporter's words to express what the speaker said, usually more concisely.

4. *Partial quotations* consist of a few words or brief phrase of a quote. They should be used sparingly.

5. *Dialogue* represents direct quotes from two people, presented as one responding to the other.

Source: Ken Metzler, *Newswriting Exercises,* 2nd ed. Englewood Cliffs, NJ: Prentice-Hall, 1987.

2. *Indirect quotations* convey what the speaker said in essentially the way he said it, but quotation marks aren't used because the quote has been altered slightly:

> The United States will find Osama bin Laden no matter how hard we must look, the president said.

3. *Paraphrased quotations* express the essence of the speaker's comment in the reporter's words:

> The president vowed to find Osama bin Laden.

4. *Partial quotations* take a fragment of the quote to preserve the color of it. Because their fragmented nature makes them distracting, they should be used sparingly, and never as a sound or video bite:

> The president said finding bin Laden would happen "even if we have to turn over every rock on earth."

5. *Dialogue* captures the drama of an exchange between two or more people:

> "We will find Osama bin Laden if we have to turn over every rock on earth," President Bush said. "All we can expect of an effort like that is a lot of pain," the Senate minority leader replied.

Gather Many, Use Few

To be effective, quotes or sound bites should be used sparingly. They should seldom be used to carry your narrative or to explain complex issues. When put on the spot, most of us are hard pressed to explain complicated matters in a coherent way, and certainly not in an efficient way. Poorly selected quotes can be tedious at best, confusing at worst. Long broadcast bites are notoriously sleep-inducing, particularly if you try to use them to explain a concept rather than convey the speaker's reaction or emotional stake in the story. For print, broadcast or the Web, use quotes to show not what happened or what the issue is, but how the participants or those affected saw it or are responding to it. Quotes should humanize our stories. Learn to listen for the quotes that will do that.

The best strategy is to fill your notebook or your video camera with quotes, then limit yourself in your story to the very best. Like carrying an umbrella, it's better to have quotes and not need them than to need them and not have them. If you gather just one quote, you are pretty much forced to use it, even if it is weak. If you gather three, you have a little more choice. If you get 10, especially from multiple sources, you not only virtually guarantee that you will use only the strongest quotes; you also ensure that you will be able to fairly represent just about every significant side of an event or issue.

Show Them Off

Because quotes convey immediacy, emotion and personality, they should not be buried in the story. If you use a long clause to introduce a quote at the end of your sentence in a print story, you will lose much of the quote's impact. Instead, in print stories use short full-sentence transitions to introduce a speaker so that the next paragraph can begin with his or her quote. In broadcast writing this same strategy leads your audience into the bite in a clear, compelling fashion. (See Box 10.3.)

> *Bad*: Replying to the president's promise, the Senate minority leader said, "All we can expect from an effort like that is a lot of pain."

> *Better*: The Senate minority leader foresees hard times. "All we can expect from an effort like that is a lot of pain."

You can see from this example that using the bad way to introduce the quote in a broadcast story would be somewhere between awkward and

Box 10.3

SETTING UP QUOTES

1. Don't bury quotes. You wouldn't be using them if they weren't strong.
2. Whether you are writing for print, broadcast or the Web, use full-sentence transitions to introduce quotes.
3. Practice writing effective full-sentence transitions:

   Bad: Reacting to the city manager, City Council Member Eaton Wise said, "I don't think Mr. Prentice has the authority to do that."

   Better: The city manager's initiative upset Council Member Eaton Wise. "I don't think Mr. Prentice has the authority to do that," he said.

impossible. The reporter would have to pause her voice-over narrative in mid-sentence for a rough transition to the quote. The nature of broadcast reporting practically forces us into good practice in setting up quotes. (Of course, you could still write a weak full-sentence transition to the bite: "Harry Reid of Nevada is the Senate minority leader.") For print and Web writing, there are plenty of opportunities to screw up; you can write weak full-sentence transitions or ignore them entirely. Practice doing it right.

When you write a transition to a quote, avoid what's called a stutter quote—introducing the quote with the same words contained in the quote:

Bad: Wise said Prentice has refused to meet with him and Bullard.

"He has refused to meet with us," he said.

Better: Wise said he was frustrated by Prentice's response.

"He has refused to meet with us," he said.

Attribution

Whether you are using direct quotes, indirect quotes, partial quotes, paraphrase or dialogue, always attribute—that is, make clear who is speaking. Identify the speaker by name. Often, other information about the speaker is relevant as well: position (*City Manager Don Prentice*); age (*4-year-old Sally Smith*), address or place of residence (*Dorothy Foster of Eden*); group membership (*Fred James, a local Democratic Party activist*), or involvement in an issue (*Sam Jones, who opposes the housing subdivision*). If you have the slightest doubt about whether your story makes the speaker's identity clear, attribute. Remember, if you have a small doubt, your audience will have a big one. Don't overattribute, though. You need not give a source for information that is readily available from any of a multitude of sources or is universally known:

> The city's proposed operating budget for next year is $15 million (*not*: the mayor said). President Bush was reelected in November 2004 (*not*: according to federal election records).
>
> *But*: Jones hit the victim over the head with a bat and yanked her purse from her, according to the arrest affidavit.
>
> *Or* (if charges have been filed): Jones is charged with robbing the victim by hitting her over the head with . . . .
>
> *Also*: The city's proposed operating budget is $15 million, but Mayor Hostetter says that's too high.
>
> *Not*: The city's proposed operating budget is $15 million, and that's too high.

Use "Said"

In print and Web stories, and when you are paraphrasing a quote in a broadcast story, generally use "said" when attributing quotes to people. Use "according to" in references to documents. Avoid trying to convey context or emotion when choosing function verbs that link a quote with a speaker. (See Box 10.4.) Often, such word choice slants the comment; it can also make your writing sound silly. Again, rather than telling, *show* the reader how the speaker reacted.

> *Bad*: "That's way too high," the mayor exclaimed wildly. "Over my dead body," Wise giggled.
>
> *Better*: The mayor jumped up and pounded his fist on the desk.
>
> "That's way too high," he said.
>
> Wise looked out at the audience and laughed.
>
> "Over my dead body," he said.

Box 10.4

USE "SAID" FOR ATTRIBUTION

1. Adjectives and adverbs can introduce bias into attribution. "Said" is much less loaded.

2. Using a full-sentence transition to a quote allows you to *show* your audience the speaker's emotion.

3. Practice showing the speaker's reaction in the transition, not in the attribution:

   Bad: "I'll file a criminal complaint if you do," Wise exclaimed wildly.
   "Take your best shot," Prentice laughed.

   Better: Wise jumped up and pounded his fist on the desk. "I'll file a criminal complaint if you do," he said.
   Prentice leaned back and laughed. "Take your best shot," he said.

Ethics

Altering and "Cleaning up" Quotes

When is it okay to alter quotes? The short answer: Never. A slightly better answer: Rarely, and only if your audience understands that altering quotes is the exception, never the rule. If we put quotation marks around a series of words in a print or Web story, they send a message to our audience that that was exactly what the speaker said. Altering quotes in broadcast stories is ordinarily a different proposition, because messing with a sound bite presents technical difficulties that simply changing words within quotation marks does not. But in deciding how much of what the subject said to leave in a bite, broadcasters are just as susceptible to altering the meaning or context of quotes.

Saying that quotes should be sacrosanct, though, presents us with a couple of problems: First, if the speaker gave us a 10-sentence response, and we can convey its essence in one of her sentences, is it misleading to use only that one sentence? Second, should we leave profanity and bad grammar in our quotes because that's what the speaker said, even though doing so might hold the speaker up to ridicule or offend members of your audience?

Most members of your audience have no expectation that what a speaker is quoted as saying is the only thing he or she said. It's all right, in fact it's desirable, to cut to the chase, to quote the most important or illustrative thing she said, *as long as the quote you use is not taken out of context.* Whether you are writing for print, Web or broadcast, you don't have to use the entire quote or bite to provide that context; ordinarily paraphrase will do a clearer, more succinct job of that. But the quote you do use should be verbatim, unless our second problem applies.

Bad Grammar, Profanity and Obscenity

Most of us, when we speak, use a more informal language than we do when we write, full of sloppy grammar and, once in a while, goddamn gratuitous profanity. As journalists, our goal should be to create understanding, not to offend our audience or hold people up unnecessarily to ridicule. As journalists in the United States pay more attention to the diversity of both audiences and the people involved in events and issues, we become more aware of people who use heavily accented or nonstandard English. Reproducing the language as they speak it could hold them up to ridicule or stereotyping by readers or viewers who think that the way people speak reflects their character, intelligence or values.

So print journalists routinely clean up poor or nonstandard grammar to avoid embarrassment to the speaker, *unless the grammar itself shows something about the speaker that is germane to the story.* (Obviously, "cleaning up" a quote presents a unique set of problems for the broadcast reporter.) Say a truck driver with an eighth-grade education is describing an accident on the interstate:

"It begun when the Chevy got sidewise, and I seen it a-comin'."

There's nothing about his grammar that's essential to that story.

Say, however, that the superintendent of schools describes a new remedial grammar program:

"Hopefully, it'll work out good, but then we ain't got nothing to lose by tryin' it."

We can argue that the grammar of the highest-ranking educator in the county is important to that story, and should be published unaltered.

With profanity and obscenity, your concern shifts to your audience. If we are writing for a general audience, we should avoid pointless or gratuitous profanity. There is no defensible reason to offend your audience just because you can. Take the example of our truck driver again:

> "Once he got sidewise it was slick as owl shit and the sumbitch behind him run right up his ass."

There is little about that language that makes it essential to the story.

But sometimes obscenity or profanity *is* germane to the story. In response to a question about Senator Edward Kennedy's intention to run for the Democratic presidential nomination in 1980, the incumbent Democratic president, Jimmy Carter, said this:

> "If Kennedy runs, I'll whip his ass."

He was quoted verbatim by most major news media in the United States. The president is usually more diplomatic and guarded when speaking publicly. The fact that Carter used that language with the press underscored his conviction.

As mentioned previously, for broadcast reporters, cleaning up sound bites is made difficult if not impossible by the limitations of the medium. Profanity can be "bleeped" out of bites for radio or TV, but bad or nonstandard grammar is probably better handled by a voice-over paraphrase of the speaker's comment.

Generally, a changed quote is going to be obvious to a broadcast audience, but a quote taken out of context will not be. Even for a quote in print, though, you do not need to show your audience that you have cleaned up bad grammar. With profanity or obscenity it's different: When you use a printed quote that has been scrubbed clean of profanity or obscenity, you need to indicate where you have actually changed or left out words. (Why the difference? I have no idea. Chalk it up to convention.)

Ask your instructor if he or she has a policy on cleaning up quotes or the use of profanity for your class. When you begin working in a newsroom, learn your newsroom's policy. If you think you need to violate that policy for the sake of using a really strong quote, always discuss the desired inclusion with your editor or producer first. In many newsrooms, such decisions have to involve top editors. (*The Philadelphia Inquirer*'s policy not only divides profanity and obscenity into three categories of words, it prescribes the level of editor who must make the ruling for each category.) Remain part of that discussion. Obviously, it's better to have those discussions as early in the day as possible, before everyone is on a tight deadline.

Box 10.5

STRATEGIES FOR DIFFICULT QUOTES

When you are confronted with bad grammar, profanity or obscenity, remember that a *paraphrased* or *indirect quote* is usually a better option than altering the quote. Depending on whether you are working for print, the Web or broadcast, other options include:

1. *Ellipsis*, the three dots that indicate something is missing, can be used in print or Web stories. Similarly, *brackets* [ ] indicate that a word has been substituted for the offensive word.

2. A *partial quote* allows the speaker's voice, but not the bad grammar or language, to reach your audience.

3. *Asking a question a second time* often yields a "cleaner" quote. Listen for possible trouble spots as you conduct your interview.

4. *Using the quote, if such use is integral to the story*. Most newsrooms have a policy against using bad grammar, profanity or obscenity gratuitously. If you think you have a compelling reason to use a quote containing any of those, it's essential that you *talk with your editor, producer or news director before you use it*.

Strategies

When you're trying to decide whether to clean up a quote, keep in mind that you have several options that do not involve altering the quote itself. Some are available to print, broadcast and Web reporters equally. Some won't work for broadcast. (See Box 10.5.) Always consider these options first.

Paraphrase the quote, or use an indirect quote. Will we lose too much by not using the quote or the bite itself?

> Honeycutt said the Chevrolet skidded sideways on the slick highway, and the pickup struck it from behind.

For print or Web reporters, *use ellipsis*, the little dots that tell your audience something is missing, to get around the profanity. Or use brackets [these squared-off things] to substitute a word for the offensive word. The brackets tell your audience that the word in brackets is not the word the speaker used:

When the Chevrolet skidded, Honeycutt said, "It was slick . . . and the [pickup] ran right up [into him]."

Use a partial quote to convey the color but not the bad grammar or language:

Honeycutt said the Chevrolet skidded sideways on the slick road, and the pickup "ran right up" into it from behind.

When you are conducting your interview, *ask the speaker the same question again.* You might get a cleaner version of the quote the second time.

If none of these solutions seems to work, and you still think the quote is compelling enough to use, *talk with your editor, producer or news director about it.* Most newsrooms have policies proscribing bad grammar and gratuitous profanity or obscenity, even in quotes. To get it into the paper or on the air, you will need to have a good argument for overriding that policy.

The exercise that follows is intended to give you practice introducing speakers and setting up their quotes. Remember to combine paraphrase and quotes, and to focus on your best quotes.

Exercise 10

Choosing Quotes

In each case that follows, assume that you have written a lede and nut graf for your story. You are trying now to write an effective transition to a quote or two, and to select the most effective sentence or two from the entire quote. Remember not to use the whole quote, and feel free to link separate quotes with an indirect quotation or paraphrase. You should also consider the options discussed above when you are confronted with poor or nonstandard grammar, obscenity and profanity.

1. Megan Leblanc is explaining why she decided not to accept a key to the city for pulling a neighbor's toddler from a burning home:

It was really, like, no big deal. I mean, everyone was all nice and grateful and so I'm like, "Okay, cool, you're really nice to do this," but I'm no hero. I was just, like, there, and I did what anybody would do. So, like, that's no reason to make this major commotion. If what the medal says is, like, "Oh, what you did was so special," then that doesn't say very nice things about what we can expect from people, does it? Am I, like, totally making no sense?

2. Retired Marine Corps Sergeant Vince Capen is asking the Blue Ridge County supervisors not to allow a zoning change that would permit five college students to rent a house adjacent to his property near Rock Falls:

I tell you, I busted my nuts for 27 years so I could retire to the kind of place I've got. Finally, after decades of service to my country, I've earned some peace and quiet. And now some rich little sons of bitches are gonna come in and throw wild parties and play their damned music at top volume all night. What they all need isn't an adolescent country club; it's a dose of Marine boot camp, and I'd be happy to provide it for them. Rezoning, my ass. Refocusing is what they need, courtesy of the toe of my boot.

chapter eleven

Sources

Chapters 1 through 10 focused on how to approach writing as a process—how to weigh the value of information to our audiences, how to organize that information in an understandable way, how to use words effectively, how to recognize the characteristics of print, broadcast and Web media and their audiences, and the basics of writing effectively for each. Starting with a discussion of sources in this chapter, we now turn to examining other skills reporters need and some types of stories that they are frequently called on to write. As you might expect, the exercises in Chapters 11 through 21 will become increasingly complex, to provide you with appropriate challenge so that your skills will continue to grow and improve, and to give you plenty of practice writing for print, broadcast and the Web.

Types of Sources

When she goes about gathering information for a story, Tori Baxter relies on two kinds of sources: the documents and records she consults, and the people she talks to. (In making this distinction, it's important to keep in mind that all documents are generated by people.)

Let's look at each kind of source in turn.

Documentary Sources

The term *documentary sources* can be interpreted broadly. In addition to the obvious—copies of lawsuits and other court filings, arrest reports, budgets, consultants' or government reports, agendas—documentary sources can include clippings or file tape of previous stories (increasingly accessed online), telephone and city directories, encyclopedias and other reference works, and

Reporters know there is no substitute for talking to people, but preparing carefully for an interview by examining documents and other resources is essential.

electronic databases. Journalists occasionally give the benefit of the doubt to a document over a quote from a person. Make sure that your documentation provides credible support or proof, not an unsupported claim. As discussed in Chapter 9, determining the legitimacy of sources has become a particular problem when relying on the Internet for information.

Human Sources

When she talks to people, Tori tries to keep in mind the type of sources she is dealing with. Examples include *witnesses* or *participants, custodians of records, experts or interpreters of information,* and *advocates.* She does not rely on a particular source for more information than that source can or should provide. For example, she would not ask a court clerk (a *custodian of a record*) who has just given her a case file why the defendant's attorney filed the motion that he did. Rather, she would call the attorney, a *participant,* or another defense attorney, who would provide information as an *expert.* She would not ask a teenager who survived a mass shooting in a restaurant (a *witness*) for the typical psychological profile of an unknown mass killer. For that, she would call an *expert* with the FBI. Experts are also sometimes *advocates,* as in the case of lawyers, doctors and some academics. In Chapter 7 we were introduced to one such advocate, Dr. Pritchard, who directs an agency for and speaks on behalf of victims of domestic violence.

In trying to be cooperative with reporters, people are often tempted to speculate about an issue or event when it would be more appropriate for them to say, "I don't know." (Police public information officers are notorious for this.) It's the reporter's responsibility both to discriminate among human sources and be discriminating about the information those sources provide.

Who and What Can We Rely On?

Whether she is talking to someone or consulting a document, Tori always keeps in mind two questions: (1) *What does this source know?* (2) *How does he know it?* Faith Palmer, her city editor, has taught her that journalists have to deal with several *levels of observation,* and that they must always keep in mind the level at which they and the source are working.

Levels of Observation

Direct or *firsthand observation* results from Tori seeing or hearing something herself. An example is what she observes at a City Council meeting. Ordinarily, audiences trust firsthand information provided by a journalist, because journalists are expected to be trained observers. *Secondhand observation* would refer, for example, to the information Tori gets from a witness. An example of *thirdhand observation* would be the account a police officer gives Tori based on the officer's conversation with a witness or witnesses. And so on. (See Box 11.1.) When she is interviewing and when she goes over her notes later, Tori must keep in mind the level of observation that the information came from. That will help her judge how much faith to have in it. It is crucial for her not to confuse levels of observation, and also for her to make clear to her audience the level of observation associated with the information. For broadcast reporters and audiences, taped interviews with sources often, but not always, make the level of observation clear. It remains the reporter's responsibility to keep it clear, both in the reporter's mind and for the audience.

Box 11.1

LEVELS OF OBSERVATION

As information moves further from firsthand observation, we should be increasingly careful about the reliability of the information:

1. *Direct or firsthand observation*: The reporter sees or hears something herself. An example would be a reporter covering a City Council meeting.

2. *Secondhand observation*: The reporter gets information from a witness.

3. *Thirdhand observation*: The reporter talks to someone who got information from a witness. An example is the account a police officer gives a reporter based on the officer's conversation with a witness or witnesses.

4. *Fourthhand observation*: Reporters occasionally receive information from spokesmen or spokeswomen, or from news releases, that is based on information that is already thirdhand. An example would be information from a police spokesman who summarized the report of an officer who had talked to witnesses.

Being Careful, and Teaching Your Audience to Be Careful

For Tori to write, "The Chevrolet ran a red light and struck the pickup truck" would be misleading unless she had seen it happen. Firsthand observation by reporters, particularly of accidents, is fairly rare.

Similarly, if Tori wrote, "Witnesses said the Chevrolet ran a red light and struck the pickup truck," that would be accurate only if she had heard this account from the witnesses themselves. If she took the witness accounts from a police report or from a conversation with the investigating officer, her story should read: "Witnesses told police the Chevrolet ran a red light and struck the pickup truck."

Sometimes participants or witnesses will confuse levels of observation themselves. Whether reporters are interviewing witnesses on tape for broadcast or are taking notes on the witnesses' answers to use in print stories, they need to ask questions carefully to make sure of the level of observation at which each witness is operating.

Finally, witness accounts of the same incident can vary wildly. Tori has learned to adopt some strategies for resolving those conflicts:

She makes sure of the level of observation of each witness. Sometimes the conflict can be resolved by determining that one witness is actually reporting information secondhand rather than firsthand, even though he thinks he observed it firsthand. For example, we see only what occurs in front or, less clearly, to either side of us. But we can hear noises behind us as well. A witness at an accident, for example, will often hear a crash, then turn and see only the immediate aftermath, missing the crash itself. But that witness might tell a reporter he saw the accident. In reality, he may be reporting what he heard first, then saw, while two other witnesses are reporting what they saw directly.

She can report to witnesses what other witnesses have said. From the responses she gets, Tori might be able to judge how sure each witness is of his or her account: "Is that what the other witness said? Oh, well, it all happened so fast, maybe . . ." or "Well, actually, I was turned around talking to my boyfriend right then, so it was after I turned around that I saw . . ." or "No, I don't care what the other witness said. I'm positive I saw the Chevy run the red light."

She can look for the commonalities in the witnesses' accounts. While each account might vary somewhat, there may well be a "nut" of agreed-on information in the accounts.

She will remind her audience of the discrepancies in the accounts: "Witness accounts varied sharply. Two said the Chevrolet ran a red light. A third said the light was yellow. A fourth thought the light was green. But all agreed that the Chevrolet slammed into the pickup truck broadside. The driver's door of the truck was crushed inward so far that it had shoved the steering column into the center of the truck's cab."

Using a combination of firsthand observation (the damage Tori saw on the pickup after the accident), secondhand observation (the witness accounts), and careful reporting of where the witnesses' accounts varied and where they agreed, Tori has given her audiences an idea of how much credence to give the information she has presented. (See Box 11.2.)

Box 11.2

WRITING DIFFERENT LEVELS OF OBSERVATION

Here are examples of how, in her story, a reporter might attribute information received at different levels of observation:

Firsthand: The Chevrolet ran a red light and struck the pickup truck.

Secondhand: Witnesses said the Chevrolet ran a red light and struck the pickup truck.

Thirdhand: Witnesses told police the Chevrolet ran a red light and struck the pickup truck.

Fourthhand: A police spokesman said witnesses told officers that the Chevrolet ran a red light and struck the pickup truck.

Combination of levels: Witness accounts varied sharply. Two said the Chevrolet ran a red light. *(secondhand)* Another told police the light was yellow. *(thirdhand)* A police spokesman said still another witness told investigators she thought the light was green. *(fourthhand)* But all agreed that the Chevrolet slammed into the pickup truck broadside. The driver's door of the truck was crushed inward so far that it had shoved the steering column into the center of the cab. *(firsthand)*

Ethics

Dealing with sources presents a number of potential ethical issues for journalists. Some of those focus on the audience, others on the sources themselves.

We will discuss levels of attribution in detail in Chapter 19. Much of that discussion centers on dealing with sources who do not want to have information attributed directly to them. For now, remember that *attributing information directly to its source is the rule*, not the exception. As discussed in Chapter 10, we should identify human sources by name and other relevant information. We should be just as careful in identifying documentary sources.

Sources should know to assume that what they say will be attributed to them in your story. We owe it to sources to identify ourselves as reporters at the beginning of a conversation, whether on the phone or in person, and to inform the source that we are working on a story. With sources who talk to news media frequently, that should be enough. With sources who are not used to dealing with reporters, we might have to be a bit clearer. Once we have done that, we must never let a source change the rule retroactively—to talk to us for 20 minutes, for example, and then say: "Now, you can't put any of that in the paper."

Broadcast reporters won't encounter this type of problem in videotaped interviews, of course, but remember that broadcast reporters talk to many sources off tape. Those sources need to be aware of the rule, because without the camera or tape recorder running, they might think they are not being quoted for attribution. If we make promises to sources—expressed or implied—we should keep them. If a source is naive or inexperienced in dealing with reporters, not making our intentions clear to the source is a form of deception.

Even though our first obligation is to provide our audiences with information they need, we must keep in mind that we can be persistent with sources and aggressive in pursuing information without causing undue harm. Belittling or insulting sources is never appropriate or necessary. Continuing to badger them after they have definitively declined to talk to us is also inappropriate. Maintaining journalistic independence does not mean we have to ignore the pain someone might be going through. If seeing people shattered by tragedy does not affect us emotionally, we should find another line of work. As CNN correspondent Anderson Cooper has said, "You shouldn't do this job if you're not willing to feel, if you're not willing to get hurt."

We owe it to sources—and our audiences—to quote them accurately, and to fairly represent what they said by not taking their quotes out of context.

For our audiences' sake we should be careful to make clear the level of observation at which a source is operating. We should also rely on sources only for the kind of information they can reliably give. We should not ask a person on the street for an expert opinion, for example. And the "stake" our sources have in the story should also be made clear, so audiences can judge a source's information against his or her agenda.

Strategies

When you evaluate information to judge its reliability and appropriateness for a story, remember:

Know where it came from—documents, or human sources? Is there a reason to give more credence to information in documents? Can human sources verify the information from documents? Can documents verify what you have gotten from people?

With human sources, *match the kind of reporting you do and the information you get to the appropriate source.* For example, don't rely on "people on the street" sources as experts to untangle a complex issue for you and your audience.

Determine the level of observation at which your human sources are working: firsthand, secondhand, thirdhand and so forth. Was the source really at the event, or is he or she reporting what someone else said who was there? Did the source really see or hear what happened? The reliability of information decreases as you move further from firsthand observation.

Make sure, by writing carefully, that your audience is as aware as you are of the level of observation. That allows your readers or viewers to make informed judgments about how much credence to give information.

Attribute carefully. Make sure your story makes clear where information is coming from. Identify people by name and other relevant information. Identify documentary sources just as carefully.

Exercise 11 calls on you to write a complete story from the facts and witness accounts you are given. Almost all of your information comes from

Box 11.3

STRATEGIES FOR DEALING WITH SOURCES

1. Stay aware of where all your information came from. Do you need human sources to verify the information from documents? Will documents verify what you have gotten from people?

2. Don't rely on the wrong human source for information. For example, a police spokesman is not the right source for how a witness is dealing with an event emotionally. Nor should "people on the street" be used as experts to explain a complex issue.

3. Make sure you know the level of observation for each of your human sources. As you move further from firsthand observation, the reliability of information generally decreases.

4. Your audiences will rely on you to help them determine the reliability of information. Write carefully to make levels of observation clear.

5. Identify human sources by name and other relevant characteristics. Do the same with documentary sources.

human sources. Keep in mind levels of observation, the type of witness you are talking to, and whether witnesses are in a position to know or are only assuming. Remember to use quotes sparingly for maximum effect, and to provide attribution. (See Box 11.3.)

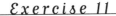

Exercise 11

Plane Crash

From the facts and witness accounts provided, write a complete story for tomorrow morning's Jeffersonville Herald, *a 30-second RDR for this evening's newscast, and a two-sentence blurb for immediate distribution on the Web. Remember to time yourself reading your broadcast story aloud, and to write the length, in seconds, at the top of your broadcast story. Whether you write the print story, the broadcast story or the Web blurb first is up to you. Think about which assignment will help you focus most easily on the other two. If you choose not to write the print story first, remember to use a key-facts outline for your RDR.*

The aircraft was a Cessna 150, a two-seat light plane piloted by Thurgood Vance, 24, who lives on Rt. 4, Culleytown. The plane crashed into a wooded area just south of the U.S. Rt. 15 bypass in Valleydale, across the road from North River Middle School. Pilot is dead. He was alone in the plane. The plane was burned and the body was inside. The craft departed from the Kupp's Creek landing strip at 11:15 A.M. Crashed shortly after noon. The crash is still under investigation. The Federal Aviation Administration will send an investigator in tomorrow to look over the wreckage and the crash site. (*Source:* Police Chief Buford Hunicut)

From Anita McLeod, teacher at North River Middle School:

I don't know anything about flying, but I think this guy is a hero. He literally gave his life to keep our kids out of danger. It looked to me like he was trying for an emergency landing along Route 15, because his engine was sputtering and the plane was balky. And then he saw we had a couple of PE classes out running the track right next to the highway. He must have been worried that he couldn't control the plane and it might career over into the kids. Next thing I knew, why, he just pulled the nose of the plane up and banked left into the woods, across the road from the kids. The plane went into the woods and exploded. Bless his heart.

From 12-year-old Lisa Kondricki, a seventh grader at North River:

I was running around the track, trying to go slow, and the coach was hollering at me to speed up, and then I heard what I thought was really loud screaming, but not like from a person, you know? More like from a motor or something, and then this big whoosh, and then I looked up and it was like the trees were on fire. I never saw an airplane, just heard these weird noises and then the woods caught fire.

From Tom Kramer, a construction worker at Virginia Department of Transportation's maintenance facility, next to the middle school and across the road from the crash site:

We had come back to the maintenance barn for some post-hole diggers, and suddenly all the guys are like "Holy shit! He crashed!" And I'm like, "What? Who crashed?" So we hopped in the truck and went hauling ass over there, but the fire wouldn't let us close enough to get him. But it was close enough to see him burning inside the plane. So I just, you know, hurled my breakfast.

From Penelope Hinds, chair of the county Board of Supervisors:

I just feel awful. I've known Thirsty since the day he was born, and I've known his mother and dad since I was a child. Such dear, dear people. What a terrible loss for them. I've been to see them, and they are devastated, of course, but I was able to tell them that their son apparently is a hero. That seemed to help a bit. I'm planning to introduce a resolution with the board to recognize him.

From Meagan LeBlanc, VPU student:

Oh, God, it was just so totally gross. The plane just, like, blew up in midair. One minute it was flying low over Kroger, and the next, you know, kablooey. I was riding my bike along the Travis Street extension, so it went right over my head and right into those trees. I think it just missed the water tower.

From Phillip Casteneda, principal of North River Middle School:

One of the secretaries in the office said, "I can hear a plane's engine cutting off," and so we ran outside, and, sure enough, this little plane was having a tough time keeping altitude and staying trim. I started running toward the track, because I saw the kids out there. I don't know what I could have done if he'd plowed into them, but then, miraculously, he veered the other way and crashed across the road. I'm pretty sure he did it on purpose.

From Valleydale Police Officer Timmy Healey's incident report:

While on patrol in my vehicle this officer witnessed an individual attempting to pilot a small aircraft, yellow in color, in the vicinity of the skies over the eastern part of the city. At which time said individual appeared to execute an intentional dive in the aircraft, however he was unable to execute a proper recovery from the dive in that said aircraft came into contact with a wooded portion of the ground. As a result the foilage became engulfed in flames. I contacted dispatch and responded to the scene in my vehicle at a high rate of speed, where I contacted several civilian witnesses who reported they were unsuccessful in their attempts to reach the pilot, who was trapped in the burning aircraft.

From Howard Kreiter, Federal Aviation Administration spokesman in Washington:

We have heard from your police chief, and will respond with an investigator beginning tomorrow. Until such time as he arrives on site and completes his investigation, we will not comment. No, I will not speculate on the cause of the crash until our investigator has had an opportunity to complete his investigation. The investigation could take one day, or it could take weeks, depending on the circumstances. I'm not prepared to speculate on that, either.

chapter twelve

Facts and Allegations

In Chapter 11 you were introduced to dealing with sources and the information they provide. In this chapter we will work on related issues: how to distinguish fact from allegation, and how to help your audience recognize each.

Tori Baxter came out of J-school thinking that her job as a journalist was to gather and present facts. With enough facts, she thought, each story could answer the fundamental questions she always keeps in mind: *What do I know? How do I know it?* When she was fresh out of school it never occurred to her that reporting a fact might not be the same as reporting the truth. In just three years, she has come to learn how tough distinguishing between fact and truth can be.

Certainly, without facts we can't hope to find the truth. But for journalists, that raises a couple of questions: Is truth just an accretion of facts? If that's the case, how do we know when we've gathered enough facts to constitute truth?

News Fact, News Truth

There is a related problem as well: the difference between what we'll call *news fact* and truth. Here's an example, similar to one presented in an earlier chapter: Say during a heated Valleydale City Council meeting recently one council member accused the city manager of adultery. Tori was there, she heard the comment. That the comment was made is a *news fact*. But is it true? And ought it to be reported, if Tori can't determine yet whether it is true or not?

The first test, before Tori even sets about trying to determine whether the accusation is true, is whether it has any relevance to her audience. It might not be worth reporting, even if it is true. Second, if the matter does have some relevance to an audience, is the news fact that one council member made the allegation in public so important that it should be reported, even if the truth of it can't yet be determined? Third, does the target of the allegation have an opportunity to respond? Fourth, what was the context for the remark? A gratuitous insult during a heated exchange? A pointed diatribe concerning the city manager's fitness for office? Long-standing bad blood between the city manager and his accuser?

The Importance of Context

Often, by carefully reporting the *context,* we can get closer to the truth, even when we can't yet determine whether the original assertion is true. In that sense, an accretion of what we *know* can help us get to where we want to be. We provide context by gathering and presenting additional relevant facts. It might be an oversimplification to say that truth is facts in context, but it's a start. For examples of how we would write a news fact and news truth, see Box 12.1.

Notice in the example in Box 12.1 that news truth does not include everything we know about the exchange—what other council members were doing at that point, what Wise and Prentice were wearing, where in the room each was sitting, and so forth. More importantly, we are not yet able to say whether the accusation itself is true. So now the reporter must ask herself: How do I know when I've got enough facts to tell the truth?

Most philosophers recognize that achieving a pure truth or a whole truth is impossible. What we as journalists are after is enough truth to keep our audience served appropriately. That's why we never disclose everything we know in news stories, even if we have the time and space to do so. Some facts

Box 12.1

NEWS FACT, NEWS TRUTH

News fact: *Valleydale Council Member Eaton Wise last night accused City Manager Don Prentice of having an adulterous affair with an employee of the city Finance Department.* (That Council Member Wise made the accusation is a fact.)

News truth: *Valleydale Council Member Eaton Wise last night accused City Manager Don Prentice of having an adulterous affair with an employee of the city Finance Department. Wise offered no evidence to support his accusation, and it could not immediately be verified. Prentice has never previously been publicly accused of adultery.* (The truth of the accusation remains to be determined. Meanwhile, the news fact of Council Member Wise's accusation has been placed in context.)

are simply not necessary to the task at hand, even though they might arguably contribute to a complete truth. The focus of most stories is narrow enough that we do not need to show everything we know about everybody in the story or every issue it addresses. For example, in a crime story in which a suspect is still at large, the physical description of the suspect—height, weight, race, clothing—is important. But in a story about a City Council meeting in which a citizen makes comments, a physical description of the speaker is almost never relevant.

For journalists, then, the challenge is to report enough to convey a truthful account of the event or issue at hand and the way it affects the people involved. As we discussed in Chapter 1, that involves a willingness by the journalist to make responsible judgments about what ought to be included in a story.

Often, when newspeople are accused of distortion, it's because someone represented in a story thought that more about him or his views on an issue should have been included, or that someone else's position should not have been. Again, the journalist needs to consider whether her audience was appropriately served by the decisions she made.

When we decide to report a news fact the truth of which cannot be immediately determined, we owe our audience—and the people involved—two duties: We must provide as much relevant context for the news fact as we can, and we must follow up on our initial reporting, so that even if we can't report in today's story whether the news fact is true, our audience can expect us to do so in the future.

Be Fair: Facts First, Words Second

As with all the other issues involved in responsible reporting, it isn't enough that we understand the difference between a news fact and the truth. We must write our stories so that the difference is clear to our audiences. Choose your words carefully. (See Box 12.2.) Watch for language that may sound compelling but leaves an unfair impression. Such writing leaves not only your subject, but you, open to criticism.

For example, newspeople frequently refer to someone who has been charged with murder as "the accused killer." Think about that. To call someone an accused killer is simply to say he is a killer who has been accused. Calling the city manager "the alleged adulterer" is the same. How can we use words more fairly? In these examples, we can use the noun or verb form of *accuse* and *allege* to put the emphasis on the accusation or allegation rather than on something we cannot yet verify. "The city manager defended himself against allegations of adultery" at least puts the emphasis on the fact that it is an allegation at this point. Similarly, "He is accused of killing" puts the emphasis on the accusation. We should avoid using *accused* and *alleged* as adjectives. Similarly, "he was arrested for killing" tells your audiences that someone was arrested *because* he killed someone. Guilt is for a jury to determine. It is fairer to say "he has been charged with," and then report the charge or charges.

When we are confronted with the necessity to report allegations of distasteful or seamy conduct, we are often inclined to try to soften the language

Box 12.2

ACCUSED, ALLEGED, CHARGED WITH

Avoid saying:	Instead, say:
The alleged killer	*He is charged with killing.*
	If no charges have been filed, say:
	He is alleged to have killed . . .
	He is facing allegations that he killed . . .
The accused rapist	*He is charged with raping.*
	If no charges have been filed, say:
	He is accused of raping . . .
	He is facing allegations that he raped . . .

we use. But as good as our intention might be, it could well cause harm. Once we've made the decision to share information with our audiences, it's usually better to let them know specifically what is alleged than to resort to euphemisms that create confusion or ambiguity. Sometimes the euphemism makes the allegation sound even worse than it is.

Ethics

We must avoid using confusing institutional terms such as *news fact* in our stories. In the example we've been using, if we determine that the comment bears reporting, we would be careful to call it an "allegation" or "accusation" until we could determine whether it was true. It's hard to imagine how an accusation of adultery could be relevant to the business of the City Council, but there are times when unsubstantiated allegations made at a public meeting cannot be ignored. Sometimes they occupy the entire focus of the meeting. Sometimes they have a direct bearing on the welfare of citizens. When that is the case, it's important to remember that nature abhors a vacuum. We must consider whether, in following our first instincts to ignore unsubstantiated accusations, we are allowing rumor to take the place of responsible reporting in the community.

For example, when a substantial part of a City Council meeting is taken up with accusations against the city manager, we can bet that those accusations will be talked about around town the next day, even if we don't report what happened. The difference is that the information will be passed along second-, third-, fourth-, fifthhand, and so on, until what the 30th person hears will be an embellished or distorted version of what was an unsubstantiated allegation to begin with. In this case, it is better for us as journalists to report what was really said and to place it in as much context as we think necessary. By doing so we help neutralize the rumor mill, and we enter into a tacit agreement with our audience that we will pursue the matter until we can determine the truth of it. That's substantially different from rushing into print or on the air with a story simply because "the guys down the street already ran it, so we're off the hook," and the decision to run a story to neutralize the rumor mill should never be entered into lightly.

Finally, you might be wondering whether our judgment will be influenced by the possibility that publishing or broadcasting such accusations could leave us open to a libel or slander lawsuit. Statements made in public meetings or proceedings, or records of them—a legislative session, a City

Council meeting, a trial transcript or minutes of a council meeting, for example—are said to be *privileged*; that is, they give news media immunity from lawsuits *provided we have fairly and accurately reported their substance.* So when it comes to reporting what goes on in public proceedings, you'll have to rely on your own judgment, not on legal constraints.

Strategies

Let's look at some strategies for *distinguishing* facts from allegations.

Remember that direct observation is best, but beware of the possibility that your own observations can be wrong or out of context.

Get people on the record. We identify the source of the information so our audience can judge how much faith to give it. We also identify the source so that the source is held accountable for what he or she tells us. Knowing that he or she will be clearly identified in a story makes it less likely that the source will lie or make unsubstantiated accusations. Those transgressions are easier to commit if we allow a source to make them anonymously.

Do your homework. For each event or issue you are called on to report, learn as much as you can about it and the players. A source who knows you have done your homework is less likely to lie to you or make wild claims.

Listen carefully, so you are sure you understand what you are being told, the significance of the information, and the level of observation at which the source is reporting.

Ask questions based on the careful listening that you do. Always be prepared to ask a source how he or she knows what he or she claims to know.

Look for ways to document a source's assertion, but keep in mind that documents can be wrong or contain falsehoods. Sometimes the document is generated by the same person making the allegation.

Now some strategies for *showing audiences* what you have learned:

The words you use to report facts and allegations are critical. Choose them carefully. Beware of the ones that protect neither you nor the subject

Box 12.3

STRATEGIES FOR DISTINGUISHING FACT FROM ALLEGATION

1. Strive for direct observation, but put your own observations to the test as well.

2. Attribute information to named sources. Proper attribution gives your audience the opportunity to judge the credibility of the source, and it keeps the source accountable.

3. Background is important. Learn as much as you can about issues and players.

4. Make sure you understand what you are being told, and how sources know what they say they know.

5. If you're not sure, ask.

6. Find documentary support for allegations if you can. But remember that documents can be wrong, too, and that one definition of *allegation* is an unsupported accusatory statement.

7. When you write about facts and allegations, take pains to distinguish them. Choose your words carefully. Many words have *connotative*—commonly understood—as well as *denotative*—dictionary—meanings.

8. Avoid using *accused* and *alleged*. To call someone *an accused killer* is simply to say he is a killer who has been accused. *The alleged adulterer* is the same.

9. Don't jump the gun. Write about arrests, not suspects. Police talk to many people who are never arrested.

10. When you write about an arrest, don't convict. Say, *He has been charged with,* not *He was arrested for.*

11. Avoid euphemisms or vague language, even when writing about distasteful allegations. Euphemisms create ambiguity, which makes everything worse.

12. Make your words serve the facts, not the other way around. Don't outrun your facts in order to use a snazzier word.

13. Keep sources on the record.

14. Where there is ambiguity, clear it up if you can. If you can't, acknowledge it, so your audience knows you are not being intentionally vague.

of the story. Be careful also of *connotative meanings*. Many words are understood by many to carry more than their dictionary—or *denotative*—meaning. For example, the denotative meaning of *deny* may simply be to declare untrue. But connotatively it can be loaded, conveying the impression that someone is refuting an accusation that *is* true. Similarly, while one denotative meaning of *admit* is simply to acknowledge as true, a more common denotative and connotative meaning is to confess to guilt or a mistake. Where that isn't the case, a less loaded word would be *acknowledge*.

Think of accused *and* alleged *as invisible adjectives.* Using them is the same as not using them. To call someone "an accused killer" is simply to say he is a killer who has been accused. "The alleged adulterer" is the same. Use the noun or verb form to put the emphasis on the accusation or allegation rather than on something we cannot yet verify. "The mayor defended himself against allegations of adultery" at least puts the emphasis on the fact that it is an allegation at this point. Similarly, "He is accused of killing" puts the emphasis on the accusation. Do not use *accused* and *alleged* as adjectives.

If you are dealing with a criminal case, it is better to avoid naming a suspect until an arrest has been made. If we didn't know that before, the 1996 Atlanta Olympics bombing case should have taught us. FBI agents leaked the name of someone they said was a suspect. His name became a household word, linked to the bombing. He was never charged, and the FBI later dropped him as a suspect. But the damage was done.

When charges have been filed, use "He has been charged with," and then report the charge or charges. The phrase "He was arrested for killing" tells your audience that he killed somebody and was arrested for it.

When you think it's necessary to report distasteful conduct or allegations of it, avoid euphemisms. Once we've made the decision to publish, it's usually better to let our audiences know specifically what is alleged than to resort to euphemisms that create confusion or ambiguity. Sometimes the euphemism makes the allegation sound even worse than it is.

Focus on facts first, words second. That means we let the words serve the facts, not the other way around. It might have seemed more stylish to say "President Clinton's alleged illicit affair with Monica Lewinsky." Until we knew it was fact, it was also patently unfair.

Attribute carefully, and keep the source or sources on the record.

Clear up ambiguity. If you can't, alert your audiences to it, so that they won't jump to conclusions. They will also realize that you know the ambiguity is there, and that you are not being deliberately or carelessly vague.

You already have some context for the exercise that follows, and some knowledge of the players involved (see Chapters 1 and 6). Keep that in mind as you write a story about this City Council meeting. And as your material gets more complex and your stories get longer, remember the *impact, elements, words* process.

Use judgment in selecting quotes. You will need to balance the value of using strong quotes to show the personalities and emotions of the council members against offending your audience with profanity, obscenity or crude characterizations.

Exercise 12

City Council Meeting

The City Council has several standing committees that consider the business of various city agencies and departments and make recommendations to the full council for action. The Finance Committee, chaired by a City Council member, is charged with weighing budgetary matters and matters of policy presented to it by the finance director or city manager. It is not charged with the day-to-day running of the department. That is the job of the finance director and his or her designees. (The city manager is the finance director's supervisor.) If, however, a city employee's conduct is in question, the committee may recommend any of a variety of courses of action to the full council, including dismissal. The Finance Committee does not itself have the power to fire the city manager or any of his department heads or employees. Council members Wise and Bullard are not on the Finance Committee, so their interest in and claims about knowledge of the city manager's involvement with the finance department are curious. Assume the following happened at the end of a routine City Council meeting last night. It is now October, one month after the events described in Chapters 1 and 6 and alluded to in Exercise 4. Write the story first for the newspaper, then as a 30-second RDR. In preparing the broadcast story, how will you handle a key-facts outline when you are dealing partly with "news facts"?

Valleydale City Council, Meeting Excerpt

Mayor Hostetter:　Anything else before we adjourn?

Council Member Wise:　I do have one matter, Mr. Mayor, if I may.

Mayor:　Sure, Eaton, go ahead.

Wise:　Thank you. For some time we have attempted to discuss some fiscal irregularities with the city manager. After one in-depth discussion two months ago, after which he promised to investigate, we have heard nothing, and now he refuses to meet with us. We are gravely concerned for the people of Valleydale. This is not appropriate stewardship of their hard-earned tax dollars.

Mayor: Hold on, Eaton. I thought we had gotten beyond all this when Don met with you. Everybody reported back to us that everything had been explained. Then four weeks ago you tried to get us to fire him, and now you're saying that somebody's got his hand in the till?

Wise: Certainly not, sir. I am saying that there are irregularities in the city budget that the city manager refuses to explain or address. We have recently lost our finance director, who resigned in frustration over Mr. Prentice's mismanagement. We think these irregularities should be aggressively pursued.

Council Member Chipps: Well, I'm just a dumb country boy, but that sounds to me like a beating-around-the-bush way of saying somebody's got his hand in the till. I don't remember the finance director giving us any such reason for leaving. If you're gonna make accusations like that against Don Prentice, Eaton, you'd better be damned sure they're right.

Council Member Bullard: Believe me, Mr. Wise would not be raising these serious matters in public if we didn't have solid evidence to support them. Why, I can't make heads or tails of the city budget, and I studied bookkeeping for a year at community college.

Mayor: Okay, folks, then I guess it's time to make your case. Do you have any particulars?

Wise: Indeed I do, but this public forum is not the place for that. I wouldn't want to embarrass the city manager unnecessarily.

Council Member Clark: Oh, for God's sake, Eaton. Same deal as last time: First you make all kinds of wild allegations in public, then when it comes time to put up or shut up, you retreat behind "I don't want to embarrass Mr. Prentice." Be fair. Let's hear what you've got. If you can back it up, let's not leave the citizens in suspense any longer. If you've got nothing, let's exonerate the man.

Bullard: Let me hasten to say here that one of the reasons we would rather discuss this in an executive session is that it gets very, very—uh—messy. My understanding is that it has less to do with Mr. Prentice's performance than with attempts to protect the job of someone in the Finance Department, a young woman who should be let go, but who is, uh . . .

Chipps: Oh, that's great. Now you're saying Don's bonking some little girl in the Finance Department, and *she's* the one with her hand in the till? But now Alice can't get rid of her because this little bimbo would squeal on Don? Oh, hell. I just noticed all the reporters out there scribbling. (*Turns toward the press table.*) That was all off the record, you guys. You can't print none of that.

Clark: I can't understand why the Finance Committee doesn't know about any of this if there is any substance to it. Even if we've got a little *Melrose Place* going on over there, we can't be talking about much money, can we? I mean, how much can one little clerk get her hands on?

Wise: *Au contraire*, Mr. Clark, my understanding is that we are talking about a substantial sum of unaccounted-for funds. And allow me to say that I am offended by the crude way Council Member Chipps has characterized the city manager's relationship with the employee, but I must reluctantly admit that he has understood Council Member Bullard and myself correctly.

Council Member Mutispaugh: Excuse me. As Finance Committee chair I would just like to make it clear on the record that, as Mr. Clark says, we have not participated in any of this. I am not at all comfortable with the accusations being made and—

Council Member Jefferson: So you're saying they're not true, Louise?

Mutispaugh: No, I have no idea whether they're true or not. I'm just not comfortable—

Jefferson: Well, hell, why don't you either look into it or resign from the committee, then? You can't just try to ignore all this. If you think there's something there, find out. If you think Eaton and Rondah are trying to crucify Don Prentice again, say so. If you can't stand the heat, get the hell out of the kitchen.

Mayor: Good job, Willie. Now you've made her cry.

Jefferson: I'm sorry if I've upset you, Louise, but—

Clark: Mr. Mayor, we're getting pretty far afield here. May I make a suggestion?

Mayor: Oh, by all means.

Clark: How about we all catch our breath for a few more weeks. I'd like the Finance Committee to look into this formally, talk to employees, find out what kind of bee Eaton and Rondah really have in their bonnet, have an outside auditor look at the books, and report back to us formally if they come up with anything. Not more wild accusations, but the real deal, with evidence, if there is any. I know that leaves you in limbo for a few more weeks, Don, but can you live with that?

City Manager Prentice: Mr. Clark, I would welcome a formal investigation to clear the air. I must say, though, that I think squandering the taxpayers' money to hire an outside auditor is completely unnecessary at this time. We ought to be able to keep our own house in order, particularly since this internal investigation will turn up nothing.

Mayor: Yeah, I see no need to call in auditors at this point.

Clark: Hang on. I'd like to get a vote on that so we—

Mayor: Oh, shucks, we don't need a vote, do we?

Jefferson: No, I'm not willing to spend money on auditors at this point, not when the Finance Committee hasn't looked at it yet.

Mayor: Are you making the request for an outside auditor in the form of a motion, Bud?

Clark: Yeah, I so move.

Mayor: Second? Anyone? Motion dies for lack of a second. Sorry, Bud, the council seems to want the Finance Committee to do the investigating. Okay, Louise, get your committee cracking on that report. Can you have it ready in four weeks, that's two council meetings from now?

Mutispaugh: We certainly can.

Mayor: Good. This thing needs to be cleared up publicly. That should make everybody more careful about making a case they can prove. Meanwhile, I will rely on the news media to handle this issue responsibly. I caution everyone here that we have no hard evidence at this point. Until we do, I don't see much of a story.

Follow-up Interviews

Subject: Council Member **Wise**

Q: What is your evidence against the city manager?

A: I am not prepared to discuss it publicly at this time.

Q: Financial mismanagement, embezzlement, inappropriate sexual behavior?

A: As much as I am sure you would love for me to, I will not respond to your taunting. We will share our proof with the Finance Committee.

Q: Did that proposal for an outside audit give you any problems?

A: You are baiting me. I'll not rise to it.

Q: Do you support Council Member Bullard's allegations of sexual misconduct?

A: This interview is over.

Subject: City Manager **Prentice**

Q: Don, can you respond to the accusations?

A: Can I? Yes. Will I? No. Except to say that the fact that the allegations are false leaves me some legal options, and I intend to explore those.

Q: You mean a lawsuit?

A: I'm not prepared to say at this time. However, if I were a member of the media I would be extraordinarily careful about what I printed, if you get my drift.

Q: What do you think the accusations are based on, then?

A: I can say that my dealings with the Finance Committee and the Finance Department over the past year have been fine, completely professional. Ms. Trump's departure had nothing to do with any of these accusations. Mr. Wise and Mrs. Bullard do not understand even the basics of municipal finance. And they show little inclination to learn.

Q: Why do you think that is?

A: I guess we'll find out in a few weeks.

Q: Why did you resist an external audit?

A: I didn't resist it. I said it was unnecessary at this time. I've just been accused publicly of misusing public funds. Isn't it equally a misuse of public funds to waste money on something we don't need?

chapter thirteen

Interviewing

In Chapter 11 we looked at sources, and how to show your audience what a source or sources contribute to a story. In Chapter 12 you worked on the issues that arise when sources make allegations against others. In this chapter you will follow up those discussions with some lessons on effective interviewing.

For many beginning journalists, the prospect of telephoning or dropping in on a perfect stranger to ask probing questions is pretty frightening. For one thing, it goes against the grain of much of what we've been told growing up: *Don't talk to strangers. Mind your own business. Don't ask rude questions.* In Chapter 1 we talked about how our obligations as journalists affect these old standbys from the parents' handbook.

Whose Advantage?

Even without all that parental advice kicking around in your subconscious, your first few interviews can be pretty intimidating. But if you think it's a gut-tightener for you, think about the person you will be interviewing, particularly if he or she isn't used to dealing with news media. Your subject goes into the interview knowing that anything he or she says might wind up in the newspaper or on the air for all to see. Or that a brand-new reporter just out of J-school won't get it right.

Now back to your perspective: The person who is quite used to being interviewed and is skilled at manipulating the media dreams of the day when an inexperienced reporter stumbles into her crosshairs. The reporter might as well be wearing a sign that says "Shoot me and mount me on your wall."

But an interview doesn't have to be a contest to see who wins. In fact, if we are to serve our audiences well, interview-as-conflict is probably not the appropriate model.

Pam Podger of *The Roanoke Times* interviews Dan Brown, retiring superintendent of the Blue Ridge Parkway. In their manner and appearance, reporters can establish the tone for interviews before they begin asking questions.

What Kind of Interviewer Will You Be?

As an interviewer, you should always convey a sense of self-assurance and professionalism. That doesn't mean you have to be cold, arrogant, unsympathetic or overly slick. Being professional means being able to judge what is required in a given situation. With the skilled media manipulator you will need to be tough and focused but still fair. With somebody who isn't used to talking to reporters, you need to be more relaxed and informal, to put the subject at ease. Your sense of self-assurance can help you do that. If one person involved in the interview feels comfortable, the other can feed off that. (This is especially true when the camera is running. The presence of a camera makes most interview subjects pretty nervous.) When it comes to the so-called grief interview, with the relative or friend of the victim of a tragedy, you need to be low-key and unobtrusive. (How many journalists does it take to change a lightbulb? Eleven—one to change the bulb, and 10 to chase the old one down the street, asking it how it feels.) Always, you need to be a good listener.

Reporters should combine open-ended and closed-ended questions to get the most from an interview. What kind of an interviewer will you be?

Box 13.1

> ## OPEN-ENDED AND CLOSED-ENDED QUESTIONS
>
> Use open-ended questions when a subject won't open up:
>
> *Tell me about your son.*
>
> *Talk about that for a minute.*
>
> *Describe what you did at that point.*
>
> Use closed-ended questions when a subject won't shut up, or is being vague or evasive:
>
> *Did you take the money?*
>
> *What was her name?*
>
> *How many hikers are missing?*
>
> *When did he graduate?*
>
>
>
> *Source:* From Douglas A. Anderson and Bruce D. Itule, *Writing the News,* New York: Random House, 1988, chapter 7.

For television interviews, plan to shoot 10 to 20 times as much tape as you will use in your story. You need to keep the camera rolling long enough to allow your interview subject to get comfortable with the camera's presence before you start asking the really important questions—the ones you expect to yield bites. Plan to spend as much time with the subject as necessary in order to get the information you need.

What Kind of Questions Will You Ask?

Journalists recognize two kinds of interview subjects: those who won't open up, and those who won't shut up. Often there is little middle ground. You'll need to use at least two kinds of questions in interviewing. In their book *Writing the News* (1988), Anderson and Itule identify these as open-ended and closed-ended. Use open-ended questions when your subject won't open up; use closed-ended questions when he won't shut up. (See Box 13.1.) Open-ended questions often don't even sound like questions: "Tell me about it." "Talk about that for a minute." It's hard to respond to such a prompt with a one-word answer. If a taciturn football coach answers questions like "How is Flurtz's arm this season?" with "Fine," try an open-ended question: "Talk about the coming season, Coach." Open-ended questions can also sound less threatening to a subject who is inexperienced, nervous or upset: "Tell me about your son."

The second kind of source won't shut up, or will try to hide or avoid honest answers with a flood of words. When that happens, used closed-ended questions to get to the point quickly and keep the interview subject focused: "Did you take the money?" "What was her name?" "How much was missing?" Often it's appropriate to elicit a one- or two-word specific answer and then let the source elaborate. Use your knife when you need your knife and your fork when you need your fork.

How Will You Go About Your Job?

Just as we have identified steps in the writing process that make it more manageable, you should approach interviewing as a process comprising several critical steps. Before we look at those, let's take a minute to talk about a mechanical aspect of interviewing.

If you are working for a radio or television news operation, you will of course be recording your interview on audio or videotape. But some newspaper reporters also tape interviews so that they can be sure to get quotes verbatim and not miss other crucial information. For print reporters, that practice raises a couple of issues. The first is time: For a reporter on deadline, finding and transcribing quotes from a tape can be overly time consuming. Second, you have to be prepared in case your tape recorder fails. Will you take a second recorder with you to the interview? If you don't realize until you return to your office that your tape recorder failed, you will have no record of the interview unless you took careful notes as well. So even if you record an interview, always be sure to take notes as a backup. Faced with taking notes as insurance, many print reporters decide not to fuss with a tape recorder, especially when they are on a tight deadline.

Now then, let's consider the steps in the interviewing process (see Box 13.2):

First, do your homework. Learn as much as you can before the interview. You'll want to know what you're likely to encounter before you encounter it. Effective interviewing starts that way. Read clips. Look at file tape. Use Google or other Internet search engines. Round up everything you can find

Box 13.2

STRATEGIES FOR EFFECTIVE INTERVIEWING

1. *Learn as much as you can before the interview.* Know what you're likely to encounter before you encounter it.

2. *Prepare a general set of questions.* It will ensure that you don't forget to ask something important.

3. *Be ready to depart from your prepared questions.* Careful listening will show you when you need to follow up on an unexpected response.

4. *Give visual cues to your professionalism.* Dress appropriately for the situation, but don't overdress.

5. *Be precise.* Ask short questions, then follow up to get the subject to elaborate.

6. *If your subject is going too fast, ask him or her to slow down.* Show the interviewee that you consider important what he or she is telling you.

7. *Watch as well as listen.* How does the subject behave? Is he or she at ease or nervous?

8. *Learn—and report to your audience—the difference between "would not comment," "did not return phone calls," and "slammed the door on a reporter."* When a source chooses not to be represented in a story, show your audience how that came about.

9. *Remember the three most important questions in journalism:* What does that mean? What does that mean? What does that mean?

10. *Make sure you have gotten appropriate identifying information about your interview subject.* Don't ever assume you know how to spell her name or have her job title right, or that you know other basic information without asking. Ask for a business card when it's appropriate.

about the interview subject and what it is that makes you want to interview him or her. Find out as much as you can about the event or issue at hand and your subject's interest or involvement in it. Knowing your topic and something about your source does several things, all of them good:

> *It helps establish rapport* when she learns that you care enough to have done your homework. Many sources won't even bother with an unprepared reporter.

> *It helps you catch lies* and discourages the source from trying to tell them.

It helps you note inconsistencies in the source's position or a change in that position over time.

It keeps you from wasting the source's time by asking questions whose answers you could have gotten elsewhere. (An interviewer once asked baseball legend Mickey Mantle what position he played.)

Second, get some questions ready based on the homework you did. You'll feel more confident going in, because you know you'll be able to control the direction of the interview and you won't forget to ask an important question.

Third, be ready to depart from your list. Careful listening will show you when you need to follow up with an unprepared question. Sometimes an interview takes off in a direction you haven't planned. If you've done your homework, you'll be better able to judge whether that change of direction will be appropriate and productive or a waste of time.

Fourth, show your professionalism. Dress appropriately for the situation, but don't overdress. And always show up on time. For a television interview, show up early to give yourself time to set up your equipment. You'll want to be ready to begin the interview at the agreed-upon time.

Fifth, keep to your purpose. Usually, you'll want to ask short questions and depend on follow-ups to get the subject to elaborate. Ask what needs to be asked—in other words, don't pull punches—but be sensitive. Avoid arguing; you're there to elicit information from the source, not express your opinion. But that doesn't mean allowing the source to get away with a vague or illogical response. You might have to ask a question several times or in several ways to get a clear answer.

Sixth, control the pace. Some subjects talk so fast you risk losing what they say. When you ask your interviewee to slow down, it shows him or her that you are interested in getting what he or she says right. That's a good idea even when the camera or tape recorder is running, for two reasons: (1) You'll want to take some notes as well; (2) a subject who talks too fast makes for lousy bites. By the way, don't accuse the source of talking too fast. Instead, put the onus on yourself: "I'm a pretty slow note-taker. Could you repeat that?" or "That sounds really important. Could you go over that again to make sure I understood it?"

Seventh, use all your senses, not just your ears. How does the subject behave? Is he or she at ease? Are some questions making him or her more nervous or ill at ease than others? Should you ask why? Remember that for television interviews you will need to shoot some "cutaways"—video shots of subject matter other than the interviewee—for editing purposes. Can you focus on something other than the subject's face that reveals something about him?

Eighth, remember that potential interview subjects can choose many ways not to be in your story. Learn—and report to your audience—the difference between "would not comment," "did not return phone calls," and "slammed the door on a reporter." Even when a source is not represented in a story, showing your audience how that came about can be informative and useful.

Ninth, keep asking, "What does that mean?" until you're sure you understand. Your interview subject might get exasperated, but eventually he or she will speak plain English. As a result, you'll understand what he or she is saying, and so will your audience. It also will give you clear quotes or bites you can use.

Finally, make sure before you write your story that you know how to spell your interview subject's name, and that you've got her job title and other appropriate identifying information right. When appropriate, ask for a business card.

Ethics

As you learned in Chapter 11, interviewing sources presents a number of potential ethical issues for journalists: quoting sources accurately, making sure information and quotes remain in context, ensuring that sources know information is on the record, properly attributing information, keeping promises to sources regarding how information will be attributed, treating sources with respect, even when we have to ask tough questions, and keeping clear the level of observation at which a source is operating. You should review that discussion before you work on the exercise at the end of this chapter.

There are at least two more ethical issues we can identify in conducting and using interviews. The first has to do with your decision whether to record the interview. Many journalists think it a matter of basic fairness to let a source know when you are recording his or her comments. Others think that the mechanics of gathering information are irrelevant—that they are under no obligation to share those methods with their interview subject. A couple of things to remember: When you are conducting a telephone interview, there is usually no way for a source to know he or she is being recorded unless the reporter acknowledges it. And a reporter who goes into a live interview with a hidden camera or tape recorder is acknowledging a form of deceit by assuming that the source would object if he or she knew the conversation was being taped. In July 2005 *Miami Herald* columnist Jim DeFede was fired after acknowledging that he had surreptitiously taped a phone conversation with a distraught source who shot himself to death moments later. DeFede said he made a quick decision that he wanted a record of the conversation because he recognized that the source was emotionally agitated. But taping conversations without consent is a violation of Florida law. Several other states have similar laws. To many observers, it was not clear whether DeFede was fired because he broke a law, because he did not tell the source he was taping the conversation, or both.

The second ethical issue is how journalists ought to respond to interview subjects' requests to hear their statements read back to them. There is no consensus among journalists on that issue, either. Some see it as a threat to journalistic independence, fearing that a source will try to amend or influence what the reporter took from a conversation. Increasingly, though, reporters are recognizing that reading quotes and other information back to sources at the end of a conversation can help fulfill the reporter's obligation to serve audiences: The practice ensures that the reporter got everything right, and gives the reporter a chance to fix what isn't right. But the reporter also must judge the difference between a source's objection that the quote is not accurate and a complaint that it simply puts him in an awkward position or makes him "look bad."

Strategies

As a warm-up to Exercise 13, your instructor might ask your class to pair off, interview one another, and to write a story based on what you found most significant in your interview. That will give you a good chance to practice many of the steps in the interviewing process.

In Exercise 13 you will assume the identity of Tori Baxter. Tori gets information from her interview with Meagan LeBlanc as well as from clips of earlier stories. (You can find references to Meagan LeBlanc in Chapter 1 and in Exercise 10.) By interviewing Meagan, Tori is changing her focus from only the most recent event, so that she can fashion a story with more impact for local audiences. Notice how she mixes open-ended and closed-ended questions for a subject who is willing and fairly relaxed, but who has an adolescent's inclination to wander off point. Note also how Tori politely challenges Meagan to explain why some things Meagan mentions—such as race—are relevant. By giving Meagan the opportunity to explain, Tori can better judge whether the information belongs in her story at all.

When you have written a story for the newspaper, try tightening it to a 30-second RDR for broadcast. Can you see why such a story would be better told as a longer broadcast "package" including bites from Meagan?

Exercise 13

Interviewing Meagan LeBlanc

Write a story for the *Herald* based on the background information presented here and on notes you will take on the one-on-one interview that you observe in class.

It is now mid-October. Meagan LeBlanc was featured this morning in a two-minute story and subsequent live interview on CNN. The subject was VPU's quadrennial mock presidential-nominating convention. Because it is celebrating its 100th anniversary—the convention has been held every four years for the past century—and because of its record for accuracy, the convention has attracted widespread media attention already. The convention is scheduled for March. Meagan is program chair. Officials at CNN estimate that the segment was seen by about four million people nationwide.

Chapter 1 refers to Meagan's rescue of 2-year-old Chandra Jefferson from a burning home in Valleydale a year ago. President Bush mentioned her in his State of the Union message in January. Meagan holds the conference record in the indoor 400 meters and outdoor 200 meters. She is co-captain of the VPU women's track team and an avid rock climber. She was the youngest woman to scale the Dawn Wall of Yosemite's famous El Capitan, a feat she accomplished with an older brother and uncle when she was 17. To reach Meagan, you leave a message on her answering machine. She calls you back later in the afternoon.

chapter fourteen

Speeches

In Chapters 1 through 10 you were introduced to the process of writing, and to basic reporting and judgmental skills every reporter needs to know. In Chapters 11 through 13 we focused on sources and responsibly handling the information they give us. In the remaining chapters you will continue to practice all those skills by applying them to particular types of reporting and stories. As you encounter each new challenge, remember your *impact, elements, words* process, and the ethical dimensions of every decision a journalist makes.

Why Cover Speeches?

News media cover speeches for one of three reasons, usually. The first is that the speaker's topic carries some potential impact for an audience. The second is that the presence of the speaker locally carries some impact. For example, we would cover a speech the president of the United States gave in Valleydale even if he talked about making yogurt. A presidential appearance in Valleydale carries emotional impact no matter what the reason is for his visit. People will tell their grandchildren about it in 50 years, over and over and over again. (If you don't believe me, ask the grandchildren.)

The third reason is the most common, and it is a combination of the other two: The advertised topic carries potential impact for readers, listeners or viewers, and the speaker has some expertise or notoriety associated with the subject. The subject's prominence or status doesn't necessarily mean that the speaker will be lucid or well-organized. Some speakers can't use plain English; others get the heebie-jeebies in front of a crowd. Still others can't organize their thoughts in a coherent fashion. As with all events or issues, the reporter is left with some decisions to make: How much of what the live audience saw should the audience for the story see, read or hear?

U.S. Senator George Allen opens the Team Virginia Military Support Center in Roanoke. Journalists covering speeches may choose to shift the story's focus from the speaker's primary topic.

Putting Your Audience There, or Not

It's the reporter's job to make sense of the speech for members of an audience who couldn't be there—your readers, viewers and listeners. The task is complicated by the fact that many speeches are scheduled at night, close to a reporter's deadlines, because that's when most people can attend.

On some cable channels, such as C-SPAN, speeches and lectures are frequently broadcast in their entirety, though not often live. Some Web sites stream video of speeches as well, though again, the Webcast is seldom live. It's rare for a major network or network affiliate station to broadcast an entire speech. It is even more rare for a newspaper to publish a full transcript. About the only exception is the president's State of the Union message. Even in that case, only a few daily newspapers will carry the full speech in addition to stories about it.

So the reporter usually must summarize the speech for the mass audience, rather than including everything the live audience heard. Keep in mind that, often, much of a speech will address the relatively narrow interests of the people who chose to attend. Its appeal for a mass audience is up to you to find and show. As a result, speech stories—whether broadcast or print—are invariably much shorter than the speech itself. As with every other story, then, focusing on the impact of a speech becomes essential.

Your Judgment, or the Speaker's?

Remember that your first job as a reporter is to keep your audience in mind. Your own political, ideological or emotional response to what the speaker says doesn't count. Hold on to your sense of professionalism, your obligation to serve your audience. What does the speaker say that will carry impact *for your audience?* Often that information doesn't come early in the speech; sometimes we don't hear it until the question-and-answer period at the end. Just as you have an obligation to change the focus of a news release to reflect what's most important to your audience, in a speech story you have a similar obligation to make sure your focus is appropriate for your audience. The speaker might emphasize something of interest to his or her live audience; something of tangential interest or importance to that audience might carry the most impact for a news audience. News stories are well-focused accounts;

there's no reason to make a reading or viewing audience sit through every-thing the live audience had to while waiting to hear the comments that carry the most significance. That's true whether you're developing the story for print, broadcast or online. Whether you're writing quotes down or taping them, you'll build your story around the most significant thing that was said.

Finding the Impact

So how do you go about making sure you serve your news audience well? First, remember that the most important thing the speaker said isn't usually the first thing. Even if you decide that your focus will be the same as the speaker's primary focus, be careful not to write a dull lede. (See Box 14.1.) A speaker's theme or topic statement can be a terrible guide for a reporter.

> Speaker: *Tonight I would like to turn my attention to the United States' foreign policy, specif-ically in the Middle East.*

In this case, the topic sentence *tells* the audience what the speaker will talk *about*. Your job is to *show* your audience what the speaker *said*.

Box 14.1

WHAT'S THIS SPEECH ABOUT?

Be wary of fashioning your story's lede from a speaker's theme or topic statement. Doing so can result in a weak lede.

> Speaker's topic statement: *Tonight I would like to turn my attention to the United States' foreign policy, specifically in the Middle East.*
>
> Weak lede: *Sen. John Kerry spoke to an audience at Princeton University last night about the United States' foreign policy in the Middle East.*
>
> Stronger lede: *The Bush administration's policies in Iraq have failed and will continue to fail, Sen. John Kerry told an audience at Princeton Univer-sity last night.*

If the most significant comment was not the speaker's theme, or if it came in answer to a question afterward, lede with it, then put it in context with a statement like this:

> *Jones's comments about Clinton came near the end of a speech to a cosmetics industry trade association about a new product line.*
>
> *Baker's characterization of Reagan was in response to a question after he had spoken for an hour to a farmers' group about federal price subsidies.*

Second, as with any story, do your homework. The more background you can gather about the speaker and his or her topic beforehand the better your story will be. Doing your homework might also give you the opportunity to write part of your story ahead of time if you know you will be facing a tight deadline. Biographical information about the speaker, the nature of his or her prominence, and how he or she came to be in town is not likely to change based on what you hear in the speech. Write that first, incorporating file tape into your package if you're working for broadcast; you can write your lede and the meat of your story about the speech itself after it happens. Sometimes speakers will release advance copies of their speeches, which can be extremely helpful. But follow closely as the speaker delivers it. Be alert to off-the-cuff remarks, which are often more engaging and revealing than prepared remarks. Former President Ronald Reagan's handlers lived in mortal fear that he would depart from his prepared text, and he often did. One of his most famous—or notorious—ad-libs was that trees cause pollution.

Third, resist the temptation to use a quote for your lede. Even in speech stories, ledes that consist of quotations—or sound bites—usually don't work. That's because quotes usually don't provide enough context for themselves. It's better to paraphrase the most significant thing the speaker said in the lede, then look for a supporting quote, close paraphrase, or sound bite to support that lede. Nut grafs are important in speech stories to provide the context. If you're working on a broadcast story, the context will probably take the form of a voice-over.

> Weak: *"This approach has my full support. I think it will settle the matter once and for all."*
>
> *That was how Valleydale Mayor Delmer Hostetter expressed his public confidence Tuesday in a plan to have the city's Finance Committee investigate allegations against City Manager Don Prentice.*

Better: *Mayor Delmer Hostetter says he supports a Finance Committee investigation of allegations against Valleydale City Manager Don Prentice.*
"I think it will settle the matter once and for all," Hostetter told a Rotary Club meeting Tuesday.

In the first example, a fairly strong quote carries immediate impact only for those of us who already know what the story is about. Practically no one in your audience does.

So rather than begin with a quote, use a strong lede to show your audience the impact. Then try to find your best quote to *support* and illustrate your lede in the second paragraph.

The Body of the Story

Bullets

Bullets are a device that can be useful to print and online reporters in writing speech stories. Often you will recognize one theme that you will emphasize, but the speaker will touch on several other topics as well. When those topics are less important than your first choice but about equal to each other, use bullets to introduce them a couple of paragraphs (or grafs) below the lede. You can then flesh them out one by one later after you've finished with the main emphasis of the story. (In broadcast stories, don't try to use a sound bite for the bullet itself. This approach is cumbersome, for you and your audience.)

A bullet graf would look like this:

While Iraq's arsenal was foremost in the president's mind, he took time to score a few political points. He advocated:

- *A constitutional amendment banning abortion.*
- *A federal hands-off policy on state laws regulating gay marriage.*
- *Mandatory college courses in drug-abuse prevention.*
- *Immediate implementation of the No Child Left Behind law, his principal public education initiative.*

Notice that the elements are set up so that, combined with the single introductory clause, the list forms a complete sentence. Limit bullet items to one or two short sentences. Remember, your intention is merely to introduce them near the lede. You can elaborate on them in turn lower in the story. For broadcast stories, that's the place to work in the sound bite if you have it. If you have fewer than three bullet items, treat them in narrative form, not as bullets. If you have more than six, the bullet format gets unwieldy.

Delivery and Response

Always notice the speaker's delivery—polished, awkward, rambling, stilted, conversational—and the audience's response. But include them in your narrative only if you think either is significant. Occasionally the audience's response becomes the focus of the story, if it is particularly strident or animated. Conversely, if the speaker put everybody to sleep, your audience should know that. Note the size of the audience as well, but keep in mind that it's usually not worth dwelling on.

Quotes

Speech stories make more use of *direct quotes* than many other kinds of stories, but you should still use quotes judiciously. Even in a speech story, most of what you write should be in paraphrase. Avoid partial quotes; as you learn to take notes, you will get the hang of getting whole-sentence quotes. As with interviewing, tape recorders often aren't much help on deadline if you're working for print. There will typically not be enough time to transcribe quotes. For broadcast stories, shoot a lot of tape or record the entire speech, but discipline yourself to use just one or two bites.

News Facts

Remember to *check assertions a speaker makes* if you can. In Chapter 12 you learned the concept of a news fact, and how it might differ from the truth. But remember that the news fact of a speaker saying something may be so compelling that it bears reporting, even when the truth of the statement can't be verified. When you have to make that decision, remember to put the comment in that context in your story:

> *Baker offered no proof or substantiation for his assertion.*
> *A legislative inquiry three months ago cleared Thompson of any involvement.*

You can see again why doing your homework beforehand can be critical.

Ethics

There is a difference between changing the focus of your story to serve the needs of your audience and misrepresenting what a speaker says. You should be able to give clear, compelling ethical arguments for deciding on a different focus than the speaker's in your story, based on the impact for the mass audience you serve. In an example from above, a speech about farm subsidies by a former member of President Ronald Reagan's cabinet will carry little immediate impact for a mass audience. But personal insights into Reagan by someone who was close to him would. A speaker might not be happy with such a decision by a journalist, but the decision is ethically defensible.

What is not ethically defensible is misrepresentation—misquoting a speaker or taking his or her remarks out of context. If the quote from Mayor Hostetter used in the earlier example—"I think it will settle the matter once and for all"—was not made in reference to the Finance Committee's investigation but to a vote against raising property taxes, we have misrepresented what Hostetter said, even if the quote itself is accurate.

Strategies

Let's summarize key strategies for finding the impact of speeches on your audience and writing compelling stories from speeches. (See Box 14.2.)

Do your homework. As with any story, the more background you can gather about the speaker and his or her topic beforehand, the better your story will be. If you will be covering a speech on deadline, you can often use the background to write part of your story in advance. That will save time later.

Remember that the most important thing the speaker said isn't usually the first thing. For example, a lot of speakers warm their audiences up with a joke. You wouldn't lede with that. In deciding what to focus on, be professional. Serve your audience, not your own political or ideological agenda.

Even in speech stories, ledes that consist of quotations—or sound bites— often don't work. That's because quotes usually don't provide enough context for themselves. Paraphrase the most significant thing the speaker said in the lede, then look for a supporting quote.

Use bullets to encapsulate important points that are separate from the focus of your story. Introduce them a couple of grafs below the lede. You can then flesh them out one by one later.

Box 14.2

STRATEGIES FOR WRITING SPEECH STORIES

1. *Be prepared.* The more you know going in, the better your story will be. Using the background you gather, try to write part of your story ahead of time.

2. *Don't lede with the first thing the speaker says.* Usually, that's "I'm delighted to be here tonight," or "Being in front of this audience reminds me of a joke . . . ."

3. *Avoid quote ledes.* Quotes don't provide enough context for themselves. You will be the only one who understands the significance of the quote.

4. *Use bullets to summarize a speaker's secondary topics.* Place your "bullet graf" a couple of grafs below the lede. You can flesh each bullet item out one by one later.

5. *Include the speaker's style of delivery or the audience's reaction only if they contribute to the story's impact.*

6. *Be stingy with quotes.* Even though the speech consists entirely of quotes, use only the best you have for your story.

7. *Watch for unsupported assertions.* If you can't check something for accuracy, remind your audience that the statement could not be verified.

Notice the speaker's delivery and the audience's reaction. But include them in the story only if you think they help show the story's impact.

Use quotes sparingly. Even in a speech story, most of what you write should be in paraphrase. As with other stories, save quotes for the most compelling stuff. Avoid partial quotes.

Treat a speaker's unsupported assertions carefully. Check them out if you can. But remember that the news fact of a speaker saying something may be so compelling that it bears reporting. In that case, remind your audience that the statement could not be verified.

Exercise 14

Speech

In class, you may be given a choice of speeches to cover, either on campus or in your community. Write a story about the speech you attend. Alternatively, write a newspaper story based on the transcript of a speech by Mayor

Hostetter presented here. Then write it as a RDR for broadcast of no more than 30 seconds.

Here is some background on the courthouse agreement Hostetter refers to: Merchants and some other city residents see a new downtown courthouse as a magnet for local businesses. Fearing a loss of potential shoppers downtown, they opposed initial plans by the county to replace the current inadequate downtown courthouse with one outside the city. The City Council approved a tentative agreement to share the cost of a new downtown courthouse with the county.

Mayor Hostetter's Address

Ladies and Gentlemen:

When we were elected to this job four years ago, the city was at a crossroads. Well, we're still at a crossroads—U.S. 50 and Route 15 still intersect right in the middle of town. But seriously, from time to time I like to advise the City Council and the citizens of Valleydale periodically on what I see as the condition of our city, its financial health, its problems, its key issues.

Let me start by saying that Valleydale is still the best place in the United States to live, bar none. Our elementary and middle schools rank near the top of the heap in the whole state. The physical beauty of our city frequently attracts filmmakers and TV producers. Retirees are flocking to the area. Our citizens are engaged and committed to community service.

But I would be lying if I said everything is hunky-dory. As a city we face daunting challenges in the years ahead. Foremost among them is how to effectively balance a reasonable tax burden against increasing demands for services and sources of state revenue that are drying up. By the way, I want to take this opportunity, since we're talking about the city budget, to give my personal vote of confidence to our city manager. Mr. Prentice is one of the most effective public servants I have ever seen, and he has withstood recent unfounded attacks upon his professionalism and character with good grace. I look forward to his being exonerated of all these scurrilous and groundless accusations.

In the longer term, though, Don and his staff face a tough job. Our aging population will need better and expanded services—health care, public safety and emergency services. But many are on fixed incomes, so property taxes will have to remain low. The key, I think, is to look for other sources of revenue. Our ever-growing tourism industry should shoulder a large share of the burden. That's why I am calling for a two-cent increase in the sales tax on restaurant food and hotel and motel rooms. It would raise, I project, another $400,000 annually.

I conclude my remarks with an observation about public service—no, wait. Before I do that, I want to mention my opposition to the planned new courthouse in the downtown area. I know we have tentatively agreed with the county on financing the thing, but I am going to do my best to see that that project dies. We should back out of that agreement. It was stupid. If the county wants a new courthouse, it can build it somewhere else, and not with city taxpayers' money. What we really need downtown is a multistory parking garage, and every merchant in town would agree with me on that. For $11 million, we could build it right where the municipal lot is now on Roosevelt Street across from Dominick's Pizza. I am going to fight for that, even if we have to raise property taxes to do it.

There is no doubt about it, Valleydale is a city whose future is ahead of it. Thank you.

chapter fifteen

Computer-Assisted Reporting

In the mid-1970s a quiet revolution began to take place in newspapers across the nation. More recently it has taken hold in broadcast newsrooms as well. The so-called "back shops" of newspapers—the composing rooms and pressrooms—began adopting computerized typesetting equipment that was faster, more efficient and less labor intensive than the old "hot type" technologies. Newspaper publishers being the mercenary folks they are, the impetus for this change was financial: Hardware replaced people, and once you've spent money up front on hardware, you don't have to pay it wages and benefits every month. Computers also take less time to set type than people do, so more income-generating work could be done in the same amount of time.

In the newsrooms, meanwhile, reporters and editors kept beating away on typewriters. Eventually they got to the point where they were writing stories and headlines on IBM Selectrics; a snazzy computerized scanner in the composing room could "read" copy from these machines and typeset it so that it was ready for the printing process.

New Technologies, New Reporting Tools

Then, about 1975, the first fairly reliable generation of word-processing computers began showing up in newsrooms. Reporters and editors took to them avidly, because word processors gave them the option of editing copy heavily without having to go through cumbersome typewriter rewrites with hard copy. And the computers had the advantage of capturing the reporters' first keystrokes and preserving them until eventually they could be printed, also using computers. Again, that meant that publishers could save money by eliminating typesetters in the back shop.

More recently, broadcast newsrooms have gotten computerized, and many are now using digital technology to shoot and edit. The Internet revolution has taken us a giant step further, providing a tool for research, communication and dissemination that is perhaps unprecedented. The rapidity of all this change is stunning to those of us who have lived through the myriad evolving generations of hardware and software. I began my news career in 1973 in a broadcast newsroom with a manual typewriter and 16 mm film. In 1976, when I moved to daily newspapers, I graduated to electric typewriters. Our first generation of newsroom computers arrived in 1978. You who were born after that have no memory of a world without powerful multiuse personal computers and desktop publishing.

Green Eyeshades and Chi-Squares

About the same time that print newsrooms started using computers, people who had had training in formal data-gathering methodologies began showing up in those newsrooms. They knew about sampling, survey techniques and inferential statistics. They envisioned a kind of reporting that relied on systematic gathering and interpretation of data from large populations rather than the old, not-very-reliable "reporter's hunch" or "some say" kind of reporting. There was some initial resistance to and distrust of these data-gathering techniques from people who had always done it the old way. Newsroom people began calling the confrontation the "green eyeshades" versus the "chi-squares." ("Green eyeshades" because editors in old newsrooms used to wear green eyeshades to keep harsh overhead light out of their eyes while they tried to read faded typewriter copy on white or yellow foolscap. "Chi-squares" because the new, science-based data gatherers often used a basic inferential statistic called the chi-square.) The initial resistance was overcome eventually by positive results, and by reassurances that the new scientific data-gathering techniques directed, affirmed and augmented traditional reporting; they did not replace talking to people face to face.

Desktop Computers and Databases

But there was another problem. The kind of data processing the "chi-squares" did required big mainframe computers. Their desktop word processors simply did not have the power or hard-drive space to do it. So they would run their programs on the same big computer that also kept track of classified advertising billing and ran the word processing and typesetting programs. (The first few times I did computer-assisted reporting projects at *The Miami Herald* in the early 1980s I had to run the programs on the mainframe between midnight and 7 A.M. so that other crucial functions, including payroll, wouldn't be interrupted. The first project took me nearly six months. *The Herald* paid for a lot of coffee.) Again, most TV stations were still in the wilderness in those days. The only time they would go near computer-assisted reporting was to report somebody else's election poll, often without regard for its reliability.

The big breakthrough came in the early 1990s, when personal computers finally were developed with hard drives that were big enough to run data processing software and had enough storage space to hold onto the output when those numbers were crunched. The new PCs had other advantages: They were more user-friendly, as was the icon-based software that had been developed by then; they were fast enough to provide access to myriad databases through the Web; and they had CD-ROM capabilities, so that databases could be imported from other sites and downloaded into individual newsroom personal computers. Having access to these data was critical for reporters, because many local governments by this time had begun computerizing operations and keeping information on disks to be manipulated by computer software. Several court challenges by news media established that those computerized records were public, just as hard copy data were.

Today, a computer-literate reporter like Tori Baxter can go out on the Web, find databases and import them. She can buy copies of local government

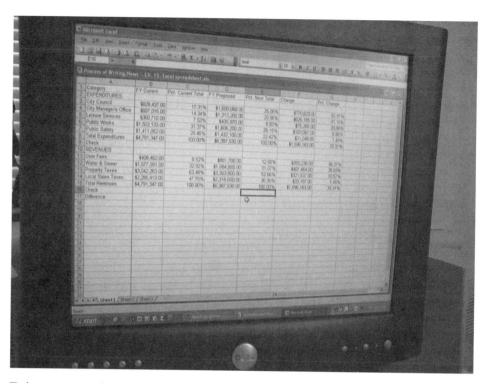

Today a computer-literate reporter with a desktop workstation can run any of several spreadsheet or statistical programs to interpret data using comparative, descriptive and inferential statistics.

agencies' data on CD-ROM and drop them into her PC. And she can run any of several spreadsheet or statistical programs to interpret those data using comparative, descriptive and inferential statistics. When she gets a copy of Valleydale's proposed budget, for example, the first thing she does is run it through a spreadsheet program to make sure all the percentage increases and decreases over last year agree with the city's raw numbers. She can also find missing items or gaps where the numbers don't add up. Then, using the Web, she can import a database from the University of Virginia that shows the municipal budgets for cities near Valleydale and for other cities statewide that are about the same size as Valleydale. From those she can run comparative statistics to see whether Valleydale's proposed budget is out of line with those of similar cities. Finally, she can use inferential statistics to compare the overall increases and decreases in the other cities with those in Valleydale to see whether anything statistically significant is going on—in other words, are the discrepancies happening by chance, or is a sustainable pattern emerging?

To do all that using a mainframe computer 15 years ago could have taken weeks, given the logistics of gathering compatible databases and begging enough mainframe time. With her PC and its data processing software, Tori should be able to do the job in a couple of hours. She can also take her data and display them graphically in fever, bar or pie charts, labeled with type in whatever point size and font she chooses. More sophisticated displays can be done by a newsroom graphic artist in Jeffersonville simply by calling up Tori's numbers and importing them into his or her own graphics software. In the broadcast or online newsroom, the same thing can happen.

Trust Your Reporting Skills

There are four things we must remember about computer-assisted reporting. (See Box 15.1.)

First, as the old computer-geek expression goes, *garbage in, garbage out.* If you plug in data that are old or wrong or improperly set up for the program you're running, you will get useless results or, worse, results that look

Box 15.1

THE COMPUTER CAN'T DO IT ALL

Remember that computers won't do your thinking for you. Some things to keep in mind about computer-assisted reporting:

1. *Garbage in, garbage out (GIGO).* If you plug in bad data, you will get bad results—useless or wrong. Get someone to help you who can catch those mistakes.

2. *Computer-assisted reporting does not replace other reporting tools; it increases their value.* Reporters still need to talk to people—a lot of them.

3. *The computer can't explain things to an audience.* As the reporter, you need to figure out the best way to do that. Often, that is through the skilled use of graphics. Avoid putting a lot of numbers in your story itself.

4. *The two-minute-mile rule.* If your data are telling you something that you think can't possibly be happening, you're probably right. Check and recheck. Don't leave your common sense in the other room.

neat and plausible until you put them in the paper and realize that you've just given Valleydale a population of 5 billion. If you are unsure about what you are doing, get some expert help. Many news operations have professionals on staff to assist in this area, if not in the newsroom then on the business side or in data processing. If you can't find assistance in-house, go to your local college or university's politics or sociology department and talk to someone who teaches statistics. He or she will know what you want to do, and how you've screwed it up.

On the front end, you can help yourself by maintaining your healthy skepticism as a reporter when it comes to finding data. If you're getting data from the Web, who is generating the data? Have they got an ax to grind? Are they spinning the data to push their cause or agenda? What did they leave out? Can you call them and get more information about them? Can you talk to a real person?

Second, *computer-assisted reporting is one tool for gathering information. It complements our other reporting tools; it does not replace them.* If your numbers tell you something is happening, go out and find the real people it is happening to, and let them show your audience the situation through their own stories. Again, the best stories are about things happening to people, not things simply happening.

Third, *when you write your story, keep numbers out of your narrative as much as possible.* Talk about increases or decreases, or trends, or developing issues, and the people who illustrate those. Look for ways to make numbers conversational: say "more than two-thirds" instead of 68.4 percent; "nine people in 10" instead of 91 percent; "about half" instead of 48.2 percent. Put the actual numbers in easy-to-read graphics accompanying the story. Winnow all the information that takes focus away from what you really want to show. Approach those graphics as you would a story: What's this story (graphic) about? What element or elements do I need to focus on to show that? Get rid of the clutter.

Fourth, *remember the two-minute-mile rule.* When he was my editor at the *Tallahassee Democrat,* Walker Lundy would tell us to trust our common sense. If we were given four affidavits from Supreme Court justices swearing that somebody had run a mile in two minutes, but we just couldn't believe that that could be true, we were probably right. With computer-assisted reporting, if your data are telling you something that you think can't possibly be happening, you're probably right. Check and recheck your data, your program, your interpretation. And get another set of eyes on it. Always remember that every computer should have a port where you can plug in common sense.

Ethics

Most of you have heard the saying, "Statistics don't lie, but people lie with statistics." There was a time when news media were too lax in reporting results of polls and surveys, failing to find out how a survey was conducted, for example, or ignoring what organization commissioned the poll. Or they simply treated all such surveys with equal skepticism, contenting themselves with simply reporting the results and who generated them, or refusing to report any poll results at all.

Today many news organizations have policies regarding such reporting. Stories about surveys or polls must include who or what organization commissioned the study, how it was conducted, and how reliable it is, including the margin of error for the findings.

When news organizations design and carry out their own computer-assisted projects, their standards for reporting the results should be at least that rigorous. As a journalist your primary moral obligation remains, as always, to serve your audience by providing accurate, fair and appropriately contextualized information. That means that you should always tell your audience how you collected and analyzed your data, whether you had help from experts, and who those experts were.

As with any other story, your words shouldn't outrun your facts. Often an opinion, belief or behavior that is not in the majority is still significant and worth reporting, but it should be contextualized to show how prevalent it is. Also, journalists might use computer-assisted reporting to try to verify a hunch, an informed opinion based on anecdotal evidence, or a formal hypothesis. But they must be prepared to find another explanation if the analysis doesn't support their assumptions.

Finally, if, as in the exercise below, your data point an accusing finger at an individual or organization, that person or group must be given an opportunity to respond. You should also seek alternative plausible explanations from other sources. That is not only a matter of fairness to the person or group, it is part of your obligation to your audience.

Strategies

Many journalists consider themselves numerically challenged. A lot of them think that their math phobia prevents them from attempting computer-assisted reporting. It doesn't. Remember that the computer and its spreadsheet and other data analysis software are another reporting tool. As the reporter, you should be figuring out what questions to ask, and what the story is about based on the answers you are getting. The computer will do the sorting and the math for you, but you still do the journalistic thinking, and the writing based on it. (See Box 15.2.)

With that in mind:

Make sure your newsroom has the resources to do the kind of computer-assisted reporting you envision.

Use experts to help you determine whether such things as surveys and computer analysis of data will answer the questions you have. Use those same experts to help you design your project and to help you interpret your results.

Put a human face on your data. Find people to interview who will show what your data are telling you. Remember that good stories are about people involved in events and issues, not just about events and issues.

Keep numbers out of your story as much as possible. Make generous use of graphics to summarize your data for your audience.

Use the impact, elements, words *process* to organize and tell your story. Focus on what's most important; leave extraneous information out. As

Box 15.2

STRATEGIES FOR COMPUTER-ASSISTED REPORTING

Remember that computer-assisted reporting is another tool in the journalist's kit. The computer crunches the numbers; you still do the journalism. Here are some other tips:

1. Don't launch a computer-assisted reporting project until you know your newsroom has the hardware, software and human resources to do it.

2. Find an expert or two to help you set up your program and analyze your data.

3. Put more people in your story than numbers. As you would with any story, interview human beings, then show your audience how they are affected.

4. Make generous use of graphics to show numbers. Keep most of the numbers out of your story.

5. *Impact, elements, words.* Show what's most important rather than reproducing every result you got.

with the reporting for any story, your audience won't see or hear a lot of your data analysis.

The exercise that follows is a fairly straightforward tutorial that takes you through a Microsoft Excel–based spreadsheet program. You will plug in hard-copy figures given to you by Valleydale's city manager showing the city's proposed budget. You will run some operations on those data once you have entered them. Following the tutorial are some guide questions to help you interpret your data. Following that are quotes the city manager gives you when you call to ask him about the budget as you have analyzed it. *Do not look at the guide questions or the interview until you have crunched your numbers once.*

Exercise 15

Analyzing Valleydale's Budget

On the day that Valleydale City Council calls for the city manager to submit a proposed budget for the next fiscal year (July 1–June 30), Tori Baxter asks for a copy. The city manager knows it's a public document at this point, so he does not quibble about releasing it. But the proposed budget isn't given to Tori until 4 P.M., and Tori is expected to get her story in the next day's paper and a summary on the Web. There isn't enough time to get anything on the evening news broadcast, but the station has expressed interest in a 30-second RDR for 11 P.M., depending on what the proposed budget shows. Tori will have to work fast, but because her computer has a spreadsheet program, she ought to be able to analyze the budget by her deadlines. Because the entire proposed budget is many pages long, she will focus only on key elements of it.

In almost every state, local governments have to balance their budgets. Unlike the federal government, they may not spend more than they take in.

This exercise walks you through part of what Tori would do to analyze those key elements of the proposed budget using her spreadsheet program. The program you will use is Microsoft Excel, but several Windows- and Mac-based spreadsheet programs share the same basic characteristics and commands. It's easy to adapt to the others once you're familiar with one. Many cities now provide their budget data online or on CD, so that the data can be imported into a spreadsheet program. But because some small communities still do not provide data in those forms, in this exercise you will learn how to enter data by hand from a hard-copy source. Make sure that you enter your figures correctly. Garbage in, garbage out.

Once you have analyzed the budget using the tools and commands that the exercise will walk you through, look at the interview with the city manager. Using both your data analysis and the interview, write a story for the *Herald* and a blurb for the Web site about the city's proposed budget. Once you have done that, your instructor might assign you to write a 30-second RDR on deadline in class.

Remember also that this is a proposed budget. It must survive several City Council work sessions and a formal public hearing before adoption. That process can take three months or more. The story you write about the proposed budget should make that clear. Assume that the release of this proposed budget comes early in November, three weeks after City Council asked the Finance Committee to investigate the city manager's handling of city finances.

A spreadsheet program can do wondrous things when it comes to crunching these numbers. What it can't do is tell you what strategy you should adopt for analyzing them. That's where looking for the impact comes into play. It seems reasonable to expect that most people in your audience will want to know whether spending is going to increase, whether taxes will go up and, if there are increases, where they will happen and why. To get those answers we will have to compare the proposed figures for next year with the actual figures for this year. Budget comparisons that show trends over the last five years are even better, but they are beyond the scope of this exercise. The two-year comparison you will do will go a long way toward helping your audience fathom this proposed budget.

Entering Your Data*

First, load Microsoft Excel by following the protocols for your personal computer or workstation. For most users, that involves clicking on the Start menu, then clicking on Programs, then going to Microsoft Excel and clicking on it. You will get a page full of empty boxes, called cells, in a grid. Rows run east–west and are numbered; columns run north–south and are designated alphabetically.

If it isn't there already, move your cursor (in Excel it looks like a plus sign instead of an arrow) to cell A1 (first column on the left, first row down) and

---

This section is adapted from Rich Gordon for Investigative Reporters and Editors, Inc. (IRE) © 2003. http://www.ire.gov. With permission.

type the word *Category.* Hit Enter. Now save your new spreadsheet so you can create a name for it. You probably know that to save you can left-click on the Save icon (looks like a diskette, same as in Word) at the top of your screen, or click on File at the top of your screen and then on Save. Your instructor will tell you what convention to use to name your spreadsheet. With my classes I use this protocol: valleybudbr. "Valley," of course, is for "Valleydale," "bud" is for "budget," and "br" are my initials. Using this protocol, everyone's slug will be the same for the first nine letters, but if your name is Tom Green, your slug would be valleybudtg; Jessica Simpson's would be valleybudjs, and so forth. As you do in Word, save often.

After you hit Enter and save your spreadsheet, move your cursor over to cell B1, just to the right of the cell you've just typed in, A1. In cell B1, type *FY Current* (for current fiscal year or budget year. Again, the fiscal year is distinguished from the calendar year in that it runs July 1 through June 30. In your stories, to avoid confusing audiences with bureaucratic terms, always call it the budget year rather than the fiscal year.).

Oops. The words *FY Current* are just a little too wide for cell B1. So let's widen your columns, and we might as well start with column A, where you typed in *Category.* Move your cursor onto the vertical line separating column A from column B at the top of the column. If you're in the right place you'll see a double boldfaced arrow pointing left and right, bisected by a vertical line. Now click, hold down, and drag to make the column as wide as you want it. Do the same for column B. You can see from your hard-copy data that there will be row headings in column A that are even longer than the word *Category,* so go ahead and make column A wide enough to accommodate the widest heading you have. You'll have to guess at the right width for column B until you have entered your data. Now go to cell C1 and type *FY Proposed,* and widen that column. Then, in cell D1, type *Change,* and widen that column.

Now, starting in cell A2, beneath *Category,* enter the budget categories from Box 15.3. Start with *EXPENDITURES,* to show that you're on the spending part of the budget, then *Public Safety* (that's the police and fire departments), and so forth. Hit Enter after you type each entry. When you try to type *Public Works* after *Public Safety,* you'll notice that the program tries to repeat *Public Safety* for you. This happens because the program thinks it is so smart that it can anticipate what you want it to do. You, of course, do not want to type *Public Safety* twice, so go ahead and finish typing *Public Works.* The program will reluctantly go along, knowing you will hit the computer with something large if it doesn't. The same thing will happen when you try to type *City Manager* after you type *City Council.* If you make an error

Box 15.3

CITY OF VALLEYDALE PROPOSED BUDGET

	Current	*Proposed*
EXPENDITURES		
Public safety	$1,411,052	$1,432,100
Public works	1,503,133	1,606,200
Leisure services	360,710	435,970
City Council	829,437	1,600,060
City manager's office	687,015	1,313,200
Total expenditures	4,791,347	6,387,530
REVENUES		
Property taxes	$3,042,263	$3,363,800
Local sales tax	2,285,413	2,318,600
User fees	408,462	801,700
Water & sewer	1,577,391	1,984,855
Total revenues	4,791,347	6,387,530

when you are typing in column heads or data, simply hit Backspace until you have erased the error, or hit Enter and highlight the cell again, then type over your error and hit Enter again. Remember to keep saving your work.

Now skip a space in column A and type *REVENUES,* your income categories. Then enter each category under Revenues. Then go to column B and enter the current actual budget figures, again from Box 15.3, corresponding to the appropriate categories of expenditures and revenues. Do the same in column C for the proposed figures. Don't worry about putting dollar signs or commas in at this point.

When you start to type in the revenue and expenditure figures, numbers like 18965491 might be converted to gibberish when you hit the Enter key. If that happens, it means your columns are too narrow, and the computer is trying to figure out a way to fit all those figures into too tight a space. Go to the top of the column, as you did with your other columns, and hold and click to widen the column. Even after you've done that, all of your figures will look like just a sequence of numbers at this point, because they won't even have commas. So let's reformat the whole block of numbers now.

Move the cursor to one corner of the top left cell showing budget figures (B3), click your left mouse button and hold it down, and then move the cursor down and to the right until you've highlighted cells B4 through C15 in a tasteful blue-gray, or maybe gray-blue. (Cell B3 won't change color for some reason.) Release the mouse button. Make sure your arrow stays inside the highlighted area, and then click the right button. You will get a drop-down box with several choices. Left click on Format Cells. You will get a series of stacked folders, labeled Number, Alignment, Font, and so forth. Click on Number if you aren't already there. You will get a drop-down list with numerous choices: General, Number, Currency, and so forth. Left click on Currency. You will also see two more choice boxes, Symbol and Negative Numbers. Relax. We are going to ignore Negative Numbers. Use the down arrow next to Symbol to get you to "$ English United States." (I know it doesn't make any sense.) Highlight it. If you do, you will get dollar signs in front of your numbers. If you click on something else, you will get the sign for Egyptian piastres or whatever. Now go to the bottom of the screen and click OK. That should give you your spreadsheet back with all your numbers converted to dollars, complete with commas in the appropriate places.

Take a second to make sure you haven't highlighted your boxes too far up. If you did, your year column headings will now look like dollar amounts. Now, left-click outside the highlighted area to get rid of the highlights, and hit Save again. Groovy.

Process of Writing News.xls

	A	B	C	D	E	F	G
1	Category	FY Current	Pct. Current Total	FY Proposed	Pct. Next Total	Change	Pct. Change
2	EXPENDITURES						
3	City Council	$829,437.00	71.13%	$1,600,060.00	25.05%	$770,623.00	92.91%
4	City Manager's Office	$684,015.00	14.34%	$1,313,200.00	20.56%	$626,185.00	91.15%
5	Leisure Services	$360,710.00	7.53%	$435,970.00	6.83%	$75,260.00	20.86%
6	Public Works	$1,503,133.00	31.37%	$1,606,200.00	25.15%	$103,067.00	6.86%
7	Public Safety	$1,411,052.00	29.45%	$1,432,100.00	22.42%	$21,048.00	1.49%
8	Total Expenditures	$4,791,347.00	100.00%	$6,387,530.00	100.00%	$1,596,183.00	33.31%
9	Check						
10	REVENUE						
11	User Fees	$408,462.00	8.52%	$801,700.00	12.55%	$393,238.00	96.27%
12	Water & Sewer	$1,577,391.00	32.92%	$1,984,855.00	31.07%	$407,464.00	25.83%
13	Property Taxes	$3,042,263.00	63.49%	$3,363,800.00	52.66%	$321,537.00	10.57%
14	Local Sales Taxes	$2,285,413.00	47.70%	$2,318,600.00	36.30%	$33,187.00	1.45%
15	Total Revenues	$4,791,347.00	100.00%	$6,387,530.00	100.00%	$1,596,183.00	33.31%
16	Check						
17	Difference						
18							
19							
20							
21							
22							
23							
24							
25							
26							
27							
28							

Near the end of your spreadsheet analysis, your figures should begin to look pretty interesting.

Calculating Spending Changes

So much for the scut work. Now for the fun stuff. Take a minute to think about what your audience will want to know about this budget. First, most will probably want to know how much spending will go up if the proposed budget is passed. Obviously, we'll want to show percentage increases at some point, but for now let's show the change in dollars. So go to your D column and click on cell D8. We'll need to put a formula in this cell to show how much higher next year's proposed expenditures are than this year's. For arithmetic functions, the first instruction you need is the equals sign: =. Then, because you want to find out how much higher next year's budget is than last year's, you'll subtract cell B8 from C8. So your command in cell D8 should look like this: =C8-B8. Hit Enter. You should get a figure expressed in dollars.

We'll look at each category of expenditures next. To save time, spreadsheet programs let you copy the formula instead of retyping it into each cell. First, highlight (click on) the cell containing the formula, or the first result you got. Then copy it by clicking on the Edit menu at the top of your screen and clicking on Copy from that menu. Now click and drag to highlight the range of cells into which you want the formula copied (cells D3 to D7). Then go back to the Edit menu and click Paste. (You can also use the copy and paste icons at the top of your screen if you are familiar with that procedure.) You will see the solutions appear in each box that you've highlighted. Now do the same thing for the figures in the Revenues columns to get the change from this year to next in revenues.

It's time to remind you that if garbage goes in, garbage comes out. Spreadsheets are powerful programs, but they can't do your front-end thinking for you. For example, if you told the program to subtract C8 from B8 instead of the other way around, you got some screwy negative numbers because you subtracted bigger numbers from smaller ones. Worse, once we get into percentage changes, you can set up a formula that gives you numbers that look plausible but are flat wrong. And if you copy one wrong formula over and over again, you simply multiply your errors. What fun.

Now look at the changes from this year to next in dollar figures. Some interesting stuff.

Calculating Percentage Changes

It's time to figure those dollar changes as percentages. We'll need to give the column a label, so type *Pct. Change* in cell E1 (you might have to widen the cell). Next, go to cell E8. Your formula for percentage change is =D8/B8.

When you type that into E8 and hit Enter, you should get the percentage by which total expenditures will go up next year, but the percentage will be expressed as a decimal. We'll convert it in a minute.

Remember also that the formula to get the percentage change from one year to the next is to take the dollar *difference* between years, shown in cell D8, and divide it by *this* year's figure, shown in cell B8. So dividing cell D8 by cell B8 will give you how much the percentage increase is in total expenditures for next year. That's why we express the formula as =D8/B8.

Be careful not to divide cell D8 by cell C8, next year's proposed figure. That would give you a meaningless figure; in effect, you'd be showing us the percentage the budget increased from next year to next year.

Now let's change that decimal to a percentage. You know how: Highlight the cell, then right click to get your Format Cells choice. Left click on it, then select "Percentage" from the list of choices. Click on OK, and you're back to your spreadsheet with the change expressed as a percentage.

Now copy the percentage change into cells E3 to E8 by using the same functions you used to get the changes expressed in dollars: Highlight E8, go to the Edit menu, select Copy, define the range of cells E3 to E7, then go to the Edit menu and select Paste. Holy moly!

Now that you've got a handle on expenditures, let's get the same percentage figures for revenues. Again, just highlight, copy, define your column of revenues, and paste. More interesting stuff.

Sorting

The Sort function on a spreadsheet program is valuable when you want to rank data, from biggest increase to smallest increase, for example. In our working sample we can pretty much eyeball those rankings, but when you've got dozens of categories, sorting can make your data much clearer. Let's sort revenues and expenditures by percentage change.

The first thing you'll need to do is use the click and drag function to highlight the range of cells you want to sort. This requires a bit of thinking. If you decide you want to see the percentage changes from highest to lowest (descending order, in other words), you'll obviously want to sort by the percentage column. *But if you highlight only the cells in column E, you'll get bad data.* Here's why: Your row headings (*Police, Fire, City Manager,* and so forth) will remain where they were. So will the figures for those headings. But because you've told the spreadsheet program to rank only the percentages, the percentages will be shuffled into highest-to-lowest order. So you'll wind up at the top with a percentage that might originally have been in the fourth row down, and it will now be next to a category and dollar figure it has nothing to do with.

What you need to do, then, is to highlight the whole range of cells in *Expenditures,* A3 to E7, and then tell the computer you want all those sorted only by the percentage column. Again, the spreadsheet program is smart enough to do that, once you tell it to. It is not smart enough to understand that that's what you want it to do if you give it vague instructions.

So click and drag to highlight all cells from A3 to E7. Notice we are not highlighting the *Total Expenditures* category, because it would make no sense to rank it when you're looking for the differences between individual categories.

Now click on the Data function on your menu bar up top. You'll get a box listing your choices. "Sort" is the first one. Left click on it. You'll see a "Sort by" slot at the top. Use the arrow to scroll down to "Column E," because that's the column you want to sort all the others by. Left click to select column E, then click on the Descending button next to the "Sort by" slot, because you want the program to rank the percentage changes highest to lowest. Ignore the other slots, which are labeled "Then by," and the buttons next to them. Now click on OK. You should see the categories, dollar figures and percentages shuffled until expenditures are ranked by highest to lowest percentage change. *Voila!* Now do the same for the *Revenues* category. Save your data and examine them.

Inserting Columns

With figures this interesting, it's hardly time to stop analyzing this budget. Let's find out what percentage of revenues is coming from each source, and what percentage of expenditures is going for each service.

To do that, you'll first have to insert a column. Move your pointer to the top of column D and click. Then go to the Insert menu on your toolbar and choose "Columns." Click on it to insert a new column D (the spreadsheet will relabel your columns automatically). Go to the top of the column and label the cell *Pct. Next* (for next year's) *Total.*

More Percentages

Remember that we're trying to find out what percentage of total revenues will be raised from each category. To do that, we're going to divide one category by the total. Go to cell D11 and type =*C11/C15.* Notice that we've added dollar signs on either side of the second C. You need to do that because we're going to copy the formula to the rest of the cells in the column. When you divide each of a range of cells by a single cell, the copying function won't work right unless you remember those dollar signs.

When you hit Enter you will see the change expressed as cents. That's because the program is reading a decimal change, not a percentage change, and then trying to express that decimal in dollars. Go ahead and highlight, copy and paste to calculate all your revenue changes. Then select a cell, right click to get Format Cells, choose "Percentage," click OK, and then copy it to all the other cells to get your change expressed as a percentage. Now create a *Pct. Current Total* column next to column C and do the same calculation for current year revenues. Then do the same for the expenditures side of both budgets, using your copy/paste function.

=SUM

Let's check a couple more things. Excel allows us to take some shortcuts that might lead to interesting data. The most common one is =SUM. If you want to check whether the city's arithmetic in the *Total Revenues* cell for the proposed year is right, for example, you could type *=D11+D12+D13+D14*. *Borrring.* But you can get the same result if you type *=SUM(D11:D14)*. Sing Hallelujah.

Okay, let's do that. In Cell D16 type *=SUM(D11:D14)*, then hit Enter. Do the same for the current year's revenues and for both years' expenditures. (You can't use the copy/paste function here, though, because you are dealing with distinct commands, not just copying a function. Be careful. You might decide to try it anyway, and you might get plausible-looking numbers. They're bogus.) If you like, you can give your rows a heading such as *Check* to remind yourself that you're checking the city officials' math.

Based on what you see, you might want to create one more label, in row 17. Call it *Difference.* Then, in cell B17, subtract the city's total revenue figure, shown in cell B15, from your total revenue figure, in cell B16. To do that, use the formula we used earlier, =B16-B15. Hit Enter. Do the same in cell D17 for the proposed budget's revenues.

Now that you've got all your data, save your spreadsheet program once again, and go on to the next part of this exercise.

Guide Questions

Use the following questions as a guide to help you organize and write your story on Valleydale's proposed budget. You might not use all the answers in your story.

1. Do the revenue totals for the current and proposed budgets check out? Do the expenditures?

2. What is the city's total projected increase in expenditures (in dollars) from the current year to next year?

3. Which category shows the biggest increase? How much was it?

4. Which category shows the smallest increase? How much?

5. What was the percentage increase in total expenditures?

6. Where were the two biggest percentage increases by category of expenditures?

7. Which category shows the smallest percentage increase?

8. What was the city's total increase in revenues (in dollars)?

9. Which revenue category shows the biggest increase? How much was that?

10. Which category shows the smallest increase? How much?

11. What was the percentage increase in total revenues?

12. Where were the two biggest percentage increases by category?

13. Which category shows the smallest percentage increase?

14. How big was the increase in user fees when expressed as a percentage increase over the previous year?

15. What percentage of its total revenues would the city get from property taxes next year?

Interviewing the City Manager

The following are on-the-record responses from Valleydale City Manager Don Prentice to your questions about his proposed budget.

Q: What do you see as the priorities in next year's budget?

A: It has been a very difficult year for us financially. Expenditures are always rising, and this city is particularly committed to staying ahead of the curve in law enforcement. Our citizens need to be safe.

Q: But our analysis shows that your law enforcement budget would go up by only 1.5 percent. The budget for your own office, meanwhile, would nearly double.

A: You're showing your ignorance. In terms of real dollars, the increase for my office is insignificant. The budget for the city manager's office and for city council are a very small percentage of the total budget. Compared to the actual dollar increases for the police, the dollar amounts of increases in both the city council and city manager budgets are not worth worrying about. Next question.

Q: How will you fund the proposed increases?

A: We're very fortunate that we've been able to hold the property tax increase to just 9 percent.

Q: Excuse me. Our figure is different, about a 10.5 percent increase.

A: What do you mean, your figure is different? You're obviously mistaken, and if you want to embarrass yourself in front of your audience, that's your business. (Laughs.)

Q: Aren't you using the wrong base year to compare—

A: Look, we are professional municipal managers. We know what we are doing. You don't. It's as simple as that.

Q: I see a substantial increase in what you plan to collect in user fees. What are user fees?

A: Huh. Believe it or not, user fees are fees charged to users. We think that's fairer than taxing everybody to pay for that stuff.

Q: Could you give us an example?

A: Hold your horses. I'm getting to that. For instance, we have parks in some of our low-income areas. Why, you wouldn't believe how those people take advantage of that. Some of those kids are in those parks all day, every day, and they don't pay a cent for it.

Q: But if you start to charge people to use the parks, won't that prevent many of them from using them? And aren't the ones who will suffer some of the people for whom those parks were built in the first place?

A: One question at a time. First, those parks were built for everyone, not just one strident constituency. And it doesn't matter who you are—rich, poor, in-between, black, white, purple. I think that if they use it, they should have to pay for it, so we're proposing a $1-a-day per-person charge for using our city's parks. And user fees are only a very small part of our budget, really. If you look, you'll see that the increase is actually very small, just a 4 percent adjustment, from 8.5 percent of our total revenues to 12.8 percent.

Q: That would be a 50 percent increase, not 4 percent. And as an actual increase from what you charged last year—

A: You know, you remind me of that old saying: Statistics don't lie, but people lie with statistics. I'm sure you'll find a way to spin these figures to fit your newspaper's agenda.

Q: Let me ask you about another area. For both the current budget year and the proposed budget, our analysis shows a substantial discrepancy between revenues and expenditures. You've got about $2.5 million more in revenue than you will spend this year, and next year is off in the same direction by about $2.1 million. There is a total over the two years of about $4.6 million in unaccounted-for revenue.

A: Again, your math has got to be wrong. The total revenues for each year do add up. There is no discrepancy. (Sighs.) This is what happens when you give a reporter a pocket calculator.

Q: We used the Microsoft Excel computer spreadsheet program for our analysis.

A: Well, if you newspeople are using a computer program designed for experts, that's your problem. Garbage in, garbage out. I am trying to emphasize how concerned we are for the citizens of this community as evidenced by the size of our police budget—more than $1.4 million next year—and you are harping on some imagined discrepancy of a few million dollars.

Q: Excuse me, Mr. Prentice, but with all due respect, this is not an imagined discrepancy. Our analysis shows—

A: You think we are hiding $2 million a year? I don't have to answer ridiculous accusations like that. You're getting very close to libelous accusations. I'd be very damned careful if I were you. (Hangs up.)

16

Police and Emergency Services

Most of the impact in stories about robberies, murders, accidents and natural disasters is emotional. Usually journalists cover them because we think it's important for audiences to connect with the human consequences of such events. When a tsunami killed more than 200,000 people in South Asia in December 2004, the news coverage was worldwide, even though the event held little rational impact for most of us half a world away.

It's true that sometimes, as a matter of public policy, we become interested in a shared problem, and the impact shifts to the rational. Terrorist acts are one example. Since President George W. Bush declared a war on terrorism after the September 11, 2001, attacks on the Pentagon and the World Trade Center, news media have provided intense coverage of terrorist acts even when they occur in other countries. An example is the summer 2005 series of bombings in London. For local news media, if homicide suddenly becomes particularly frequent in a certain area of town, or a car wreck is the fifth in six months at a particular railroad crossing, the impact also shifts to the rational.

As isolated events, though, most of the crimes and emergencies that we report on carry minimal rational impact. We don't know the participants or their families, and the chances that something similar will happen to us remain remote.

Where's the Impact?

That presents us with a dilemma: If we limit our reporting to summaries of police reports, we deal in statistics, not human beings. We write about things happening, not things happening to people. That has the long-term effect of either dehumanizing our crime stories, making them merely titillating and almost cartoon-like, or of overemphasizing crime as a problem in a given community, especially if a news organization adopts an if-it-bleeds-it-leads news strategy. (Studies show that older people who read, watch and listen to a lot of news believe that their world is becoming increasingly dangerous, even though nationwide the violent-crime rate has been dropping steadily for more than a decade.) The temptation of doing this kind of reporting is about more than a cheap readership or ratings boost. Let's face it: Racing to the scene of a murder carries an adrenaline rush of excitement tinged with fear that make most other kinds of reporting seem pretty mundane, particularly for a beginning reporter. And as reporters we have the advantage of standing apart from it, divorced from emotional involvement.

But if we insist on writing about human beings, as we should, we must contact the people involved in or affected by crime or tragedy, or those close to them, to learn about who they are or were, and to try to portray them or their relatives as people very much like the rest us. Often, that kind of reporting can be awfully intrusive, and reporters are criticized for being insensitive at such times. It is particularly difficult for television reporters, because video cameras are seen as intrusive even in the best of circumstances. If we are to write crime stories, we must seek the balance between humanizing the victims and remaining sensitive to their needs.

Don't Victimize Twice

When I was called on to contact the victims of accidents or crimes, or their families, I was surprised by how often they chose to cooperate. I would explain that my reporting so far was based on a summary provided by police, but that I wanted people to know the person involved as a human being. Usually, by the time reporters try to contact a family, their friends and relatives will already be on hand to screen telephone calls and visitors. Relatives will often talk about the victim, and will agree to pass along questions to a spouse or parent of the victim, or at least ask the spouse or parent whether he or she wants to talk with you. Sometimes the first person you talk to will be a family friend who is determined to protect the relatives from unnecessary intrusions. Edna Buchanan, the Pulitzer Prize–winning former police reporter for *The Miami Herald*, said she would call a family twice. If the first person hung up on her, she would wait a minute and call back, often getting a more cooperative person the second time. If the second person hung up, she would not call a third time. That, she said, would be harassment. Most reporters never get comfortable with making those contacts, and that's good. If wading into the middle of a family's grief ever becomes routine for a reporter, he or she should find another line of work.

Dealing with Police and Fire and Rescue Workers

As you deal with police officers at a crime scene or investigating a crime, remember that they have a job to do, as you do, and that often your jobs will conflict. You are trying to collect as much information as you can, so you can weigh what is appropriate to put into your story. Police often want to withhold most of what they know so an investigation is not compromised. Be polite, professional and persistent, and if you are on the police beat regularly, get to know the officers. Once they know which information they can trust you with, your working relationship will be easier because it will be more clearly defined. For example, sources and reporters who trust each other will occasionally swap information to save each other time. As a reporter you want to make sure that what you will be getting is at least as valuable to you as what you will be sharing, and your police sources are operating under the same guideline. You can be assertive with police without resorting to hostility.

Fire and rescue workers ordinarily do not have to worry about compromising an investigation of a crime by what they tell you, but they have an even bigger concern: trying to save lives and prevent risk to others. Their focus will be on that; if your timing is bad you will be distracting them from it. That does not mean you always have to limit your contacts to public information officers. But you need to use common sense in approaching frontline emergency workers. You will earn their trust if you don't force them to choose between saving lives and talking to you.

Dealing with Hospital Workers

At one time, obtaining information about people who had been or were being treated at your local hospital was relatively straightforward. All but the smallest hospitals have designated people to deal with news media. Sometimes they are public relations professionals; in other cases they might be shift supervisors, the director of nursing or the chief of staff. Most hospitals are still willing to provide specifics about the meaning of the several patient conditions you hear in news stories: good, satisfactory, fair, poor, serious, critical, grave, guarded or stable.

But relations between hospitals and news media changed with the passage of the Health Insurance Portability and Accountability Act of 1996, or HIPAA. While the primary purpose of the law was to help provide health insurance protection for workers who changed jobs, as with many laws there were some other provisions that had substantial impact. One of those provisions dealt with patients' confidentiality rights. On the advice of their lawyers, numerous health care providers have interpreted the law to mean that they can no longer release any information about a patient without the patient's consent.

Remember Levels of Observation

When you are trying to sort out what you know from what you or others may be assuming, remember your levels of observation. (See Box 16.1.) As you move further and further from firsthand observation, be more and more careful about judging the value of information, and be sure to attribute your information to a particular source. Be careful as well to determine whether your source is in a position to know the information he or she is giving you, or whether he or she is speculating.

Remember also that police officers make mistakes, just as reporters and the rest of humanity do. Always check names and addresses against your City Directory in the Appendix. If a police report contains information that you don't think can be correct, challenge it. Call the reporting officer or run it by witnesses. For example, several years ago, on the campus where I teach, a frater-

Box 16.1

HE SAID THAT SHE SAID THAT HE SAID . . .

In Chapter 11 you learned the importance of keeping *levels of observation* clear to yourself and your audience. The more removed someone is from direct observation, the more we need to verify the information. To review briefly:

1. *Direct* or *firsthand observation*: The reporter sees or hears something herself. An example would be a reporter covering a City Council meeting.

2. *Secondhand observation*: The reporter gets information from a witness.

3. *Thirdhand observation*: The reporter talks to someone who got information from a witness. An example is the account a police officer gives a reporter based on the officer's conversation with a witness or witnesses.

4. *Fourthhand* observation: Reporters occasionally receive information from spokesmen or spokeswomen, or from news releases, that is based on information that is already thirdhand. An example is information from a police spokesman who summarized the report of an officer who had talked to witnesses.

nity member was thrown from a Homecoming float against a parked car when the driver of the float turned a corner too sharply. Police insisted the young man had been thrown 46 feet, even though the street itself was not that wide, and the width of the parked car and the float narrowed the distance even more. If you cannot resolve an apparent anomaly in your reporting, acknowledge that uncertainty to your audience when you write your story. (See Box 16.2, page 210.)

Ethics

In Exercise 16 you will need to exercise your ethical judgment about your professional responsibility as a journalist to your audience and the people about whom you write. Information that is included in a police report might or might not be relevant to your story. Having information available to give to audiences does not necessarily mean we should share all of it with audiences. For example, in offering a description of a robber who is still at large, the lawbreaker's race is often included. In most other contexts, though, the race of someone in a story is irrelevant. But when we as journalists look at

Box 16.2

"THAT'S WHAT HE SAID"

Practically every editor who has challenged a reporter on a dubious fact has gotten this response at least once: "Well, that's what he said."

No wonder editors contemplate homicide occasionally. To keep yourself alive and your editor out of jail, remember:

1. An editor's job is to try to clear up both ambiguity and incredulity. As a reporter, it's your job too. Don't drive your audience crazy.

2. When a source—even somebody "official" like a police officer—tells you something that doesn't sound right, keep asking questions.

3. If you—or your sources—can't ultimately explain, acknowledge that to your audience.

> Bad: *Police said the student was thrown 46 feet from the Homecoming float onto a parked car.*

> Better: *Police said the student was thrown from the slow-moving Homecoming float onto a car parked along the two-lane street. An investigating officer reported that the float was going about five miles per hour, and that the student was thrown 46 feet. It was not immediately clear how the student traveled that far on the narrow street.*

crime as an issue rather than as a series of isolated and unrelated events, we may see a pattern of crime in a particular neighborhood. If most or all of the victims of a series of crimes are of the same race, or if a category of crime appears to victimize the poor disproportionately, race or socioeconomic status might become relevant. Over the long pull, though, news media must be careful to present a full picture of a community. If the only time a particular race or ethnicity is mentioned in a news medium is when an at-large criminal is being described, or if one group is exclusively portrayed as poor, downtrodden or victimized, both the group and the news audience are being ill-served.

Most states have laws that dictate special treatment of juvenile offenders—usually defined as those younger than 18. There is a separate court and corrections system for juveniles, and to release their names is usually against the law unless they are charged as adults. It is important for you as a reporter to remember that while those laws prohibit *release* of the juvenile's name, they cannot prohibit *publication* (including broadcast) if a reporter learns the name. Most news media do not routinely publish or air the names of juveniles involved in or charged with crimes, but they sometimes make exceptions. Those exceptions most often have to do with the seriousness of the crime. It is important for you as a reporter to know your newsroom's policy, and to initiate or be part of a newsroom discussion before anyone decides to violate the policy.

Be careful with the words you use to report arrests and the treatment of suspects. Be sure you are right before you tell your audience that someone has been arrested. He or she might have been taken in only for questioning. Not all suspects are charged with crimes, and naming someone before he or she has been arrested is usually a bad business. Similarly, if you say Jones was arrested for murdering Smith, the implication is that Jones did it. Guilt is for a court to determine. Say instead that *Jones was charged with* murdering Smith. Don't say "charges" unless it is more than one charge. And remember not to use certain words as adjectives or adverbs: *alleged, allegedly* or *accused.* They are invisible modifiers.

We often see news media report the maximum sentence someone who has been arrested could face. Doing that is almost always both unfair and misleading. For one thing, an arrested person enjoys—or should enjoy—the presumption of innocence. He or she will face no sentence at all unless found guilty. For another, practically all states now have sentencing practices that mean a conviction almost never carries the maximum sentence. Talking to defense lawyers and prosecutors—particularly those not directly involved in the case—can give you a better idea of a likely sentence.

Finally, a reminder to be particularly sensitive to what the victims of crime or tragedy—and their loved ones—are going through. Fair, persistent questioning in any other interview can constitute badgering with people who have just been through something awful. "How do you feel?" is a pretty stupid question, and downright insensitive. Remember the value of open-ended questions: "Talk about your son." "I'm sure this must be difficult, but describe, if you can, what that was like for you."

Strategies

In reporting on crime, accidents and other emergencies and unexpected events, remember (see Box 16.3):

> *The impact will usually be emotional.* Most of us are not directly affected by crime, accidents or natural disasters. But crime, accidents and disasters

are not just exciting events. They have human consequences. Show their impact on the people involved.

When interviewing victims, their friends and relatives, don't make them feel victimized again by your interview. Use open-ended questions to be more sensitive.

Develop a working relationship with police, firefighters and rescue workers. Understand the demands of their jobs, and let them know the demands of yours. You can be an appropriately thorough reporter without getting in the way or distracting them at a crime or rescue scene.

Be aware of confidentiality rights. The Health Insurance Portability and Accountability Act of 1996 (HIPAA) has had a profound effect on hospital workers' willingness to share patient information. Learn how your local hospital staff and administrators believe they are constrained by the law.

Be careful with the words you choose when reporting arrests and charges. Remember our legal system's presumption of innocence, and leave guilty verdicts to the courts. Similarly, avoid reporting the maximum sentence

Box 16.3

STRATEGIES FOR COVERING CRIME, ACCIDENTS AND EMERGENCIES

1. Few of us are directly affected by the crime, accidents or natural disasters reported in the news. But we connect with the people who are. Focus your story on the emotional impact by showing the human consequences.

2. Use open-ended questions when interviewing victims, their friends and relatives. "How do you feel?" is a stupid question to ask of someone in emotional pain.

3. Understand the demands of the job for police, firefighters and rescue workers, and make sure they understand your job.

4. Many hospitals will no longer release patient information because of the Health Insurance Portability and Accountability Act of 1996 (HIPAA). Ask to meet with executives of your local hospital to discuss your needs and their constraints.

5. The presumption of innocence is a fundamental legal right. Don't use your story to convict someone who has not been tried. Leave guilty verdicts to the courts. Similarly, avoid reporting the maximum sentence that someone who is under arrest could receive. Wait until he or she has been convicted, then report the actual sentence.

that someone who has been arrested could receive. For one thing, he or she hasn't been convicted yet. For another, practically all states have sentencing practices that in most cases prevent the maximum sentence from being handed out.

In Exercise 16A you will have both a police report and a subsequent interview to work with. The interview will take place in class; take notes on it. Even with the benefit of the interview, carefully examine the police report for revealing or humanizing information, and include it in your story if you judge it to be relevant. Be careful with attribution; make sure you accurately represent what police say the victim or witness told them.

In Exercise 16B you will not have the benefit of interviews with witnesses and participants. The information in your story will come from the police report, but you will need to provide appropriate context for it. For that, look at previous exercises, including Exercise 16A.

For both exercises your instructor might assign stories for print, broadcast, and the Web, or you might be asked to write one story for one medium, the second for another. Or you might be assigned to write one story outside of class and write the second on deadline in class.

Exercise 16A

Police Report

Write a story for print, broadcast or the Web, or all three media, based on the police report presented here and on the follow-up interview conducted in class.

CASE NO. XX-1374

DRUG ARREST—137 N. Randolph St.

ARRESTEES: Topping, Courtney Ann
Age: 21
137 N. Randolph St.
Possession of Narcotics (Crack Cocaine, Class II Felony)
Possession of Controlled Substance (Oxycontin, Class III Felony)
Resisting Arrest w/o violence (Class II Misdemeanor)
Possession of a Deadly Weapon (Class III Misdemeanor)

Hunter, Meriwether Chase (Chip)
Age: 22
209 Woodland Terrace
Chevy Chase, MD
Sale of Narcotics (Crack Cocaine, Class I Felony)
Sale of Controlled Substance (Oxycontin, Class II Felony)
Possession of Narcotics (Crack Cocaine, Class II Felony)
Possession of Controlled Substance (Oxycontin, Class III Felony)
Resisting Arrest w/Violence (Class II Felony)
Possession of a Deadly Weapon (Class III Misdemeanor)

LeBlanc, Meagan Lucille
Age: 21
137 N. Randolph St.
Possession of Narcotics (Crack Cocaine, Class II Felony)
Possession of Controlled Substance (Oxycontin, Class III Felony)
Possession of a Deadly Weapon (Class III Misdemeanor)

Smythe-Wilhoit, Brittany Davis
Age: 20
137 N. Randolph St.
Possession of Narcotics (Crack Cocaine, Class II Felony)
Possession of Controlled Substance (Oxycontin, Class III Felony)
Possession of a Deadly Weapon (Class III Misdemeanor)

Brelsford, Tiffany Belle
Age: 21
137 N. Randolph St.
Possession of Narcotics (Crack Cocaine, Class II Felony)
Possession of Controlled Substance (Oxycontin, Class III Felony)
Possession of a Deadly Weapon (Class III Misdemeanor)
Obstruction of Justice (Class II Misdemeanor)

WITNESSES: Jefferson, Naomi
Age: 34
139 N. Randolph St.

Jefferson, Joshua (juvenile)
Age: 14
139 N. Randolph St.

McNab, Shereen (juvenile)
Age : 13
237 Fulton St.

DETAILS: While on patrol in the area of 139 N. Randolph St. at approximately 14:17 P.M. in the afternoon of 10/28 this officer was approached by BF Naomi Jefferson outside her home at 139 N. Randolph St. Mrs. Jefferson informed this officer that an individual residing next door to her at 137 N. Randolph St. had been dealing "crack cocaine and something else" to her son, BM juvenile Joshua Jefferson. Mrs. Jefferson stated that she was acquainted with the individuals living at 137 N. Randolph St., being four WF VPU students and that she had "never had trouble" with them. However she further stated that a WM had recently occupied the premises and had approached her son Joshua offering to sell him drugs.

This officer then contacted the Blue Ridge Regional Drug Task Force (BRRDTF) in the person of Sgt. Wiggins to alert him of suspected drug activity. Pursuant to further conversations involving Mrs. Jefferson, Sgt. Wiffins, and myself, it was decided that a BRRDTF plainclothes officer would "tail" Joshua Jefferson for a few days. On the afternoon of 10/30, as Joshua approached his residence after walking home from Howard Lynton Middle School, plainclothes officer XXXXX and this officer observed suspect HUNTER approach Joshua. There insued a brief conversation, after which Joshua handed suspect HUNTER what appeared to be U.S. currency in an undetermined amount. Suspect HUNTER then handed Joshua a small packet and walked away in the direction of the VPU campus. Officer XXXXX and this officer then waited for Joshua to enter his home, whereupon a few minutes later Officer XXXXX and this officer approached the front door. At this time Mrs. Jefferson arrived home from work. Officer XXXXX and this officer had a conversation with Mrs. Jefferson on her front porch, reporting to her what we had observed transpose between Joshua and suspect HUNTER. Mrs. Jefferson then became upset and gave Officer XXXXX and this officer permission to question Joshua. At which time Officer XXXXX and this officer entered the Jefferson residence and began a conversation with Joshua.

At that time Joshua denied knowing suspect HUNTER, but when confronted said that suspect HUNTER had approached him outside his home for the first time that afternoon, wanting to know directions to the university (VPU). Pursuant to further questioning, however, Joshua became upset (i.e., crying) and very remorseful and admitted to buying "downers" from suspect HUNTER on three occasions. He then stated that on the first two occasions he was accompanied by his girlfriend, BF juvenile Shereen McNab, and that she had "bought some too." At that time Joshua produced from his trousers pocket the substance which he said he had bought from suspect HUNTER. Later tests confirmed the substance to be Oxycontin, a prescription-type controlled painkiller. Joshua stated that he had purchased the drugs for $30. Pursuant to further conversations with Mrs. Jefferson, it was decided not to arrest Joshua. Officer XXXXX and this officer then contacted Shereen McNab at her residence, 327 Fulton St. In the presence of her parents, she confirmed Joshua's story. Shereen McNab stated that she had paid suspect HUNTER a total of $60 for her drugs. It should be noted that the juvenile's father, Rev. McNab, at that time began stating in a loud voice that the police department had for a long time ignored "leeches" praying upon people in the Love Hill community by selling drugs. He also stated that the neighborhood was being ruined by VPU students, stating that "first they took away our housing, now they are taking away our children's lives." Rev. McNab challenged officers to "lock up that blood-sucking college boy." This officer urged Rev. McNab to contact the chief or the city manager if he wished to file a compliant about law enforcement in the Love Hill area. Officer XXXXX and this officer then secured a warrant for the arrest of suspect HUNTER and allowing a search of the upstairs rear bedroom of 137 N. Randolph St., which on information and belief was the last known residence of suspect HUNTER.

As Mrs. Jefferson had reported at least five unrelated individuals living at 137 N. Randolph, and because she said she was "almost sure" but could not confirm that they did not have weapons in the home, it was decided that the arrest of suspect HUNTER be executed by the full BRRDTF with backup provided by the VPD Special Weapons and Tactics (SWAT) team because of the potentially highly hazardous nature of the operation.

At approximately 0600 hours on 11/05, the BRRDTF with backup provided by the VPD SWAT team entered 137 N. Randolph St. and executed the arrest of suspect HUNTER. Suspect HUNTER was apprehended in the upstairs rear bedroom, where he was sleeping in the company of WF Courtney Ann Topping. At the time of his arrest suspect HUNTER began shouting at members of the BRRDTF to "leave her the hell alone" and attempted to forcefully push an officer away from suspect TOPPING. Suspect TOPPING had became hysterical and attempted to exit the upstairs bedroom window, whereupon she was restrained by officers, whereupon suspect HUNTER assaulted officers. Suspect HUNTER was restrained and suspect TOPPING was then allowed to put a bathrobe on (she had been in a state of complete undress when officers arrived in the bedroom to execute the arrest of suspect HUNTER). A weapon in the form of a red Swiss Army type knife was discovered on top of the dresser near the entrance to the bedroom door. Suspect HUNTER admitted that it belonged to him. Other weapons located in the kitchen of the residence were three kitchen-type knives with approximate seven-inch blades. WF suspects later admitted that the weapons belonged to them but insisted they were intended "only for cooking with."

At this time other officers with the BRRDTF and VPD SWAT team reported that they had secured the residence and had located three other individuals, WF Tiffany Brelsford, WF Brittany Smith-Wilhoite, and WF Megan Leblanc, all of whom appeared to have been asleep. All suspects were then placed in the living room of the residence under armed guard by VPD SWAT team officers. At that time WF Brelsford began shouting at officers, taking the Lord's name in vain and saying the suspects should be allowed to "put something decent on" and should not have to be observed "in our nighties." However after a brief conversation with Sgt. Wiggins it was decided that because no drugs had yet been located in the residence it would be necessary to execute a body-cavity search of all suspects. There was fear that in the process of being allowed to dress outside the presence and observation of male officers the WF individuals would be able to dispose of contraband. At that time a female Virginia State Police Officer was summoned to execute the body-cavity searches of the WFs.

Trooper Melody Parker of the Jeffersonville barracks arrived on scene at approximately 10:20 A.M. and proceeded to search the WF suspects. By this time BRRDTF officers had executed a body cavity search of suspect HUNTER, which was negative. Suspect HUNTER repeatedly insisted on calling a lawyer or his parents in Chevy Chase, Maryland. However it was explained to him that he would not be allowed to make a telephone call until such time as he was processed at the Blue Ridge Regional Jail Facility (BRRJF). Body cavity searches of the WF suspects were likewise negative. However a search of the laundry room subsequently revealed approximately 30 white pills and a small bag of what appeared to be crack cocaine in a pair of blue-jeans type trousers, male size 33/34. The trousers also contained approximately $88 in U.S. currency in the left front pocket. Later tests confirmed crack cocaine. The pill substance was revealed to be Oxycontin, a controlled substance prescription painkiller-type drug. Suspect HUNTER denied that the substances were his or that the trousers belonged to him.

All suspects were transported to the BRRJF at approximately 12 o'clock noon on 11/05, where WF suspects each posted $2,500 bond. WM suspect HUNTER remains at BRRJF under a $40,000 bond.

Alan W. Grant
Patrolman, VPD

Exercise 16B

Traffic Accident

Write a story for print, broadcast or the Web, or all three media, based on the police report presented here, supplying context based on information given in previous exercises, including 16A. You might find it helpful to refer to the map of Valleydale at the front of the book for help with this exercise.

CASE NO. XX-2004

Fatal MVA—West Trafalgar and Inverness St.

PERSONS INVOLVED: BOWERS, Randy (deceased)
                                                Age 21
                                                Southern Military Academy

                                                Le Blanc, Meagan Lucille
                                                Age 21
                                                137 N. Randolph St.
                                                Valleydale

                                                TOPPING, Courtney Ann
                                                Age 21
                                                137 N. Randolph St.
                                                Valleydale

                                                HUNTER, Meriwether Chase (Chip)
                                                Age 22
                                                137 N. Randolph St.
                                                Valleydale

WITNESSES: DOBBINS, Howard F.
                                                Age 62
                                                1910 John Wesley Rd.
                                                Blue Ridge County

                                                DOBBINS, Dorcas M.
                                                Age 60
                                                1910 Joan Wesley Rd.
                                                Blue Ridge County

FINE, Seymour K.
Age 47
211 Wall Faulkner Highway
Inverness

DETAILS: While investigating a report of a disturbance in the area of Trafalger and Roosevelt Streets (The Breeze restaurant) at approximately 02:31 A.M. in the morning of 12/15 this officer was alerted by a passing motorist to a "serious" accident near the intersection of West Trafalger and Inverness Streets. This officer responded immediately, arriving on the scene at approximately 02:32 A.M. Upon arrival this officer witnessed two damaged vehicles, still appearing to contain several occupants. Vehicle 1, a late-model Ford Explorer SUV, black in color, was resting against the northern concrete abutment of the footbridge that crosses over Trafalger St. By observing the damage to the front end of the vehicle, this officer concluded that the vehicle had struck the abutment at a high rate of speed. Vehicle 2, an older-model Chevrolet Sierra pickup truck, light brown and white in color, was resting on the southern shoulder of Trafalger St., pointing in a westerly direction. It had sustained damage to its right front fender. This officer immediately radioed Valleydale Fire Rescue and VPD dispatch for backup. I then proceeded to render assistance to the occupants of the vehicles.

At approximately 02:35 A.M. this officer was joined by Officer Healey of VPD and by units of Valleydale Fire Rescue, who subsequently confirmed that BOWERS, an occupant of the rear seat of Vehicle 1, was deceased. TOPPING and LEBLANC were transported by Fire-Rescue personnel to JSH.

HUNTER, who appeared to have been driving the vehicle, appeared to be uninjured but was sitting in the driver's seat of Vehicle 1 in a dazed condition. He reported that Vehicle 2 "came out of nowhere." He made no further statement, instead he asked to be allowed to call a lawyer, although he had not been placed under arrest. This officer then asked Officer Healey to detain HUNTER pending completion of a preliminary investigation.

Occupants of Vehicle 2, Mr. and Mrs. DOBBINS, did not appear to be injured. Mr. DOBBINS reported that they were proceeding into the intersection of Inverness and Trafalgar Streets, attempting to execute a right turn after having come to a full stop at the end of Inverness, when Vehicle 1, traveling west in the eastbound lane of Trafalger Street at a high rate of speed, struck their right front fender and spun Vehicle 2 in a counterclockwise direction until it came to rest in the position this officer first observed it. Mr. and Mrs.

DOBBINS stated that the driver of Vehicle 1 then appeared to lose control of his vehicle and struck the northern abutment of the footbridge at a high rate of speed.

At this point in time, as this officer was concluding his interview with Mr. and Mrs. DOBBINS, an older-model Honda Civic 4-door, light gray in color, appeared at the accident scene. The driver, FINE, then approached this officer and said he had witnessed the accident. This officer inquired of FINE why he had left the accident scene, and FINE informed this officer that he was the one who had first driven to Trafalgar and Roosevelt streets to inform this officer about the accident.

FINE stated that he had been traveling westbound in the westbound lane of Trafalger Street and had been accelerating up the hill adjacent to the Post Office after having stopped for the traffic signal at Trafalger and Lee Avenue. As he drew abreast of McLaren Street, FINE stated that a black SUV-type vehicle "roared" past him headed westbound in the eastbound lane of Trafalger Street at a high rate of speed. He observed the vehicle "clip" the right front fender of a brown pickup truck that was just turning eastbound into Trafalgar Street from Inverness Street. FINE stated that the pickup truck appeared to have been at a complete stop before entering the intersection. FINE further stated that subsequent to striking the right front fender of the pickup, the SUV-type vehicle proceeded to swerve back into the westbound lane of Trafalgar Street ahead of FINE and strike the northern abutment of the footbridge at a high rate of speed. FINE stated that as he did not possess a cell phone he believed it the best course of action to proceed for help rather than stopping to aid the victims himself. FINE further stated that he turned around and proceeded in an easterly direction on Trafalger Street because he remembered seeing "a cop outside The Breeze" (that being this officer) as he drove past a moment earlier.

At this point in time, based on the statements of HUNTER, Mr. and Mrs. DOBBINS, and FINE, Officer Healey and this officer executed the arrest of HUNTER on charges of reckless driving and negligent homicide. HUNTER was then transported to JSH for tests. Following such tests, HUNTER was then transported to BRRJF, where he made no further statement and was incarcerated. A further charge of vehicular manslaughter is pending.

Officer Healey and this officer then proceeded to JSH, where we were informed that LeBLANC and TOPPING had been treated for numerous injuries and were hospitalized. At approximately 07:30 A.M. this officer contacted LEBLANC who was in her hospital bed with Officer Healey. The nurse reported that LeBLANC was in a heavily sedated condition. LEBLANC stated that they had been proceeding to a party at "a student house" in the country when the accident occurred. She further stated that she and her friends, including HUNTER, TOPPING, and the deceased BOWERS, had been partying at 137 N. Randolph St. for several hours before leaving for the second party. She further stated that she had not been drinking because she was the evening's designated driver, but when they decided to leave for the second party, HUNTER grabbed the keys from her and insisted on driving and would not surrender them. At this point in time LEBLANC became too sleepy to interview further. Officer Healey and this officer then proceeded to the bedside of TOPPING but were told by a nurse that TOPPING was "out like a light" and due to her injuries would probably remain heavily sedated for several days.

Alan W. Grant
Patrolman, VPD

chapter seventeen

Covering Local-Government Meetings

In Chapter 12, as you dealt with distinguishing facts from allegations for your audience, you waded through part of a Valleydale City Council meeting. For that exercise you didn't need to know a great deal about how city governments work beyond the background that was provided at the top of the exercise. The goal of this chapter is to prepare you to cover a real government meeting in your community. The exercise at the end of this chapter is just such an assignment.

Who Cares about Local Government?

Most of us pay at least some attention to what goes on in Washington, D.C.— the domestic agenda and foreign policy that the president and executive branch set for the nation, the way Congress carries out—or thwarts—that agenda with legislation, the way the courts modify or reject laws through their rulings. We worry about the impact Washington will have on our pocketbooks, on our safety and on the welfare of our families.

But many of us pay far less attention to the workings and actions of state and local governments. There is an irony there, because the government actions that affect us most directly, day in and day out, are enacted and carried out by local government. If you are a college student living on a campus far from home, you could be forgiven for thinking that what the city council in your college town does has nothing to do with you. But when you remember that local governments pass property tax increases, noise ordinances and laws governing the sale and consumption of alcoholic beverages, the connection might become a little more obvious.

As a reporter, you need to learn how your local government works even if you don't see much personal connection to the community you are in. Almost everyone in your audience is directly affected by what local government does. Your audience members own property, send children to public schools and pay taxes locally. To be able to monitor local government for our audiences, we must first understand how that government is supposed to work. We must understand the system, the players and the major issues. Carl Schierhorn of Kent State University has said that governments do simple things in complex ways, but that in our stories, we should focus more on the simple things than on the complex ways. Unfortunately, we can't explain things simply for our audiences if we don't understand the complexity.

Local-Government Structure

In New England, a number of small towns still practice *direct democracy*. That means that every registered voter may attend periodic *town meetings* to propose and vote directly on local laws—usually called ordinances—tax rates and other matters. Just about everywhere else in the United States, localities operate as the state and federal governments do, through *representative democracy*. Citizens elect representatives—variously called council members, commissioners, aldermen, supervisors or some other title—to govern on their behalf. These elected governments can represent as few as a few hundred people or as many as several million, as with New York City. There are other elected groups as well—local boards of education, or school boards, water and sewer management boards, hospital boards and conservation district boards, to name a few. There are also other elected officials in many localities—the county sheriff, the local prosecutor, the tax collector.

One of the challenges of covering local government is the need to understand that one geographic area might comprise numerous governmental jurisdictions. One county I worked in in South Florida consisted of 28 elected municipal governments in addition to an elected county government and school board. And the interests of those myriad governments sometimes conflict. An example of conflicting interests was given in Exercise 14, when Mayor Hostetter called on the Valleydale City Council to back out of an agreement with Blue Ridge County's government to build a new courthouse.

Your instructor might choose to discuss with you the roles of elected officials in your area. Because your assignment at the end of this chapter will be to cover a local-government meeting, we will focus on the primary units of local government, the ones most familiar to citizens—city governments, county governments and, in many areas in the North and Midwest, township governments.

The elected representatives for each govern within their geographic boundaries according to powers granted them by their state in a charter. They are not allowed to reach beyond those powers in passing laws. For example, most city or county charters allow localities to set local property tax rates, but those rates may have a limit, or cap, imposed by state law or a state's constitution. Local governments cannot trespass at all in some areas. As another example, local governments can pass some ordinances regulating open containers of alcohol in public. But if the city council in a college town yielded to local pressure and reduced the drinking age to 18, the law would be quickly struck down by a court, because state constitutions allow only the state government to set the legal drinking age.

City and township governments are usually one of two types—the mayor/council form, or the manager/council form. In the mayor/council form, citizens elect a mayor and several council members, usually five to seven. The mayor acts as the chief executive of the city, and can wield substantial power. Like the council members, the mayor must stand for election periodically, usually every four years. The mayor and his or her staff usually establish their vision for the city and try to persuade the council to approve it by adopting ordinances, setting tax rates, approving plans for private development, and so forth.

In a manager/council form of government, voters elect council members but council members hire a professional city or county manager. The manager serves at the pleasure of the council, not the voters. Council members usually elect from among themselves a mayor to preside at meetings and represent the city at official functions—the ribbon cutting for the new big-box discount store, for example. But the mayor in a manager/council form of government

Box 17.1

CITY AND COUNTY GOVERNMENTS

Most regions in the United States have separate governments for cities and counties. Some areas have other forms of government as well, including the township government. City and county governments are generally one of two types:

1. *Mayor/council.* The locality is governed by several elected *council members* (they may also be called commissioners, supervisors, aldermen or some other title), and a separately elected *mayor* who serves as the locality's chief executive. The mayor wields substantial power. Most localities elect from five to seven council members, whose terms are usually four years.

2. *Manager/council.* The locality is governed by several elected officials who select a mayor or chair from among themselves. The mayor or chair's duties are largely ceremonial, and his or her power is limited. The chief executive of the locality is a professional *city or county manager* hired by the elected officials. As in the mayor/council form, there are usually five to seven council or commission members, who usually serve four-year terms.

has little power. Most county governments are of the manager/council or manager/commission type, depending on what the county's elected representatives are called. (See Box 17.1.)

Elected representatives in both types of local governments may be elected *at large*—by all voters in the locality—or *by district*—by only those voters in designated districts within the larger locality. Whether elected officials represent only a district or all the voters in a locality has a substantial impact on how they vote on many issues. For example, there may be consensus among members of a county commission who are elected at-large that the county needs an airport. But with district representation, you can almost guarantee that the commission member from the district where the proposed airport would be built will oppose it.

Local-Government Functions

The city or county's elected officials meet periodically—usually once every two weeks—to conduct the locality's business. They will closely follow an

AGENDA
ROCKBRIDGE COUNTY BOARD OF SUPERVISORS MEETING
Monday, October 25, 2004 at 7:00 pm

7:00—Call to order, Devotional and Pledge of Allegiance

7:05—Items to be added to agenda, if any

7:05—Citizen comments

7:05—Chairman and Superintendent of Schools—Funding for Effinger School and waiver of fees

7:30—Public hearings:
    (1) Hevener Modile Homes—amend proffers 1, 3–9
    (2) Radon Resistant Construction—one and two family dwellings 1, 3, 10–13
    (3) Tourism Corridor Overlay District—change of final approval authority and membership of TCO Board 1–3, 14–27

      —End public hearings

8:00—Other planning and development issues:
    (1) Special exception review:
      —Martin Landing Strip—extend permit for five years 2, 28–33
    (2) Subdivision Review:
      —Longview Meadows—final review 2, 34–36 +Inserts
      —The Summit at Woods Creek—final review 2, 37–38 +Inserts

8:15—Other items for consideration:
    (1) Appointments:
      a. Community Services Board—to fill unexpired term 39
      b. Regional Library Board—to fill unexpired term 70
      c. Regional Tourism Board—term of Tom Osella expires 12/31/04 three-year term 41
    (2) Request for joint session with School Board
    (3) Proposals on Real Estate Reassessment

—Adjourn—

An agenda for the Rockbridge County, Virginia, Board of Supervisors shows the many ways local government affects our lives.

agenda that is prepared by either the manager or the mayor, depending on the kind of government. The meetings are almost always open to the public. Some items are relatively straightforward—approving several thousand dollars for a new photocopier, for example. Others may prove highly contentious, particularly when citizens understand how a proposal would affect them and come to the council meeting to be heard on the matter. Examples of often-controversial matters include passing local tax increases, approving a new housing development or factory near other homes, or passing a local ordinance governing certain types of behavior—prohibiting skateboarding on city streets, say.

Meeting agendas almost always include a few wild cards as well. Most localities allow time in the meeting for citizens to bring up matters that are not on the agenda. Under a New Business category on the agenda, the elected representatives often have that opportunity, too. That's what happened in Exercise 12, when Council members Wise and Bullard launched yet another attack against City Manager Don Prentice. Sometimes such matters carry a lot of weight. But I once covered a meeting at which the council members got into a shouting match over who was going to offer the opening prayer. (The issue had nothing to do with the constitutional separation of church and state; it was purely political. There had just been an election in which several new council members had been voted in, and the citizen who usually offered the prayer had been a supporter of the "old guard.")

When considering most tax increases, new ordinances (local laws) and some types of developments, the elected officials must hold at least one *public hearing*. A public hearing is a formal proceeding that has been advertised in the local newspaper for a particular time and date so that people know when to come and be heard. The elected board cannot vote until the required public hearings have been held. Local council or commission meetings almost always set aside other time for citizens to be heard as well. During those times citizens may comment on any matter, whether it is on the agenda or not.

Whether you are dealing with a county or city government, the elected board will rely on the staffs of various departments in the local government, as well as committees and subcommittees comprising council members and citizens, to prepare and give first consideration to matters that will eventually come before the council. Typical committees include public safety (including police, fire, and ambulance/rescue services), public works, planning and zoning, finance, and transportation. There might be others as well, depending on the locality's size and needs. The committees meet regularly, usually in the two weeks between council or commission meetings. Through the mayor or manager, city or county departments will bring matters to these committees before the matters go before the full council or commission. Sometimes the process works backwards: Things come up at council or commission meetings—issues raised by citizens or council members—that are referred to a committee or a city department for examination. To use Exercise 12 again as an example, the council decided to have the Finance Committee look into the allegations against the city manager.

As with the federal and state governments, one of the most important functions of local government is passing a budget—a plan for raising and spending public money each year. The budget process usually takes months, beginning with requests for spending and estimates of income from each city department and ending with the local elected government's formal vote to adopt the budget, sometimes with accompanying tax increases. In Exercise 15 you wrote a story about City Manager Prentice's *proposed* budget for Valleydale for next year, at the point it was made public but well before any committee work or public hearings, and weeks before the final vote.

Let's look at another example of how an issue would make its way through city government. If a developer wants approval for a new housing subdivision, he or she would first file a set of plans with the staff of the appropriate department, often called the Planning Department. After reviewing the plans, the Planning Department staff would take them to the Planning and Zoning Committee. The committee would review the plans as well in a public meeting, often conducting its own public hearing. The committee members would then vote on whether or not to recommend approval of the development to the full council or commission. Remember that the committee's vote is only a recommendation. It is not final.

You might have figured out by now that by the time a matter comes before a city council or county commission it might have been under consideration by department staff and a committee for three months or more. As my former colleague Professor Ron MacDonald used to say, "Local governments never do anything for the first time." Depending on how conscientious local reporters are, citizens might or might not have had plenty of opportunity to learn about and form an opinion on the matter and make that opinion known to their elected representatives.

At the council or commission meeting, the council or commission may be required to hold another public hearing. After that the members can vote to accept the recommendation of the Planning and Zoning Committee, reject the recommendation, or send it back to the staff or committee for more work or other options. To citizens and reporters, these votes can be confusing. Here's why:

Say, in our example above, the Planning and Zoning committee voted to recommend *against* the new housing subdivision. At the council meeting, it would probably come to a vote in the form of a motion by a council member to accept the committee's recommendation. If council members vote yes on the motion, citizens—and some reporters—might confuse that yes vote for approval of the subdivision. What the council did was vote yes on the committee's recommendation, which was to reject the subdivision. As a reporter, you need to be careful.

Who Are Those Other People?

In addition to the city manager or mayor and the other elected representatives, you might encounter several other officials at a local-government meeting. (See Box 17.2.) The city, county or township attorney is a lawyer hired by the

Box 17.2

WHO DOES WHAT?

Elected officials comprise only some of the people at a local-government meeting. In addition to the mayor or chair and the council members, the meeting may include:

1. *The city or county manager*, the chief executive of the locality, who is hired by the elected government and serves at its pleasure. The manager usually prepares the agenda and makes a brief presentation about each item.

2. *The city or county attorney*, a lawyer hired by the locality full- or part-time to give legal advice on pending matters.

3. *The clerk*, responsible for the official record of the meeting, including minutes, votes and other decisions by the elected officials.

4. *The planning and zoning director*, who makes recommendations to the elected body on requests for approval of construction projects or certain uses of property.

5. *Department heads*, including the police chief, utilities director and finance director.

6. *The audience*, which usually comprises citizens and journalists.

locality, either part-time or full-time, to give legal advice to the manager and elected representatives. The attorney might be called on several times during a council meeting. The clerk is the employee responsible for creating an official record of the meeting, and will keep minutes and record the result of votes and other actions.

Key city departments are often represented at the meeting by their heads—the finance director, the director of planning and zoning, the police chief. Remember that none of these people can vote or otherwise substitute for elected officials; they are there to provide information or expert advice only.

Stories from Local Government

If you read, watch or listen to local news media over the course of a year, you can probably identify several types of stories about local government. How many of each kind of story you see or hear depends on the locality, how good its government is, and whether the reporters covering the local government are as good as they ought to be. Among the types of stories you might recognize, in about the order of frequency with which we see them:

The record. The stories that simply tell audiences what the local government did at its latest meeting. "Valleydale's City Council last night voted 4–1 to approve the city's budget for next year." We see these stories most frequently, often with ledes as dull as this one, with no hint given the audience of the impact of the vote.

The analysis. Stories that go beyond the action of the elected government to try to show audiences the significance of it: "Property taxes will go up an average of about $50 next year for Valleydale residents as a result of City Council action last night." You worked on an analysis story in Chapter 15 with your computer-assisted reporting exercise.

Somebody screwed up. Stories that report a costly mistake or improper action by an individual or body: "Valleydale will have to spend $20,000 on a special election because someone got the math wrong on a ballot item in Tuesday's election." Obviously, reporters usually have to find those stories on their own or thanks to a tip. Public officials don't often trumpet their own failures.

The system is screwed up. Someone suffered, or taxpayers will foot the bill, because of the nature of government: "Blue Ridge County will have to raise $3 million in local taxes for a new sewage treatment plant because of new federal requirements that are not fully funded by federal dollars."

Obviously, this is not an exhaustive list. What's important for you to understand is that the more you know about how local government is supposed to work, and the more you can learn about your own local government, the better you can serve your audience. In addition to learning how your local govern-ment works, before you attend a council meeting, get a copy of the agenda and study it. Check clippings and file tape. Have there been recent stories about anything on the agenda? Talk to the city, county or township manager, council or commission members, and department heads for an idea of what is likely to happen and the significance of pending items. Focus only on one or two. You don't want to write a story summarizing every item—some will not be worth writing about.

As you get to know the players, you can also determine which initiatives—and the responses to them—reflect elected officials' campaign promises, big donors, personal or political ideologies, constituents' needs or desires, or even squabbles among elected officials, some of them personal.

Ethics

Covering a city, county or township government regularly can help you immensely in serving your local audience. You will have the opportunity to become something of an expert on ongoing issues. You will become comfortable enough with jargon, technical language and bureaucratese to translate it for your audience. You will develop sources who will tip you to events and issues that your audience needs to know about but that may not be reflected in public documents, schedules or agendas. You might even uncover stories that help expose and correct wrongdoing, waste or inefficiency.

But there is a potential ethical dilemma inherent in covering just about any beat, not just local government. Put bluntly, you might forget who you are there to serve. In trying to serve your audience, you will get to know local officials—elected or not—well. Some of them may become friends or close acquaintances. You will depend on them for tips, explanations and quotes. Because it is human nature to like some people more than others, you might find yourself talking to some more often than others. That has the potential to slant your stories if you are not giving a fair hearing to all sides of an issue. Because some people are more quotable than others, the same thing happens when you decide whom to interview and whose quotes or bites to put in your story.

Because you will become so familiar with their jobs and the tasks and issues facing the people you cover, you might also develop more empathy with them than is healthy for serving your audience. You might become overly sympathetic to their contention that some things should be trusted to experts rather than scrutinized for your audience. In the worst case, you might be tempted to ignore wrongdoing by someone you have become close to.

These things don't happen because reporters want to be co-opted. They happen because we get to know the people we report on as human beings. Practically everyone in our audience remains a faceless stranger, so it can be harder to maintain empathy with an audience you don't know than with government officials and employees whom you do.

News organizations recognize this potential problem. Some attempt to solve it by rotating reporters' beats every couple of years. The problem with that approach is that it ensures that there is little institutional memory and limited expertise on the part of whoever is covering the beat at a given time. If a reporter becomes intimately involved with someone on his or her beat, though, the appropriate solution is usually to move the reporter to another beat to preserve his or her independence and avoid betraying the trust of both the audience and the person the reporter is involved with.

It should be possible for a reporter to be well connected with people on his beat—short of an intimate relationship—and still maintain the necessary independence. It is up to the reporter to make clear to people with whom he becomes friendly that the reporter's professional responsibility comes first; associates should clearly recognize when the reporter is "wearing the reporter hat." A conscientious reporter draws a clear line between shooting the breeze with sources and talking about a department head who is being investigated over his expense vouchers for an out-of-town trip. I once covered a city in South Florida whose city manager was fond of meeting with reporters at a local bar after City Council meetings. He often gave us valuable perspectives on issues before the city. That, in turn, allowed us to serve our audiences better. Then one night he was arrested on a charge of drunk driving on his way home from the bar. I felt bad about it, but I also wrote a story about his arrest.

Strategies

When you are assigned to cover a local government meeting, keep the following general points in mind (see Box 17.3):

Do your homework. Get an agenda to see what items are on it.

Let impact on your audience be your guide. The order of the agenda has nothing to do with the importance of each item. The number of people wanting to be heard on a particular issue might not reflect its importance either. For example, a city budget can take so many months to adopt that no citizens show up for the final vote, even if it includes a tax increase. On the other hand, an entire neighborhood might show up to oppose a request by someone to operate a hair salon in the basement of his or her home. No one outside that neighborhood is likely to be affected by the decision.

Check your own news outlet and others for previous stories about any of the items. Talk to the players before the meeting. Understand going in what the significant items are about.

Box 17.3

STRATEGIES FOR COVERING LOCAL GOVERNMENT MEETINGS

1. Get a copy of the agenda before the meeting.

2. Review the agenda using impact as your guide. The order of items on the agenda often has nothing to do with their importance.

3. Get the background. Check for previous stories. Talk to the city manager, council members, department heads and involved citizens before the meeting.

4. At the meeting, listen closely so that you are able to accurately quote citizens. Make sure you get the correct spelling of their names.

5. When you put your story together, focus on only one or two items. Consider doing separate stories about other significant actions.

6. Translate jargon, technical terms and bureaucratese. Help your audiences understand the significance of what happened.

7. Quotes show the human face of the issue. Choose quotes that do that effectively, but don't clutter your story with them. Use paraphrase to provide background and explain the issue.

At the meeting, *listen closely to and record accurately the comments of citizens*. Seek speakers out after the meeting for follow-up questions and to verify the spelling of their names.

Try to keep the focus to just one or two items. If other significant decisions were made or issues arose, consider a separate story.

Write so that your audiences can understand what happened, and its significance in their lives. Translate jargon, technical terms and bureaucratese into plain English.

Use quotes sparingly to show the depth of feeling by elected officials and citizens about the issue. Use paraphrase to provide background and explain the issue.

Exercise 17

Covering a Meeting

Attend a local-government meeting. After you have written a newspaper story and a Web blurb about an issue from the meeting (your instructor might allow you to do more than one draft), write the story on deadline in class as a 30-second RDR.

chapter eighteen

News Conferences

If you have ever watched a news conference, you were probably amazed, impressed or disturbed by the often rough-and-tumble nature of them. Many of us recall Secretary of Defense Donald Rumsfeld's frequent news conferences during the Iraq War, for example. Even the highest-ranking government officials can be subjected to probing, abrasive, sometimes downright rude questions by a gaggle of aggressive reporters. As a result, we sometimes see officials become defensive or even "lose their cool," giving in to confusion, frustration or anger. At such times it looks like the reporters have the official cornered, or on the run. Why on earth, you think, would anyone subject himself to that?

It might surprise you to learn that many reporters hate news conferences. That's probably more because of what news conferences aren't than of what they are. When someone in the public focus calls a news conference, it usually means that individual reporters are not going to get a one-on-one interview during which the reporter could ask all his or her own questions and

Box 18.1

WHY DO PEOPLE CALL NEWS CONFERENCES?

1. News conferences are a good way to publicize a product, issue, event or agenda.

2. News conferences allow a source to control how information is released. Even a contentious news conference gives a source better control than many interview situations do.

3. Because the subject is often a surprise, news conferences can allow sources to "spin" information to their advantage. Reporters often are not prepared to ask probing questions.

4. By putting a source in contact with several reporters at once, news conferences save the source time.

press the subject for responses to them. Sometimes, in a news conference, an individual reporter might not be recognized at all. And often there is little opportunity for follow-up questions. During the Vietnam War, reporters came to call the military's daily 5 P.M. press briefing "the five o'clock follies" because of their frustration with official evasiveness, information control and sometimes downright lying.

Sources call news conferences in order to better control the release of information and their responses to questions, while at the same time getting publicity. (See Box 18.1.) A news conference can also save a source a lot of time; instead of sitting down for a series of time-consuming individual interviews, the source can take care of all those reporters at once. So even if a televised news conference looks pretty rough on the person in front of the room, the format almost always favors the source. And most news conferences are far more sedate than the raucous ones we remember seeing. By the way, until the advent of broadcast news, news conferences were always called press conferences. Some people still use that convention, believing that "press" can be a generic term encompassing all news media. In this book we'll use "news conference."

How Do News Conferences Serve Your Audience?

As with anything you do as a reporter, you will need to determine whether and how your participation in a news conference will serve your audience.

There are a number of decision points. The first is whether to go at all. Public relations people and "handlers" pursue two strategies when announcing news conferences: They might announce in advance what the news conference will cover, especially if they know the topic will attract a lot of attention. Or they might insist on keeping the topic secret until the reporters show up. Often, secrecy surrounding the topic of a news conference is a good indicator that reporters will not be much interested; the only way the source can get reporters to attend the news conference is to keep them in suspense.

Another decision point comes when, as sometimes happens, sources put conditions on the news conference. For example, a source might say in advance that he will not discuss a certain topic or will not answer questions about that topic. This reflects the old tension between the agenda the source thinks is important and the agenda you think is most important to your audience. If a source puts conditions on a news conference, you as a reporter

News conferences may be called in unlikely places—sometimes to highlight a candidate's political agenda. Here, a hunting supporter introduces Tim Kaine during his successful campaign for governor of Virginia.

must decide whether it's worth agreeing to those conditions just to get access to the source for comments on what the source does want to talk about.

A third decision point comes when you consider whether you can get your job done in the format of a news conference. You must consider the possibility that the speaker will not call on you to answer the questions you want to pose. You must also consider whether other reporters are apt to keep the speaker on point. You have little control over what other reporters want to ask the source about. And do you want to tip other reporters off about a story you're working on by asking questions in their presence?

For you to have any chance of reaping benefit from a news conference, and for you to deal effectively with these decision points, getting the background is essential. Again, do your homework. Find out all you can about what is apt to happen at the news conference before it happens. Find out about the source: Why is he or she in a position to call a news conference? Current popularity or notoriety? Why? The point person for a hot topic? What's the topic? What do we already know, and can you anticipate the next development? What happened recently to precipitate the news conference?

Roanoke Times reporters Aaron McFarling, left, and Reed Williams wait to interview basketball star Shaquille O'Neal about his support for a law enforcement program. Sometimes the only access to celebrities and high-ranking officials is in a news conference.

Check your clips or file tape. Talk to other people close to the source or close to the issue that precipitated the news conference. Look for documents or on-line resources that can fill you in.

When you get into the news conference, remember that the source's answers to all questions are fair game to all the reporters there. You don't have to ask the question to be able to use the response. Sometimes the source will want only to read a statement, and will say that he or she will not take questions. Try to ask some anyway. Challenge the speaker. Try to corner him or her afterward to ask the questions you need answers to. Many sources who say they won't answer questions find it hard to walk away when reporters start asking them. After the news conference, phone the source or his or her representatives to ask more questions. Often you can get more information that way.

If you are reporting for broadcast, it's usually best to tape the entire news conference and pick the bites you want later. Remember, it's better to have it and not need it than to need it and not have it.

Remember also that your story might well focus only on one subject among several covered in the news conference. Just as the source's agenda might not be your audience's, so other reporters' agendas might not coincide with your own news judgment.

Ethics

Reporters occasionally ask questions about a topic that the source has already said he or she won't discuss. In that case, whether to answer or not is still up to the source. If he or she chooses to answer, you may use the response, despite what the source said previously about what he or she wouldn't answer.

Be sure to place what you get at the news conference in the appropriate context. Here again, your background becomes crucial to the story. Do your homework.

Sometimes a source or his or her representative will tell you the topic of a news conference only if you agree to an *embargo*; that is, you agree not to publish or broadcast a story before the news conference takes place. If you make a promise, keep it, but before you make any promises, see if you can find out from other sources what the news conference will be about. Remember that your primary obligation is to serve your audience, not a corporation or public official. If your audience will benefit from knowing the information before it is announced at a news conference, and you can share the information without breaking a promise, write the story. Finding out beforehand what the news conference will be about also helps you to decide whether it's even worth going to.

Strategies

To help you turn a news conference from the source's to your audience's advantage, remember (see Box 18.2):

Get the background. Find out all you can about what is apt to happen at the news conference before it happens. What precipitated the news conference? Can you anticipate the next development?

Check your clips or file tape. Talk to other people close to the source or close to the issue. Look for documents or online resources that can fill you in.

If you decide to attend, *remember that the source's answers to all questions are fair game* to all the reporters there. You don't have to ask the question to be able to use the response.

Box 18.2

STRATEGIES FOR COVERING NEWS CONFERENCES

1. Do your homework. Find out all you can about what prompted the news conference.

2. If the person calling the news conference is trying to keep the subject a secret, talk to other people who might tip you. You don't want to waste time going to a news conference that offers no real news. If you do go, you want to be prepared.

3. All the answers you hear are fair game for you to share with your audience, no matter who asked the question. You don't have to "own" the questions to use the responses.

4. Try to tape the entire news conference if you are working for broadcast. That ensures that you will have the bites you need later. You might consider archiving for later use the material you don't put in today's story.

5. Don't take no for an answer—not at first, anyway. If the speaker says he or she won't take questions, try asking some just the same.

6. If you are using the news conference to get access to a hard-to-reach source, stick to your agenda, not the source's, with your questions.

For broadcast stories, *tape the entire news conference* if you can. You can pick the bites you want later.

If the speaker says he or she won't take questions, ask some anyway. Try to follow up after the news conference as well.

The news conference might cover several topics, but *other reporters' agendas might be different from yours.* Be alert for surprises you need to follow up on, but otherwise, stick to your agenda on behalf of your audience.

Exercise 18

Chief Honeycutt's News Conference

You have already watched several one-on-one interviews in class. This time, we have scheduled a news conference so that you can practice your questioning skills. You will base your questions for Chief Honeycutt on the statement he makes and on what you know from Exercises 16A, 16B and earlier exercises. Make sure your story focuses on any new information you obtain from the news conference. Just as you will use information supplied in earlier exercises to help you formulate questions for the chief, use those exercises to provide background and context for your story. Assume it is December 20, five days after the accident described in the police report in Exercise 16B.

chapter nineteen

Courts, Trials, Indictments, Lawsuits

Many reporters flee for the bathroom when the assignment editor starts looking for someone to cover courts. The reporters' reluctance—or fear—about walking into a courtroom is based partly on their assumption that they will be tied down for hours or days while the justice system moves at its glacial pace. But the bigger reason is their misconception that nobody but a lawyer would ever understand what was going on. In Chapter 17, when the assignment was to cover a meeting of your local government, you learned to focus your story mostly on the simple things governments do rather than the complex ways in which they do them. Follow the same advice in covering the judicial system: Learn and understand the complexity, but translate it simply.

Lawyers and judges are always careful to tell potential jurors that what goes on in the courtroom is nothing like what they see on TV. Actually, often it's a great deal like it is on TV. What's different is what goes on *before* cases come to trial. For nine cases out of 10, civil or criminal, the period prior to a trial is when a resolution will be made, so pretrial activity is critically important.

It is also critically important to know where you are in the judicial system, so you can make sure your audience understands the context for what is going on. Again, once you know a few basics, it's not hard to keep yourself and your audience oriented. The simplest way to look at how courts are organized is as a series of bifurcations.

A Primer on the Courts

In the United States, all courts fall broadly under either the *federal court system* or a *state court system.* Each of those systems has two types of courts: *courts of original jurisdiction*—courts that try cases—and *appellate courts*— courts that hear appeals of rulings and verdicts made by lower courts. Within the courts of original jurisdiction there are two types of cases: *civil,* involving disputes between private individuals or companies, and *criminal,* in which the state or federal government, in effect, charges an individual or individuals with endangering or harming others and violating the peace and security of all members of society. (See Box 19.1.)

Let's look at a couple of examples. If your doctor determines you have gangrene in your leg but accidentally amputates the wrong leg, you may sue your doctor in civil court for harming you, but in most circumstances the doctor's behavior would not result in criminal charges. But if somebody robs a gas station, charges are brought in criminal court, because theft and threatening someone's life are looked on not as a financial transaction between private parties but as offenses against all of society. Whether you are in civil or criminal, state or federal courts, *most court proceedings, and nearly all trials, are open to the public.* The principal exception, as you learned in Chapter 16, is criminal cases involving juvenile defendants and, in some states, civil matters of family law, including divorce, child custody and adoption and settling a will. (But when I worked for *The Miami Herald* in Florida, covering courts in Palm Beach County, divorce cases were public. You can imagine the media coverage some of the high-profile breakups among the superrich in Palm Beach attracted.)

In most jurisdictions, for both criminal and civil cases, there are two levels of courts of original jurisdiction. The lower civil court handles *small-claims* cases (the kinds of things you see on *The People's Court* on TV). The upper civil court handles lawsuits in which much more money is at stake.

Box 19.1

HOW COURTS ARE ORGANIZED

1. Both the *federal government* and each *state government* maintain a system of courts.

2. Each system has *courts of original jurisdiction* (trial courts) and *appeals courts*.

3. Courts of original jurisdiction include *civil* and *criminal* courts.

4. Many jurisdictions also have separate *family courts* (including divorce cases), *probate courts, juvenile courts* and *traffic courts*.

5. Most systems have a lower trial court that hears relatively minor matters—civil *small claims* and criminal *misdemeanors*.

6. A second, upper-level trial court hears civil cases in which large amounts of money are at stake, and serious criminal cases, called *felonies*.

(The names of the courts or divisions differ from state to state. In Virginia, where Tori Baxter works and where our fictional community is located, lower courts, both civil and criminal, are called general district courts. The upper courts are called circuit courts.) The lower court for criminal cases handles *misdemeanors*—things like public drunkenness or simple vandalism—as well as most traffic cases. Misdemeanors are punishable by less than a year in a local jail, a fine, or both. The upper court, the *felony* division, handles more serious crimes—armed robbery or murder, for example. A felony is a crime that can result in a sentence of more than a year in a state prison.

Civil Cases versus Criminal Cases

Sometimes a single incident will give rise to cases in both civil and criminal court, and the outcome of each can be substantially different. An excellent example is the O.J. Simpson case. Simpson was found not guilty of criminal charges of murdering his ex-wife and another man. But in a separate civil case later he was held responsible for their deaths and was ordered to pay substantial damages to both families. How did that happen?

It's important to remember that civil courts apply a less stringent standard of proof than do criminal courts. In civil court, the person bringing the suit, or plaintiff, must prove his or her case by *the greater weight of the evidence*.

In criminal court, the prosecution must prove the defendant guilty *beyond a reasonable doubt.*

The O.J. Simpson cases were atypical in that both civil and criminal cases were taken to trial. Again, about 90 percent of both civil and criminal cases are resolved by some sort of pretrial settlement. In civil cases, the parties often compromise, and such settlements are often allowed to be kept secret. In criminal cases, defendants often *plea bargain*, agreeing to plead guilty to a lesser charge to avoid a trial and the possibility of a longer sentence for conviction on a more serious charge. Unlike civil settlements, criminal plea agreements usually must be public unless the defendant is a juvenile.

Within broad limits, a civil case can be brought by anyone who thinks another person is responsible for causing him harm—usually financial harm or damage to reputation. Similarly, a plaintiff can ask for any amount of damages. For those reasons, it's often advisable to de-emphasize the amount that a lawsuit asks for unless a solid foundation for it can be established.

Most states now allow still photography and video coverage of trials and many other judicial proceedings. The federal court system does not.

The Visual Story

While most court proceedings are public, there are still restrictions governing photography and video cameras in courtrooms. Most states now allow cameras at all public proceedings, but *the federal court system does not.* In the state courts, judges still have a lot of latitude in deciding how many cameras to allow and where they may be located. In cases that attract a lot of interest, photographers and videographers might have to agree to a pool arrangement that allows just one of each in the courtroom at a time. The tape and photos must be shared with other interested newspapers, television stations and online news outlets. It is always a good idea to let the judge or bailiff know in advance that you plan to have a photographer or videographer in the courtroom.

The Charging Process for Criminal Cases

The *charging process in criminal cases* can be complicated. It is designed to ensure that the rights of the accused are preserved and that people are not unjustly accused of crimes. We need to distinguish the charging process and pretrial procedures from the process of a trial. Covering a trial is beyond the scope of this book. Remember, though, that about 90 percent of cases will be resolved sometime during the pretrial process.

Because Exercise 19A deals with an *indictment,* we will go into some detail about the charging process here. The process differs somewhat from state to state, but generally follows a typical course.

When police believe a crime has been committed, they may arrest and charge the person they believe committed it. In most jurisdictions, within 24 to 48 hours of the person's arrest, he or she must appear before a judge or magistrate, a court official with limited judicial powers. The judge or magistrate reviews what is called a probable cause affidavit to determine preliminarily whether there is enough evidence to justify the arrest. The judge or magistrate then either sets a bond or denies bond, depending on the seriousness of the crime, how dangerous the defendant is seen to be and the likelihood that he or she will flee. The bond amount is *not* a reflection of whether the judge or magistrate thinks the accused is guilty. The accused is also told that he or she has the right to a lawyer, and a *preliminary hearing date* is set. If the defendant cannot afford a lawyer, the judge may appoint one.

Later—sometimes several weeks later—*at the preliminary hearing, the prosecution presents its case before a judge,* who decides whether there is enough evidence to send the case to a grand jury. A defendant is never determined to be guilty or not guilty at a preliminary hearing, unless he or she decides at that point to plead guilty. The preliminary hearing is also a chance for the defense to see the prosecution's case, and see what they're up against. The defense can but usually doesn't present any evidence. (In some states, some criminal cases do not have to be reviewed by a grand jury. A prosecutor can review the case prepared by police and file charges with the court by *information,* a formal charging document.)

If the judge determines after the preliminary hearing that there is enough evidence to take the case to a grand jury, the grand jury is convened. A grand jury is a body of 18 citizens brought together in a *secret* meeting to hear evidence against someone. This meeting is not a trial, and usually only the prosecutor's evidence is heard. (In different jurisdictions, prosecutors are variously called state attorneys, district attorneys or, in Virginia, commonwealth's attorneys. They represent the people in criminal cases.) If a grand jury decides there is enough evidence to charge the accused, it will issue an *indictment*. The indictment is a formal charge, not a finding of guilt, and your story should make that clear.

Once an indictment has been returned, a series of court proceedings and pretrial hearings will usually ensue. Most of these proceedings are public, and you can usually find out much about the case by attending them. The nature and outcome of these proceedings often shows you whether the case is likely to go to trial.

To use the O.J. Simpson criminal case again as an example, early pretrial motions filed by Simpson's attorneys indicated to veteran court reporters that the defense would focus on how evidence was gathered and on the behavior of police officers in conducting the investigation. Sure enough, at trial, much of Simpson's defense focused on allegations that evidence had been poorly gathered or maintained, and that at least one of the key officers in the investigation was racist.

Writing about Court Cases

As with crime reporting, *the impact in court stories is often emotional.* As part of our obligation to monitor institutions of power, news organizations should keep up with how well our judicial system works and trends in the justice system. Those stories may carry rational impact. But when you are reporting on individual cases, most of the impact is emotional. Look for the elements that give you that impact. Just because a story originates in court, it does not have to be laden with jargon, nor should it emphasize the process at the expense of the result. In explaining the case and its outcome to your audience, use plain English, not legalese. And remember that sometimes the bringing of a lawsuit or a criminal case is not the real impact we are looking for; it tips us to that impact.

Remember also that, as discussed in Chapter 16 with respect to reporting arrests, you must be careful with the words you use to report legal matters. Guilt is for a court to determine, so avoid saying "Hunter was arrested for possessing cocaine." Similarly, we should say "indicted on a charge of" instead of "indicted for" or "indicted with." Don't say "charges" unless it is more than one charge. In criminal cases, a defendant is found *guilty* or *not guilty*. There is no such thing as finding the defendant innocent. That's because the defendant does not have to prove his or her innocence; the prosecution must prove guilt beyond a reasonable doubt.

When a defendant is found not guilty, it means only that there was not enough evidence to meet the prosecution's burden of guilt. People who are found not guilty are not necessarily innocent of the crime. Because our legal system is structured to protect the rights of the accused, such a verdict is not necessarily a miscarriage of justice. We are willing to put up with letting people "get away" with wrongdoing occasionally for the sake of protecting other defendants from being wrongly convicted.

Occasionally charges are dismissed against a criminal defendant because police did not tell him of his right to remain silent and to talk to a lawyer, or because police used improper questioning or search methods. Defendants also occasionally go free because of mistakes made at their trials. In such cases we sometimes see or read in news stories that a judge released the defendant "on a technicality." Defense lawyers point out that that language is true only if you consider fair-trial guarantees in the United States Constitution "technicalities." "Released on a technicality" may also imply that the defendant was guilty, and that any ruling that afforded him or her the same rights as other citizens is a miscarriage of justice. You should avoid loaded language in your story, and remember your obligation to your audience to put facts in context.

Public officials will often decry the practice of plea bargaining, particularly when they are running for office. Allowing a defendant to plead guilty in return for a lighter sentence is frequently portrayed as being "soft on criminals" and cheating society out of justice. In some cases, the process is arguably unfair, but as a reporter you need to remember that a defendant who is willing to plead guilty before trial could also be found not guilty at trial. Even with a guilty verdict at trial on a more serious charge, judges and lawyers know that sentencing guidelines in many states would not permit a substantially longer sentence than a defendant might accept in a plea bargain. And without plea bargaining nearly every criminal case would have to go to trial, causing an enormous backlog of cases in most jurisdictions. As a reporter, you should explain the reasons for the plea bargain to your audience. Avoid writing about plea bargaining in a way that implies that the defendant "got off easy," unless you have evidence that a finding of guilt on a more serious charge was practically assured. That evidence is nearly impossible to nail down when you consider that a jury trial could have resulted in a not guilty verdict.

As with reporting requested damages in civil cases, it is often misleading to report the maximum sentence for the crime with which a person has been charged. You learned that in Chapter 16. Even if there is a conviction, defendants are seldom sentenced to the most severe punishment the law allows. If you do report the maximum sentence, you should also report the most common or most likely sentence for the crime. In many states, including Virginia, these are fairly easy to determine, because the states have set *sentencing guidelines* for judges to follow. The guidelines take into consideration not only the crime but the defendant's prior criminal record.

Remember, finally, that in civil cases there is no prosecutor, just the plaintiff's attorney and the defendant's attorney, and no charges, just a suit or complaint. Prosecutors represent the people only in criminal cases.

Ethics

Most court proceedings and related records are open to the news media and the public so that we may preserve constitutional guarantees. Giving citizens the ability to monitor their justice system helps prevent miscarriages of justice, abuse of people accused of crimes, and power grabs by ambitious public officials. England's infamous and highly secret Court of the Star Chamber was much on the minds of the framers of the United States Constitution in the 18th century.

But for journalists, having access to all manner of court proceedings and records does not mean we must report everything we see and hear. As with much of journalism ethics, *can* does not necessarily equal *must* or *should*. The most frequently cited example of journalistic restraint is the policy of most news organizations not to name rape victims in stories without the victim's consent. Similarly, when a rape victim testifies at a trial her identity is almost always kept from our audiences. While journalists routinely name the victims of other crimes, the argument is that rape carries a stigma for the victim that other crimes don't. In other words, even though journalists could provide the information to an audience, they make a reasoned decision not to.

Even where there are legal restrictions on disclosing information, it's important to remember that those legal constraints may not offer much guidance for journalists who have to make ethical decisions. For example, as you learned in Chapter 16, most jurisdictions prohibit court officials and police from releasing the names of juvenile defendants. The idea is to give youngsters a chance to mend their ways without having to endure a public stigma. The law sometimes carries criminal penalties for people who release the names of juvenile offenders. *But there are no legal prohibitions against journalists publishing the information if they manage to obtain it.* For journalists, then, it becomes a matter for ethical reasoning: Does the need of my audience to know the identity of a juvenile charged with a crime override our reluctance to make public the names of youngsters in trouble?

If legal proceedings are public because we as a society want to make sure that they are properly monitored, our professional responsibility as journalists includes not just *publicizing* those proceedings but also *explaining* them. The way good journalists do that, as you learned in earlier chapters, is to *show*, not *tell*. An audience that doesn't understand what it reads or watches cannot evaluate the justice of our system.

Strategies

Before you are sent to cover a trial or a pretrial proceeding:

Make sure you understand the judicial system in your state. Get an expert to explain it to you. Many state bars—the licensing authority for lawyers—publish guides or primers for journalists. The primer often includes a glossary of legal terms translated into audience-friendly language.

Remember the importance of pretrial proceedings, from arrest to trial. They can provide you with a preview of how the case will unfold. More importantly, about 90 percent of both civil and criminal cases are resolved without a trial. So if you ignore the pretrial activity in a case, chances are nine in 10 that you will miss the resolution of the case.

Make sure you understand—and explain to your audience—the nature of the judicial proceeding. Is it a criminal or civil case? Is it being reviewed by a grand jury, or about to go to trial?

Are still or video cameras allowed in courtrooms in your judicial system? If they are, *let a judge or bailiff know that you are planning to shoot a court proceeding.*

Understand the purpose of the proceeding you are covering, and make sure your audience understands as well. Is a defendant being formally charged, or is he pleading guilty? Are lawyers and court officials simply deciding on a timetable for the rest of the case?

Translate legalese and jargon into plain English, and avoid loaded language.

Avoid dwelling in criminal cases on the maximum sentence or, in civil cases, on the amount that a lawsuit demands. Most often those figures are meaningless. Sentencing is up to a judge; damage awards are up to a jury.

Focus on impact for your audience. Most often in court cases the impact for a mass audience will be emotional. Frequently that emotional impact depends not on the filing of criminal charges or a lawsuit but on what underlies that filing. (See Box 19.2)

Box 19.2

STRATEGIES FOR WRITING ABOUT COURTS

1. Understand your state's judicial system. Talk to an expert, such as a law professor, or obtain the primer for journalists published by your state bar.

2. Remember that about 90 percent of both civil and criminal cases are resolved without a trial. Stay on top of pretrial proceedings.

3. Explain to your audience where the case is in the judicial system—civil case or criminal? At a procedural stage, or substantive?

4. Find out whether cameras—still or video—are allowed in courtrooms in your judicial system.

5. If you don't understand the proceeding you are covering, find a friendly lawyer to explain it to you. Then explain it to your audience.

6. Use plain English in your story, not legalese or jargon. Stay away from loaded language like "he was released on a technicality." Show what happened.

7. Write about likely sentences rather than maximum sentences. Similarly, don't dwell on the amount a civil suit asks for. Wait until the amount is decided by a judge or jury.

8. Remember that the impact of most court cases on a mass audience will be emotional. Make your story reflect that.

In the following exercises, keep in mind where in the court system each case originated, and look for the real impact of each. In each, you will need to use earlier exercises for background.

Exercise 19A

Indictment

From the background information and indictment presented here and using contextual information presented in earlier chapters, write a 30-second RDR and a Web blurb.

Background

Police read the indictment to Hunter this morning at 9:45 at the Blue Ridge Regional Jail, where he has been jailed since the accident, unable to make a preliminary bail of $25,000. His new bail has been set at $250,000. He is scheduled for arraignment tomorrow at 9 A.M. in Blue Ridge Circuit Court. Witnesses examined by the Grand Jury in reaching its decision were Alan W. Grant, Timmy Healey, Howard F. Dobbins, Dorcas Dobbins, Seymour Fine, Meagan Lucille LeBlanc and Courtney Ann Topping.

> **In the Circuit Court of the Commonwealth of Virginia for the Blue Ridge Circuit**
>
> THE PEOPLE
>
> v.
>
> MERIWETHER CHASE HUNTER,
> defendant
>
> An Indictment
>
> Your Grand Jurors, in session in the above styled case this 29th day December, do hereby accuse the above named defendant MERIWETHER CHASE HUNTER by this indictment with the crimes of RECKLESS DRIVING, NEGLIGENT HOMICIDE, and VEHICULAR MANSLAUGHTER.
>
> Committed as follows:
>
> The said MERIWETHER CHASE HUNTER on or about the 15th day of December, in the City of Valleydale, then and there being the driver of a motor

vehicle westbound on Trafalgar Street, a public thoroughfare in the City of Valleydale, did then and there willfully and unlawfully drive said motor vehicle carelessly and heedlessly in reckless disregard of the rights and safety of others in a grossly negligent and criminal manner, in support of which we allege, to wit:

1. That defendant failed to keep a proper lookout for other traffic upon or crossing a public highway;
2. That defendant illegally and recklessly crossed into the left traffic lane in a no-passing zone;
3. That defendant did fail to obey the legal and duly posted speed limit;
4. That defendant did drive his motor vehicle at a speed greater than reasonable and prudent under conditions then and there existing, and in violation of existing laws;
5. That defendant drove said motor vehicle while in a state of intoxication, in violation of state law.

As a direct and proximate result of the defendant's driving said motor vehicle in the manner and under the conditions aforesaid, defendant HUNTER did thereby then and there lose control of his motor vehicle, damaging the private property of citizens, to wit, HOWARD and DORCAS DOBBINS and VIRGINIA PRESBYTERIAN UNIVERSITY, and causing to be inflicted grievous bodily injuries on the person of RANDY BOWERS, who as a result of said injuries did die on the 15th day of December, contrary to statute and against the peace and dignity of the Commonwealth of Virginia.

Dated this 29th day of December in Circuit Court, Commonwealth of Virginia.

Joshua A. Taliaferro
Commonwealth's Attorney

Exercise 19B

Lawsuit

From the background and lawsuit presented here and contextual information provided earlier, write a story for the *Jeffersonville Herald*.

Background

Assume it is now three months after the accident described in the police report in Exercise 16B. At a pretrial hearing a month ago, a judge dismissed the criminal charges against Hunter because Officers Grant and Healey neglected to read Hunter his Miranda rights when they questioned him after the accident. He has been living in Blue Ridge County since he was released from jail. He no longer lives with nor is dating Courtney Topping. On the advice of her lawyer, LeBlanc will not talk about the lawsuit.

In the Circuit Court of the Commonwealth of Virginia for the Blue Ridge Circuit

MEAGAN LUCILLE LeBLANC
    Plaintiff

v.

MERIWETHER CHASE HUNTER,
    Defendant

Comes now the Plaintiff, by and through her undersigned attorney, and alleges:

I

For the purposes of the above-styled action and at all times material hereto Plaintiff was a resident of the Commonwealth of Virginia by dint of her attendance as a full-time student at Virginia Presbyterian University in the City of Valleydale, Virginia.

II

Plaintiff brings this action as an adult under the provisions of the laws of the Commonwealth of Virginia.

III

At all times material hereto Trafalgar Street was a paved, two-lane, two-way street upon which traffic moves in an easterly–westerly direction, within the duly and legally constituted boundaries of the City of Valleydale.

IV

On or about December 15th, Plaintiff was riding as a passenger in a Ford Explorer sport-utility vehicle then operated by Defendant and traveling west on Trafalgar Street. At the time and place aforementioned Defendant was negligent in one or more of the following particulars:

1. In driving in excess of the legally posted speed limit.
2. In driving in the left, eastbound lane of Trafalgar Street in a clearly marked no-passing zone, in violation of the traffic laws of the Commonwealth of Virginia.
3. In driving with a blood-alcohol level of .25, more than three times the legal limit under the laws of the Commonwealth of Virginia.

    4. In failing to keep and maintain an adequate lookout for the other traffic upon and entering into Trafalgar Street.

    5. In failing to keep the Ford Explorer vehicle under adequate control.

V

Because of the manner of the Defendant's willful and negligent operation of said motor vehicle, Defendant did then and there cause said vehicle to strike another vehicle, being operated by Howard F. Dobbins in a safe and legal manner.

VI

As a result of said collision, Defendant lost control of his vehicle and did cause it to crash into a concrete bridge abutment owned by Virginia Presbyterian University.

VII

By reason of the negligence of the Defendant in one or more of the particulars alleged herein, the collision occurred and Plaintiff was caused to suffer serious and extensive bodily injuries, including an injury to the head with concussion of the brain and injury to the central nervous system, lacerations of the face and head, injury to the left leg with multiple fractures to bones of said leg, injury to the right arm with a compound fracture of the upper, or humerus, bone; and multiple bruises and abrasions about the head, body, and limbs, and was caused to suffer physical and emotional shock. Said injuries were permanent in nature, and by reason of the injuries, Plaintiff has and will continue to suffer pain, discomfort, inconvenience, disfigurement, disability, and mental anguish.

VIII

By reason of the injuries, Plaintiff has been required to have an ambulance, to be hospitalized, and to have the services of physicians, nurses, technicians, and the use of special medical and physical therapeutic equipment, medicines, and supplies, all at the reasonable expense of $227,894.14, and claims compensatory damages in that sum. Plaintiff will by reason of her injuries continue to require medical and dental care for an indefinite period of time in the future, including costly and painful reconstructive surgery about her face and mouth. The total of her future medical expenses is unknown at this time. This Complaint will be amended when the full amount of her compensatory damages is known.

IX

By reason of the injuries, Plaintiff has been and will continue to be unable to participate in intercollegiate athletics.

X

As a direct and proximate result of the Defendant's negligence as alleged elsewhere herein, Defendant did cause the death of Randy Bowers, a passenger in the same vehicle driven by Defendant and in which Plaintiff was also a passenger. Plaintiff and deceased Bowers had been engaged and had made plans to be married upon Plaintiff's graduation from Virginia Presbyterian University. As a result of Defendant's negligence in causing the death of Bowers, Plaintiff has suffered egregious emotional distress and mental harm and anguish, as well as loss of consortium and companionship.

XI

Prior to the accident, Defendant had been living in the same domicile as Plaintiff by dint of being in a relationship with one of Plaintiff's housemates. By engaging in illegal activities, Defendant did cause his own arrest on drug charges and the arrest of several innocent parties in the house, including Plaintiff. As a result of Defendant's illegal behavior which led to the arrests, Plaintiff suffered public humiliation, embarrassment, and damage to reputation, and was forced to withdraw as a candidate for Valleydale City Council.

WHEREFORE, Plaintiff prays this honorable court for judgment against the Defendant for compensatory and punitive damages in excess of $2 million, for costs and disbursements incurred as a result of this action, and for such other and further relief as to the court may seem proper.

Teresita L. Sanchez-Rodriguez
Attorney for Plaintiff

chapter twenty

Working from Background and Other Levels of Attribution

Journalists are often criticized for rushing into print or on the air with every scrap of information, rumor and innuendo that they hear. There is some validity to that criticism, of course, but there is also irony, because every journalist I know learns far more than he or she will ever tell an audience. A critical role of the journalist is to weigh both the reliability of information and the appropriateness of sharing it with an audience.

Almost always, if we intend to share information with an audience, we should attribute it to a particular, named source. Audiences should expect that; careful attribution helps them decide how much faith to put in the information. Attribution also holds each source accountable for what he or she says, and discourages sources from taking "cheap shots" at others. So in the discussion that follows, *remember first that "on the record" is the rule; any other arrangement is an exception to the rule.* We should not break that rule without a very good reason.

When the microphones are out and the camera is rolling, interview subjects should know they are on the record.

When Journalists Won't Identify Sources

On occasion, however, a journalist will agree not to identify his or her source of information. The usual criterion for that decision is that there is no other way audiences will learn necessary information without such a guarantee by the reporter to the source. This privilege is too frequently abused by reporters, particularly those covering Washington. For example, many early stories about then-President Clinton's involvement with White House intern Monica Lewinsky relied heavily on unnamed sources speculating about what might have happened.

More recently, using information from an unnamed source, columnist Robert Novak identified a CIA operative, a potential violation of federal law. As part of her investigation of that case, *New York Times* reporter Judith Miller went to jail rather than reveal one of her sources despite a court order to do so. Miller was jailed even though she had written no stories about the case. Another news organization, *Time* magazine, and reporter Matt Cooper, decided ultimately to obey the court order. In Miller's case, she and *The Times* made an ethical decision that journalistic independence, protecting her source and preserving the value of confidential source relationships were worth going to jail for. Eventually, after discussions with her source, Miller, too, decided to obey the order. Whether—and under what circumstances— journalists should be allowed to protect sources despite a court order is a classroom discussion worth having.

Levels of Attribution

It is important in any discussion of attribution to recognize and define the levels at which reporters receive information. The following typology is not universally shared, but it encompasses most of the types of promises reporters make to sources. (See Box 20.1.)

Box 20.1

LEVELS OF ATTRIBUTION

Here are the *levels of attribution* most journalists recognize. Remember that on the record is the rule; other forms of attribution are exceptions.

1. *On the record.* The source is named and his or her involvement in the issue is identified. On-the-record information may include direct quotes, indirect quotes, partial quotes, dialogue and paraphrase.

2. *Not for direct attribution.* The reporter may use the information, and may even use quotes, but agrees not to identify the source. The reporter and source agree on how the source will be referred to.

3. *Background.* Information that is presented in the story without attribution, often from an expert who does not want to be associated with a particular story but who agrees to provide context for it.

4. *Deep background.* Information that will not be used directly in a story. Often it is used to guide reporters or to confirm information obtained from other sources.

5. *Off the record.* To reporters, information that is not usable in any way. To sources, it may mean anything from not-for-attribution to deep background. The reporter should make the difference clear to the source.

On the record is the most frequent way reporters present information to audiences. The source is named and his or her involvement in the issue or expertise in it is discussed briefly. On-the-record information can be in the form of direct quotes, indirect quotes, partial quotes, dialogue or paraphrase.

Not for direct attribution means that the reporter may use the information, and may even use quotes, but agrees not to identify the source. There is a lot of room for negotiation between reporter and source over how the source will be referred to in the story to give the audience some idea of his or her credibility. The reporter wants to get as specific as possible; the source wants to remain unidentifiable. Often the attribution will look something like this: "a source close to the mayor said." Remember that your agreement is not to *identify* the source. If you do not name the source but decide to get cute and include so much identifying information that everyone will know who the source is, you have still broken your promise.

Background is information that is presented without attribution. Sometimes that happens because the information is available from numerous sources. For example, in a news story there is no need to say "President George W. Bush was reelected in November 2004, according to *The Encyclopedia Britannica*." But some information might be well known by people in a particular field or profession but not by the public, and we need someone in that profession to guide us. Say we were checking a tip that patients were dying at a local hospital because there was no clear-cut chain of command or treatment protocols in the emergency room. We would probably interview emergency room physicians at other hospitals for general information about the organization of and job responsibilities in a typical emergency room. That information might be presented to an audience without attribution: "In many emergency rooms, a designated triage officer evaluates incoming cases for severity and decides who must be treated first."

Deep background is information that not only will not be attributed; it will not be used directly in a story. The most celebrated example of a deep-background source is the Watergate scandal's Deep Throat. When Bob Woodward and Carl Bernstein of *The Washington Post* were pursuing the Watergate story, which eventually led to the resignation of President Richard Nixon in 1974, they needed someone familiar enough with the Nixon White House and the Committee to Re-Elect the President to point them in the right direction. They used Deep Throat for that. Sometimes Deep Throat would let them know whether a path they were pursuing would be productive. Sometimes they would run information they thought they knew past Deep Throat for his reaction. Deep Throat occasionally confirmed what other sources had told them. At other times his information gave them the perspective and direction they needed to question other sources. Never in their stories did they attribute information to Deep Throat, nor did they directly present information Deep Throat gave them. Woodward and Bernstein promised not to reveal Deep Throat's identity until his death, but in late spring 2005 his family revealed him as W. Mark Felt, deputy director of the FBI during the Watergate investigation. While still alive when his identity was revealed, Felt was in his 90s and in fragile health.

Off the record, to many reporters, means that the information is not usable in any form. But sources will frequently say "off the record" to mean anything from not-for-attribution to deep background. It is important for the reporter to clear up that discrepancy. When a source tells a reporter that information the source is about to give the reporter must be "off the record," the reporter will frequently respond: "That means I can never use it. In that case why do you want to tell me? You know I'm a reporter. Why would you give me information I can't use?" Usually, at that point, a source will respond with something like, "Well, I do think it's important that people find this out. I just can't have it known that it came from me." For the reporter, that's not the same as "off the record." Taking a hard line on the meaning of "off the record" is usually a good strategy for a reporter because it sets clear parameters and gives the reporter a chance to negotiate how to get information to an audience.

Negotiating Attribution with Sources

How does the fundamental and very important negotiation of attribution work? The reporter wants the information to be reliable and credible, so he or she tries to get it as closely associated with the source as possible. The source wants to distance himself or herself from the information as much as possible. It is critical that the reporter and source strike the agreement *before* the information is given, that both understand the level at which they are operating, and that the reporter keep that promise. As long as a reporter has identified herself appropriately to a source and said that she is working on a story, she and the source should assume that information will be on the record unless they strike a prior agreement to the contrary. *Never let a source talk to you for 20 minutes and then say, "Of course, that was all off the record."*

Again, remember that sources should almost always be on the record. Anything else is an exception to the rule. So as a reporter, you must find out and report why a source does not want to be on the record. There are legitimate reasons—fear of losing a job or other retribution, fear of physical danger to oneself or one's family—but never let a source deviate from being on the record just so he or she can take cheap shots at somebody else. You should always tell your audience why your source is not identified: "One witness said the assailant shot three times from only a few feet away. The witness asked not to be identified because the killer is still at large and the witness fears retribution." (Notice here that we did not even identify the witness by sex.)

Always *verify* information that is not on the record.

Keeping Sources Unidentified in Broadcast Media

You have no doubt seen the various ways television reporters handle bites from sources who are not on the record. Those techniques include silhouetting, "blue-dotting," voice masking and so forth. Whichever technique you as a television journalist might use for a particular source or story, remember that the negotiation and the promise arising from it come first.

Ethics

Because this entire chapter has been about decisions you make when you decide to break the rule of keeping sources on the record, it has been about ethical decision-making. To help clarify your ethical reasoning, think about the decisions you face in terms of both your audience and your source, and what you owe both.

Ordinarily, we owe our audiences trustworthy information about matters of importance. That means that they should know where information is coming from. Giving information to them that hasn't been fully attributed means that we have judged the information to be so important that audiences must have it even if they cannot know its source. That is certainly an appropriate way to judge competing ethical demands. Remember, though, to stay open to other approaches to ethical decision-making. The obvious one in this case is determining whether the information you want is available from any other source on the record.

What we owe our sources, simply put, is to keep our promises. A promise of confidentiality should be seen as a kind of *moral contract*, and all parties to a contract should understand its provisions before they agree to it. Your source should understand what you are promising by "not for attribution," "background," "deep background" and "off the record." He or she should also know the lengths to which you are willing to go to keep your promise.

Making such a "contract" may sound relatively straightforward, until you consider that, like Judith Miller, reporters sometimes break the law, violate a court order, and even go to jail rather than break the promises they make to sources. With so much at stake, your source should know whether you are prepared to go that far. It is also fair to ask your source whether he or she would be willing to be identified to keep you out of jail.

Strategies

Reporters should get information on the record. Let that be your rule. Careful attribution helps audiences decide how much faith to put in a story. *Any arrangement with a source other than on the record is an exception to the rule.* (See Box 20.2) But on the rare occasions when you are about to decide that a source cannot be identified:

Make sure first that there is no other way your audiences will be able to learn necessary information on the record.

Make sure your source understands *not for attribution, background, deep background,* and *off the record.*

Make the agreement about how you will identify your source before the source gives you information. Sometimes the source will want to remove himself or herself as far from direct attribution as possible. You will want to get the source as close to on the record as you can. Don't let a source try to renegotiate after he or she tells you something.

Remember, and let your sources know, that off-the-record information is virtually useless to a reporter.

Always verify information that is not on the record.

Keep in mind the ways of keeping sources in broadcast stories unidentified, even when they are on tape.

Tell your audience why you have agreed not to identify a source.

Keep your promises.

Box 20.2

STRATEGIES FOR ATTRIBUTING INFORMATION

1. Keep sources on the record unless there is no other way your audiences can learn essential information.

2. Go over *not for attribution, background, deep background* and *off the record* with your source to make sure he or she understands the difference.

3. Negotiate with the source over how the source will be identified before the source gives you information. Don't let a source try to renegotiate afterward.

4. Off-the-record information is usually of no value to a reporter. Make sure your source knows that.

5. Verify information that is not on the record.

6. Even when they are on tape, sources in broadcast stories can be kept confidential. Make sure they understand and agree with how you will do that.

7. When sources are not on the record, tell your audience why not.

8. Keep promises you make to sources.

Read the Finance Committee's report, the rebuttal from Council members Wise and Bullard, and the transcript of the city manager's news conference presented here. Remember that the Finance Committee comprises one City Council member and two members appointed from the community. Remember also that the information in the report and in the city manager's news conference is all on the record. City Council is expected to discuss the report and the rebuttal at its next meeting Tuesday. You might also want to refresh your memory by reviewing Chapter 6, the "Resignation" and "Goodbye Luverne" scenarios in Exercise 4, and the information contained in Exercises 12 and 15.

Whether or not your instructor has assigned separate stories for Exercise 20A, the Finance Committee report, and 20B, the city manager's news conference, use the information in those, and what you find out in the interviews below, to write your story for Exercise 20C.

Exercise 20A

Finance Committee Report

CITY OF VALLEYDALE
Finance Committee
MEMORANDUM TO: Honorable Mayor and City Council
FROM: Finance Committee—Louise Mutispaugh, Preston Allen, C.D. "Tarheel" Davies
RE: Special Report

This is a special report of the Finance Committee in response to the Mayor's special request on Oct. 15. In it we report on and discuss concerns raised by Council Members Wise and Bullard relating to the activities of the City Finance Department and the City Manager. It should be pointed out at the outset that the Committee received cooperation from the City Manager in its investigation. It should also be pointed out that Council Members Wise and Bullard object strongly to the Committee's conclusions and recommendations. Their dissenting report is appended hereto.

Approximately one year ago Council Members Wise and Bullard began alleging that there were certain irregularities in the methods by which the Finance Department accounted for the city budget, including but not limited to property tax revenues and expenditures for the City Manager's office. The allegations began as a "whispering campaign" but soon were being made on the record in open City Council meetings. At one such session, the Finance Committee was asked to investigate the allegations. We were asked to report back to the City Council in three weeks. We apologize for not meeting that deadline. The substantial delay was due to our desire to give those with evidence against the City Manager every opportunity to come forward. With the exception of Council Members Wise and Bullard, no one has.

We repeatedly asked Council Members Wise and Bullard to provide evidence substantiating their allegations. To this date, they have failed to do so, other than to repeat their earlier allegations. The sole piece of evidence they have presented consists of a newspaper article in the *Jeffersonville Herald* based on a computer analysis of the current and proposed city budgets. We do not find the article either persuasive or sufficient as evidence of wrongdoing.

Therefore, we consider this matter to be closed. We suggest to Council Members Wise and Bullard that an apology to the City Manager and the Finance Department employees would be appropriate.

Respectfully submitted,
Louise Mutispaush, Chair
Preston Allen, Member
C.D. "Tarheel" Davies, Member

Council Members Wise and Bullard Respond:

We believed at the time we presented our evidence initially, almost a year ago, and our further investigation has since proven, that irregularities in the management of city finances not only exist but are serious and possibly illegal in nature. We realize that these are serious allegations, and we would not be making them if we did not believe them to be true as proven by our evidence. Of equal concern is the City Manager's open defiance of our authority. We have been told by several members of the Finance Department staff that they were ordered by the City Manager not to cooperate in our own investigation, which we conducted independently when it became obvious to us that the Finance Committee was biased in favor of the City Manager. Accordingly, much of the evidence we offer will be in the form of comments from anonymous workers.

Our investigation has concluded:

1. The City Manager is both unconcerned and overly concerned with the day-to-day running of the Finance Department. On the one hand, employees tell us that he is inclined to micromanage certain accounts. On the other hand, other employees say that he is unconcerned about the size of overall budget increases in recent years. "He's got his grubby hands all over my books," one told us. But another said, "I don't think he's even aware what the city budget is. I've never seen him walk through that door." Clearly, something is the matter.

2. According to a newspaper account from the *Jeffersonville Herald*, the city's revenue and expenditures have not balanced for the current and next budget years, leaving more than $4 million unaccounted for. Unfortunately, our own investigation was unable to track the missing and unaccounted-for funds. The City Manager has denied that such a discrepancy exists, even though, for once, the media has gotten the story right.

3. The City Manager has openly exhibited inappropriate and immoral behavior toward certain staff members of the Finance Department. In particular, he has entered into an obviously adulterous relationship with one female staff member, showering her with flowers and other expensive gifts. (The staff member denied the relationship but was obviously not being truthful.) As further evidence, we submit that the City Manager has gone in the past year from little concern for his physical appearance to an overly fastidious attitude, including designer haircuts and expensive outfits. This is a radical change from the individual whom we criticized two years ago for being unconcerned about his physical appearance in a highly public job. There is obviously no other explanation than that he is trying to attract and keep the attention of the opposite sex.

4. The City Manager intentionally presents proposed budgets that council members are unable to fathom. It is obviously his strategy to "keep us in the dark." Using highfalutin terminology such as *disbursements* and *ad valorem* and numbered categories to correspond to the different funds are two examples of

his obfuscation. Indeed, in the words of one Finance Department staff member: "We had a perfectly simple system here for years. Then two years ago he insists that we adopt some 'standard' system out of some accounting textbook that the state supposedly was requiring cities to do. I'll bet. None of us can understand it except him and his bimbo."

5. Following the resignation in disgust of the previous Finance Director, the City Manager went out of his way to bypass the authority and effectiveness of the Acting Finance Director. While we believe the Acting Finance Director should have been more forceful in her dealings with the City Manager, and should have reported all questionable behavior on the part of the City Manager directly to City Council members, this report is in no way intended as a criticism of her. For example, the City Manager ordered flowers, at city expense, for the secretaries in all city departments on National Secretaries' Day. It was an obvious ploy to disguise the individual in the Finance Department whom he really wanted to give flowers to. Yet the Acting Finance Director never informed the Finance Committee or City Council of this obvious evidence of the City Manager's inappropriate involvement in the "affairs"—pardon the pun—of the Finance Department.

As a result of these myriad transgressions by the City Manager, morale has reached rock-bottom among employees of the Finance Department. "This has become an awful job," according to one. "We used to come and go as we pleased. Now there always has to be at least one person around in case somebody from the public walks in with a stupid question, and we are required to take our coffee breaks and lunch hours at prescribed times. And he's taken away the Internet access from our computers. Do you know how much easier the Internet made shopping in this town?"

Admittedly, we joined other City Council members in being among the City Manager's most ardent supporters when he was hired five years ago. We believed he would bring a sense of professionalism to city departments. Instead, he has brought distraction and discord. It is with deepest regret but also a sense of concern for the citizens of Valleydale, then, that we, Council Members Wise and Bullard, respectfully reject the Finance Committee's conclusions and urge the City Council to adopt the following resolution:

WHEREAS, City Manager Ron Allen "Don" Prentice has openly defied the Valleydale City Council, and

WHEREAS, the City Manager has engaged in activities that can only be deemed morally reprehensible, and

WHEREAS, under his stewardship questionable accounting practices have been adopted in the city's budget, leading to large amounts of missing or unaccounted for funds, and

WHEREAS, as a result of the City Manager's actions morale in the Finance Department has plummeted and citizen confidence in the Department has disappeared,

NOW BE IT THEREFORE RESOLVED that the following actions be taken by the council:

1. That the Council terminate Ron Allen "Don" Prentice as City Manager, or, if it so chooses, give him an opportunity to resign voluntarily.

2. That City Council assume direct authority to oversee employees of the Finance Department on a day-to-day basis, and that Committees of Council be given similar responsibility for other city employees, including the full power to hire and fire department heads.

3. That the council in its wisdom accept and review this report in executive session and order it forever sealed to avoid embarrassment to the City Manager, the former Finance Director, and the Acting Finance Director, and that no recording or minutes of that session be taken.

Respectfully submitted,
Eaton Wise, Council Member
Rondah Bullard, Council Member

Exercise 20B

City Manager's News Conference

Prentice: I have no opening statement. Let's get right to your questions.

Q: (Bill Williams, Channel 9, Wilson) Mr. Prentice, how do you feel about the Finance Committee's report?

A: It's what I expected. They found nothing because there was nothing to be found.

Q: (Tori Baxter, *Jeffersonville Herald*) What about the rebuttal from Council members Wise and Bullard?

A: It's garbage. Next question.

Q: (Mel Looney, WHIC-FM, Beausoleil) Don't you think you'd better elaborate, Don? There are a lot of—

A: Maybe you didn't hear me. It's garbage. That's elaboration enough.

Q: (Williams) What about the accusations that you and a Finance Department employee—

A: Pure sleaze. I'm not even going to dignify it with a response. Look, doesn't anybody want to ask me about the Finance Committee's findings? They're the ones that matter.

Q: (Baxter) Mr. Prentice, Council members Wise and Bullard in their report cited a story in the Herald regarding inconsistencies in budget figures—

A: Well, that shows how confused they were if they believed what was in the newspaper. You listen to me, little lady, you're lucky you didn't get your butt sued over that story. Remember that the committee put no faith in the story whatsoever. I don't know how you can continue to show your face around here. I'd be too embarrassed.

Q: (Baxter) Sir, there seems to be little substantiation for Wise's and Bullard's other claims, including—

A: Well, now you're talking. I'm surprised you of all people noticed that. The long and short of it is that Council members Wise and Bullard don't understand anything about municipal finance, and the Finance Committee does. That explains about 98 percent of the problem.

Q: (Ellen Harper, Channel 7, Jeffersonville) What's the other 2 percent, Mr. Prentice?

A: That's a smart-ass question. I was speaking figuratively. Look, this whole business was the result of misunderstanding on their part. After some initial, frustrating, futile attempts to explain to them how city finances work, I gave up. Maybe that was my only mistake. I probably should have kept trying, as useless as that seemed. So let them take their best shot. I have ultimate faith in the other City Council members. Again, I'd like to point out that the official report, the one done by the only appropriate body to conduct the investigation, couldn't find a single thing to criticize. The other two just don't like me. Why else would they get on me about the way I dress? They were the ones who were on my case a year ago about me looking sloppy. Go figure.

Q: (Looney) Don, it sounds like there are a lot of disgruntled Finance Department workers.

A: Yeah, and all of them anonymous. Even if you assume that Wise and Bullard didn't make up those quotes, I'm not surprised the people didn't want to be identified, since they were complaining that I've forced them to act more professional.

Q: (Baxter) What do you think will happen Tuesday night?

A: As I said, I have ultimate faith in the other council members. I'm not going to comment further at this time. That concludes this press conference.

Q: (Baxter, shouting after him) Will you resign?

A: Hah! You'd like that, wouldn't you? Well, write this down, little lady, and stick it in your newspaper: There is no goddamn way I'll quit.

Exercise 20C

Levels of Attribution

In this exercise, you are working on a longer story, a "weekender" in newspaper parlance, trying to figure out what is at the heart of the conflict between council members Wise and Bullard and City Manager Prentice. Writing the story for print presents one set of challenges; writing it for broadcast presents those same challenges, plus others. Your instructor might ask you to augment your story with an outline or shooting script of how you would tell the story visually, including presenting interviews with people who do not want to be identified.

Some of the information given is not on the record. Note how Tori Baxter deals with sources who do not want to be on the record, and how she negotiates the agreement before she gets any information. You will need to determine whether and how to use and attribute the information those sources provide. You will need to provide context from the Finance Committee's report, from the dissent by Wise and Bullard, and from the city manager's news conference. All the material in both is on the record. Assume it is now late March, and that the report came out three days ago, more than five months after the City Council meeting at which Mayor Hostetter asked for it. Remember that the Finance Committee had promised it in about four weeks. Assume that Prentice's news conference was two days ago, the day after the report was released. Assume that you did a daily story about the release of the report and one about Prentice's news conference. Remember that City Council has scheduled an executive session Tuesday to discuss the Finance Committee's report and the rebuttal. Assume also that you are able to find and read the City Council minutes referred to below by Luverne Trump.

When Tori Baxter gets to her office Thursday morning, there is a brief handwritten note in her mailbox: "Tori—This is all so hateful. Why can't everyone just get along? Please don't call me. I have no further comment. Louise Mutispaugh." Tori is hoping to have more luck with the other players.

Q: Hi, is this Alice Turpin? Hi, this is Tori Baxter with the *Jeffersonville Herald*. Sorry to bother you at home.

A: Better here than at the office, Tori.

Q: Well, that's what I figured. I know we haven't had much contact with each other recently, but I'm trying to get a handle on this business with Mr. Prentice, the Finance Committee and Council members Wise and Bullard.

A: Yeah, join the club. Look, I've generally been impressed with your budget stories, because you seem to have a basic understanding of stuff and an ability to get that across to ordinary citizens. And as far as all this business, I sure would like folks to know what's really going on. But it all has to be off the record.

Q: Off the record isn't useful to me or my audience, Alice. It means I can't use anything you tell me. Is that really what you mean?

A: No, I didn't realize that. I'd like to point you in a couple of directions, direct your inquiries a little, but nothing that winds up directly in the story. And if my name ever got used, unless and until they fire Don Prentice, I'd be history. I'm in between a real rock and a hard place. Can we work something out?

Q: What you've described to me is called deep background, Alice. Can we get any closer to on the record than that? I'd like the story to include some of what you tell me.

A: Sorry, no way. There are things I know that would be traced right back to me if they were reported directly. I've got to stay with what you call deep background. Okay?

Q: Okay.

A: You might get in touch with Luverne Trump. I think she's working in Mountain City now. She always played it pretty close to the vest, but she might have some things to say on the record. She was pretty upset when she left here.

Q: Thanks, I'll definitely give her a call. Meanwhile, you'll talk on deep background, right?

A: Right. I hope you understand how much I'm trusting you. Here goes: Your budget story last fall hit the nail on the head. There is one hell of a lot of money unaccounted for in the city budget—more than you said, actually— and it wasn't an arithmetic error. Bullard smelled a rat, but she hates Prentice so much personally that she's blind to what's really going on. Plus she's dumb as a sack of rocks, as you might have surmised.

Q: Why does she hate Prentice?

A: I have no idea. Ask her.

Q: What about Wise?

A: He obviously hates Prentice, too, but for a different reason. As nearly as I can tell—and I *am* pretty bright when it comes to the city budget, Wise was a part of Prentice's little scheme until a couple of years ago. It was pretty cozy for a while, but then it blew up. If you check council minutes from about two years ago you'll discover a budget work session at which Wise kept insisting that the City Council's office budget be increased even more. That was code for him wanting a bigger slice of the unaccounted-for money. They got into a shouting match right there. After that, Prentice froze him out, and Wise has been retaliating ever since.

Q: Let me make sure I've got this clear: You're saying that the unaccounted-for money in the city's budget over the last couple of years—

A: Longer than that.

Q: Okay, in the couple of years that I've been covering the city, the unaccounted for money is going into the city manager's pocket? And before that into Wise's pocket, too?

A: Not all of it, but yes, that's it.

Q: Why are Louise Mutispaugh and the Finance Committee backing Prentice, then?

A: She isn't, necessarily, she just doesn't like to fight. The smoother things go, and the more people get along, the happier she is. She's a non-starter in all this. Her head's in the sand. The Finance Committee's so-called investigation was bogus. They talked to Prentice a couple of times, and nobody else as far as I can tell. Not to me, anyway. They accepted what he told them. The other two committee members went along with whatever Mutispaugh wanted to do.

Q: Okay. Wise and Bullard also accused Prentice of having an affair with one of your employees.

A: God, that would be funny if it wasn't so pathetic. All Rondah Bullard can think of is Don Prentice bonking some stupid kid and then sending her flowers and candy. Smell the coffee, Rondah.

Q: What do you mean?

A: I mean the kid is as sharp as a tack. She isn't in love with Prentice, she's blackmailing him. She figured out what was going on, and instead of going to Luverne or me with it, she went to Prentice. If you get my drift.

Q: I think so, but you'd better make it clear.

A: She told Prentice she knew what he was up to, and that he'd better cut her into the deal if he knew what was good for him.

Q: You know this?

A: I haven't confronted her. But, like I said, I'm smart enough to figure it out. I have seen the books, I know her salary, and I've seen where she goes on vacation and what she wears to the office now. She's definitely getting a piece of the action.

Q: What's her name?

A: I'll give it to you, but for God's sake be careful when you talk to her. If she figures out that I've been talking to you, she goes straight to Prentice, and I'm hanging from the nearest light pole 10 minutes later. Try asking her about being accused of having an affair. That might flush her out of deep cover.

Q: Okay. Who is she?

A: Mary Quillian. Lives in Beausoleil. She graduated from Tech a couple of years ago with an accounting degree. She went to work for the city about a year and a half ago, supposedly just for a little while, while she studied for her CPA exam.

Q: How long have you suspected all this was going on?

A: I'm a professional finance manager, for God's sake. If several million bucks disappears from the city budget over several years, I'm gonna know about it.

Q: Then why didn't Luverne Trump know about it?

A: I'm sure she did. Why do you think she quit?

Q: Did you talk to her about it?

A: Nope. You've got to understand the culture of the Finance Department. Prentice was in there snooping around constantly. When I figured out what was going on with him and Quillian, I was afraid to talk about it with anybody. The walls might have ears.

Q: But you didn't talk about it with Trump before Quillian arrived, either.

A: I didn't know for sure that anything was wrong until after Quillian arrived. I suspected stuff, but before my last promotion I never got to see enough of the books.

Q: But if you've known about it for as long as you have, why haven't you blown the whistle?

A: Because you know what happens to whistle-blowers. Look, it's one thing to discover the bottom lines don't match, like you did. It's another to figure out where the hell it went. Whoever does blow the whistle on this is only gonna get one shot, so it had better hit the target. Otherwise they're dead meat.

Q: Couldn't you have quietly gone to City Council with any of this?

A: Same problem. If they'd mishandled it, I'm history. And there's definitely an old-boy network among city managers. By the time Prentice got through with me I'd be lucky to find a job mopping city hall bathrooms in South Succotash.

Q: Why do you think council would mishandle it?

A: For one thing, I'm not sure enough of them have the stomach to finish the kind of fight it would start. Prentice is tough. He'd fight hard, as you probably already know. Then there's the intelligence factor. Do you know what the department heads call Bullard?

Q: You mean the Frosted Flake?

A: Okay, you've heard that. Only two of the council members are really dim, including Bullard, but that's still too risky as far as I'm concerned. And neither the council nor I have subpoena powers, which I suspect it would take to do the job right. You'd have to be able to look at personal bank accounts, offshore deposits, stuff like that.

Q: Are you saying—

A: I'm saying every dog has his day. Or in this case, her day.

Q: You know, I've never understood what that meant.

A: Okay, I'll put it another way. *Stay tuned.*

Q: Well, if you're not going to try to resolve this through City Council, how—

A: Like I said, stay tuned. City Council isn't the only way to go with this.

Q: I need to know when I'll be able to get what you've told me on the record.

A: I'll tell you when it's all right. Probably when Prentice is standing on the scaffold with the noose around his neck. Good luck with your story. Bye.

Q: Wait a minute. How about after the City Council makes a decision on Prentice? Can I go on the record then?

A: Good lord, no. I'd still be dead meat, especially if they vote to keep him, which they'll do.

Q: When, then?

A: Look, there is still another shoe to drop. You'll know when that happens, if it happens. Then call me, and I'll tell you then that you can go on the record. Bye.

Q: Hi, Ms. Trump? It's Tori Baxter from the *Jeffersonville Herald*.

A: Hey, I told you you'd be calling me back someday.

Q: How about that.

A: Don't tell me the Prentice business has finally been resolved.

Q: Hardly. The Finance Committee finally released its report this week, and that cleared him. But Council Members Wise and Bullard included a dissent that still calls for his resignation.

A: No new evidence, though, I'll bet.

Q: Just a story I wrote a couple of months ago about the current and proposed budgets. Did you see that?

A: Somebody sent it to me. Interesting.

Q: You're not going to tell me you were surprised.

A: Are we on the record?

Q: Yeah.

A: Okay. Give me a second. (Pauses.) Right. On the record: It is troubling that some of the city's elected officials and their city manager still have not resolved their differences. It is fair to say that the controversy had a lot to do with my decision to resign.

Q: That's it?

A: That's not enough?

Q: You're not worried that people will interpret that to mean you were partly responsible for the irregularities?

A: Okay. I'll add this: Part of my frustration had to do with Mr. Prentice's insistence on being heavily involved with the day-to-day management of the budget and the Finance Department employees.

Q: Would you like to comment on whether you think any of the accusations against Prentice are true?

A: Not on the record.

Q: Ah. How about not for attribution?

A: Depends on how you will refer to me.

Q: How about "someone familiar with the workings of the Finance Department"?

A: That could point to Alice. Surely you don't have her on the record.

Q: Okay. How about "a source familiar with the city budget process"?

A: That'll do. That could mean anybody on council or the Finance Committee, I suppose. Okay, then, from someone familiar with the city budget: There is money unaccounted for in the city budget. There has been for some time. Where it went is what isn't clear. Good luck finding that out.

Q: Not for attribution, does Wise know about this?

A: Council Member Wise is aware that the specific problem has to do with un-accounted-for revenue, and the fact that it has exceeded spending for several years. The fact that he will not say that publicly is curious. His problem with the city manager appears to be due partly to the revenue problem and partly to personal animosity.

Q: Wise used to support Prentice. Do you know when that changed?

A: Again, not for attribution: It appeared to begin after he and Prentice crossed swords over the City Council's allocation in a budget work session about two years ago. Look in the minutes.

Q: I need to ask a couple more questions on the record. How do you think this will be resolved?

A: I have no idea how it will be resolved. I'm fairly sure that Tuesday night's meeting will not be the end of it, though.

Q: How do you—

A: That's all I'll say, Tori. Good luck with your story. (Hangs up.)

Q: Hello, Ms. Quillian? This is Tori Baxter with the *Jeffersonville Herald*.

A: Sorry, I don't want a subscription. I watch the news on TV.

Q: No, Ms. Quillian, I'm not selling home delivery. I'm a reporter with the paper. I cover Valleydale and Blue Ridge County.

A: Oh. Oh. Uh—

Q: Ms. Quillian, I'll say up front that I need to talk to you about something rather distasteful for a story I'm working on. But it's important to you that you hear me out.

A: What do you mean?

Q: I'm sure you've heard of the criticisms Mr. Wise and Ms. Bullard have made about Mr. Prentice and your department.

A: Good Lord! Has that been in the paper? They told me it would all be kept secret!

Q: Who told you that?

A: Mr. Wise and Mrs. Bullard, when they talked to me about—uh, no comment.

Q: Ms. Quillian, Mr. Wise and Ms. Bullard have accused Mr. Prentice of having an adulterous relationship with someone in the Finance Department. I have been told that that person is you.

A: That's a lie! Don—Mr. Prentice—and I have a strictly professional relationship. Those people are just being hateful. And if you print it I can sue you, right? Because it isn't true?

Q: Ms. Quillian, I'm confused. You say your relationship with Mr. Prentice is professional. I thought that staff-level employees report directly to a department head, who reports to the finance director, who reports to the city manager. Why would you have a professional relationship with Mr. Prentice?

A: I, uh . . . Oh, this is *so* not happening! No comment. I'm out of here. (Hangs up.)

Q: Hi, Mr. Prentice. This is Tori Baxter.

A: And what can I do for you, young lady? I hope you're not going to grill me some more about those ridiculous comments from Mr. Wise and Mrs. Bullard in their so-called report.

Q: Actually, sir—

A: I thought I made it pretty clear at the press conference that I'd said my piece.

Q: In that case, can we talk about what's likely to happen Tuesday?

A: I thought I was pretty clear about that, too. No further comment.

Q: Well, then, what about after Tuesday?

A: What the hell do you mean?

Q: Do you believe that whatever happens at the council meeting Tuesday will be the end of this controversy?

A: There's no controversy. There are just two very confused City Council members. And I don't know what the hell you're talking about. Tuesday will be the end. Goodbye.

Q: Mr. Davies, it's Tori Baxter with the *Jeffersonville Herald*. I'd like to talk to you about the Finance Committee's report.

A: Oh, you'll have to get with Louise about that. That whole thing caught Preston and me both at a really busy time, so we agreed to just let Louise handle it and sign off on whatever she came up with.

Q: You can't comment on whether Mr. Wise's and Ms. Bullard's accusations have any validity?

A: Nope. I mean, I didn't do any investigating of my own. Louise was sure they were groundless, so Preston and I took the easy way out. Like I said, we didn't have the time to roll our sleeves up. You'll need to ask Louise. (Hangs up.)

Q: Ms. Bullard, this is Tori Baxter with the *Jeffersonville Herald*.

A: Oh, yes, Miss Baxter. Eaton told me you might be calling. I have no comment beyond what is in the report.

Q: Ms. Bullard, are you sure the city manager is having an adulterous affair with Ms. Quillian?

A: Well, nothing else would explain his behavior, would it? I have a duty to all the Christian people in our community, whom I consider my constituency, and I take that duty very seriously. I believe they are sick of this sort of behavior in our public officials, ever since President Clinton. I may not have been able to do anything about Mr. Clinton's immorality, but I can set our own house in order. There is no place in public life for immoral people. Now this is off the record, but—

Q: Excuse me, ma'am. We are on the record. Is there a reason why you want to go off the record now?

A: I didn't realize—I guess I should have known when you said who you were. Well, I have nothing to hide about my Christian faith. But I do want to talk off the record now, because I don't want to harm the young lady unnecessarily.

Q: Okay. You're off the record now.

A: Thank you. I feel badly for Miss Quillian. Perhaps there is time for her to see the error of her ways. And as our Lord taught us, I would not be the one to cast the first stone.

Q: Back on the record. What about the budget irregularities you and Mr. Wise are alleging? You got no support from the Finance Committee in its report. Do you think Mr. Prentice is directly responsible for those?

A: Oh, you'll have to talk to Eaton about that. God bless you. Goodbye.

Q: Hi, Mr. Wise, this is Tori Baxter with the *Jeffersonville Herald*.

A: Well, I *told* the mayor this would happen if we made the report public. You media vultures swooping down to pick over—

Q: Yes, sir. I noticed that you relied exclusively on my earlier budget story to support your accusation in the report of financial irregularities in the city budget.

A: My, we do have a big ego for such a little girl, don't we?

Q: Sir, my story merely pointed out that the revenues and expenditures didn't match. The tone of your addendum to the Finance Committee report was that that discrepancy was intentional and directly the responsibility of the city manager. Are you saying—

A: What we are saying is in the report. I'd be very careful about putting words in our mouths if I were you.

Q: I'm not about to do that, sir. That's why I called. I want to hear in your own words why you think those discrepancies exist.

A: I'm not prepared to speculate at this time.

Q: Are you saying it could be an honest mistake?

A: I'm sure anything is possible.

Q: And yet you thought it was grounds for recommending the dismissal of Mr. Prentice.

A: You media people are all afflicted with tunnel vision. That was just one transgression we cited in our report. Let it speak for itself.

Q: But you offered little substantiation for any of the accusations in the report, sir.

A: What substantiation do you media people need beyond the word of honest public servants who conducted a thorough investigation and want to do right by the citizens of Valleydale?

Q: Sir, you were once a keen supporter of Mr. Prentice. What happened?

A: It's outlined in our report.

Q: But your change of heart about him was quite abrupt. It appeared to take place pretty suddenly about two years ago.

A: Nonsense.

Q: Sir, how long have you been aware of what you call the irregularities in the city budget?

A: I'll have to admit I first became aware when I read your story in November.

Q: You had no inkling earlier? At at least two council meetings before that story was published, you made allegations of irregularities.

A: I did no such thing. You are confused about the time frame.

Q: Sir, didn't your animosity toward Mr. Prentice begin with a disagreement over the City Council's allocation during a budget work session about two years ago?

A: That's a rude, impertinent comment! You weren't there! I was. I remember distinctly what happened. I won't respond to such a vicious allegation!

Q: Why are you characterizing it as a vicious allegation?

A: This interview is over! (Hangs up.)

Q: Mayor Hostetter, this is Tori Baxter.

A: Talk to me Tuesday after the council's executive session, Tori.

Q: Executive session? Why are you holding a closed meeting about this?

A: Tuesday. I'll talk to you Tuesday. Bye-bye, Tori. (Hangs up.)

chapter twenty-one

Bringing Multiple Elements Together

Many issues that journalists cover cannot be dealt with in a single story. The issue continues to evolve, sometimes over several months, new events associated with it keep happening, and the journalist's understanding continues to increase. Her clip file in such cases might run to dozens of stories by the time a resolution is reached.

City Manager Don Prentice's standoff with Council members Wise and Bullard is just such an issue. You and Tori Baxter have been dealing with it since the beginning of this book.

How Did We Get Here? Where Do We Go Next?

Reporters who cover such ongoing issues often keep a running, often chronological account of them. They certainly keep their own stories in a file for easy reference. Many keep an updated written summary in their computers to copy and paste into their next story as background. That saves time and helps ensure the accuracy of the background information. Usually, reporters who do that can even recite the salient elements of the issue and the chronology of events from memory.

As an issue evolves, they also think about how the latest development or event "fits in." Does it resolve part of the issue or conflict, or does it complicate or aggravate it? Does it bring additional players into the fray, or expand the audience affected by the issue? How does it affect the list of people the reporter should be interviewing for the story, or the experts or records she needs to rely on?

A reporter will also try to anticipate what will happen next. Often, the reporter can't be sure enough to work such a prediction into the story, but thinking about it can help her plan her continued coverage.

Is the Audience Keeping Up?

When I covered courts for *The Miami Herald*, my file on a big case often ran to a dozen or more stories by the time the case was resolved. For the cases that went to trial, the first day of jury selection was always an education for me. After devoting hundreds of hours and thousands of words to reporting the pretrial activity, I would watch as prospective jurors, one after the other, would tell attorneys they knew nothing about the case and could not recall watching or reading any stories about it. That was probably good for the judicial system: The taxpayers didn't have to pay the expense of moving the trial elsewhere so an unbiased jury could be found. But it taught me that I couldn't make many assumptions in any story about what my audience already knew.

Eventually, to help my reporting and writing, I came to think of two kinds of approaches to stories: the martian approach and the stranger in town approach. The martian approach was for when I knew I had to explain everything, as if a martian had just landed and needed to know what we mean by the United States, the state of Florida, democracy and a jury trial. The stranger in town approach meant I could assume that my audiences would know where they were and what a trial was but knew nothing about a particular case. After watching jury selection a few times, I became convinced that I should use the stranger in town approach no matter how much I had written about a case previously. About the only exception was when I decided I needed to be even more basic; then I used the martian approach.

I tried to keep in mind, though, that even though my audiences might not know anything about a story, that did not allow me to talk down to them. In an earlier chapter I referred to writing coach Don Fry's comment that audiences aren't stupid, they just don't know much. That's especially worth remembering when you have to explain ongoing and sometimes complex issues.

Ethics

In Chapter 1 you read about framing stories, a way of providing the appropriate context for them. One way journalists frame stories is as conflict. Conflict—between people, political ideologies, conceptions of what is good—is a relatively easy way for audiences and reporters to understand both events and complex issues. But conflict is certainly not the only way to frame stories, and often it's not the best way. Sometimes part of a story is indeed about conflict, but framing the entire story that way would mislead your audience.

The issues surrounding Valleydale's budget and accusations against City Manager Don Prentice certainly involve conflict. There is an intense battle raging between Prentice and Council Member Eaton Wise, for example. But until you read Tori's interview with Alice Turpin, you probably imagined the conflict was rooted in egos and personalities, classic sources. You tried to imagine how it could be about differing political philosophies—another potential source of conflict.

But now we know that what is between Prentice and Wise has more to do with greed than personal or ideological conflict. Because Turpin talked to us on deep background, we are still waiting for an opportunity to show our audiences what this story is really about. Meanwhile, we need to be careful not to oversimplify the story. There is a difference between turning a complex issue into an overly simple story—by insisting it is all about conflict, for example—and explaining complex issues in a straightforward way. As ethical journalists whose primary obligation is to serve our audiences, we should strive to do the latter.

Strategies

The action from the Valleydale council meeting summarized below is straightforward. Many ongoing issues reporters face appear to conclude in such a cut-and-dried fashion, almost anticlimactically. But remember the following:

Because some issues go on for so long, *your story must include extensive background* to provide appropriate context for your audience.

Few if any in your audience will have seen all of your previous stories, and even those who did will need reminding of some of the events that have taken place.

When you are dealing with a complex issue, high-profile players, and a series of events leading to an apparent climax, *consider using the hourglass story format* discussed in Chapter 7. Last night's events, along with a nut graf and some quotes from the players, would go in the first, top-heavy section. The narrow neck of the hourglass could be a chronological summary of the events that preceded last night. The bottom bulge of the hourglass could include more from the participants, plus an explanation of what is to happen next, if you know.

Even if the people involved in an issue believe it to be resolved, *include in your story any questions that still have not been answered* or that they ignored for the sake of reaching some compromise or conclusion. (See Box 21.1)

In Chapter 20, several people you interviewed appeared to agree that a resolution to an issue that first arose in Chapter 1 might be at hand. The City Council meeting summarized here happens on a Tuesday night. At the meeting, council members go into executive session. Remember that in many states—Virginia is one—governing bodies may convene such secret meetings to consider real estate purchases or personnel matters. They may not cast a

Box 21.1

STRATEGIES FOR WRAPPING UP AN ONGOING ISSUE

Covering an ongoing issue to its conclusion might involve writing multiple stories over several months or longer. Remember:

1. Include extensive background in each story for context.

2. Your audience will need reminding of what has happened so far. A chronology of events is often a good idea.

3. When you are trying to explain a complex and ongoing issue, you might find the hourglass story format useful. See Chapter 7 for a refresher.

4. Show your audience any questions or issues that remain unanswered, even if the participants think they have been resolved.

formal vote in those meetings, however. If they take action, it must occur afterward, in a public meeting.

Wise, Bullard and Prentice

Assume that the release of the Finance Committee's report, the rebuttal from Council members Wise and Bullard, and the city manager's news conference were on successive days last week, and that the newspaper story you wrote in Exercise 20C ran in Sunday's *Jeffersonville Herald*. Write a story for print weaving the events from the City Council's executive session and whatever background from earlier assignments you think appropriate. Then think about what still isn't resolved. Then—and here's a challenge—write the whole thing as a 30-second RDR for broadcast.

The Valleydale City Council went into executive session last night. Two hours later council emerged, went into public session, and voted unanimously to endorse Ron Allen "Don" Prentice's performance as city manager. Council Member Eaton Wise then read the following statement:

For several months, Mrs. Bullard and myself have attempted to call attention to what we perceived as certain conditions in the City Finance Department. It is clear to us now that we do not have the support of our colleagues on the City Council nor on the Finance Committee in this matter. Accordingly, in the interest of civic harmony, we rescind our request for Mr. Prentice's termination and hereby resign from the City Council, effective immediately.

We apologize to the citizens of Valleydale for whatever friction has resulted from our continued efforts to ensure good government. Cities should run smoothly, and friction hinders that smooth operation. We also extend our regrets to Mr. Prentice. We hope that this apology concludes this unfortunate episode in the life of the best city in the United States, and we pray that the media does not continue to blow this minor disagreement out of proportion.

The remaining council members vote unanimously to accept the resignations of Wise and Bullard. Mayor Hostetter instructs the city attorney to report back to council at its next meeting on the procedures for appointing interim council members and on whether the city needs to hold a special election. Several council members praise the Finance Committee and chair Louise Mutispaugh for their work, but Mutispaugh resigns from the committee, citing the stressful nature of being a member. The mayor then appoints Council Member Clark chair of the Finance Committee.

Prentice addresses the meeting briefly, reading a statement:

I am pleased and relieved to have this unpleasantness behind me. Maybe now we can all—including the media—focus on the business at hand, serving the citizens of Valleydale. Mr. Wise and Mrs. Bullard, I know you were trying to serve your constituents, and I realize that elected officials operate under constant political pressures, including reelection. As for the news media, I fully intend to pursue in another forum what I consider certain published libelous statements. I assure the council that that will in no way affect my continued performance as city manager. Thank you.

Despite his promise, Mayor Hostetter refuses to speak to reporters after the meeting. So do the other council members and Prentice.

Exercise 21B

Finishing the Story

When Tori interviewed Valleydale Acting Finance Director Alice Turpin a week or so ago (Exercise 20C), Turpin said she would not consider any City Council action on City Manager Don Prentice to be the end of the matter. She would not elaborate then except to say (1) Tori should "stay tuned" and (2) if she (Turpin) was right and something else happened ("the other shoe dropped"), Tori could call her back when it did happen and ask her to go on the record with her earlier deep-background comments.

In Exercise 21A you had to consider what questions remained unanswered, what issues remained unresolved. Will they all be addressed in Exercise 21B? Remember the stranger in town approach: Even though you included extensive background in your story for Exercise 21A, you will need to provide that again for your audiences in Exercise 21B.

Write a story for the *Jeffersonville Herald* and, on deadline in class, a 30-second RDR.

Background: It is two days after the City Council meeting at which Wise and Bullard resigned. Prentice and Wise surrendered themselves at the Blue Ridge Regional Jail at 4 P.M. today, a few hours after the indictment was made public. Each was accompanied by his attorney, but they arrived separately. Neither spoke to the other, nor would they or their attorneys speak to reporters. Each was released without bond to await resolution of the case, but Prentice was required to surrender his passport. Arraignment is set for 9 A.M. tomorrow, at which time each will enter a plea. Each crime is a Class II felony, punishable by up to 10 years in prison.

Commonwealth's Attorney Taliaferro would not comment on the indictments, made public this morning, but he did provide a list of witnesses who testified before the grand jury. The list comprises Alice Turpin, Mary Quillian and Luverne Trump. Taliaferro does confirm that Quillian was granted immunity from prosecution for her testimony.

Police Chief Buford Honeycutt also confirms a tip that a magistrate has ordered Prentice's office and the Finance Department offices sealed and a 24-hour guard posted outside them. He also tells you that officers executed a search warrant at Wise's home on Marshall Street. He will not discuss what was removed, if anything.

In a brief statement read over the phone, Mayor Hostetter announces that city council met in an emergency executive session this afternoon. Council suspended Prentice without pay pending resolution of the criminal case. It also appointed Alice Turpin acting city manager. Turpin's first action was to suspend Mary Quillian without pay, again pending resolution of the criminal case against Prentice and Wise.

Write a story based on the following, incorporating appropriate context and background.

In the Circuit Court of the Commonwealth of Virginia for the Blue Ridge Circuit

THE PEOPLE

v.

RON ALLEN PRENTICE
and
EATON WISE,
defendants

An Indictment

Your Grand Jurors, in session in the above-styled case, do hereby accuse the above named defendants RON ALLEN PRENTICE and EATON WISE by this indictment with the crimes of CONSPIRACY, GRAND LARCENY, EMBEZZLE-MENT, and BREACH OF PUBLIC TRUST.

Alleged as follows:

1. The defendant Prentice was at all times material hereto, and remains, the City Manager of the City of Valleydale, a City of the Second Class as defined by the Code of the Commonwealth of Virginia.

2. The defendant Wise was at all times material hereto a duly elected Member of the City Council of the City of Valleydale, a City of the Second Class as defined by the Code of the Commonwealth of Virginia.

3. The defendant Prentice was hired as City Manager of the City of Valleydale on or about March 1, 1998, by unanimous vote of the City Council, including defendant Wise.

4. That defendant Wise has been a duly elected member of the City Council of the City of Valleydale since on or about May 1, 1994.

5. On or about Jan. 1, 1998, and continuing until approximately two years ago, defendants Prentice and Wise did engage in a conspiracy to embezzle public moneys from the treasury of the City of Valleydale and convert them to their own use. The total sum embezzled by defendant Wise was approximately five hundred thousand dollars.

6. Approximately two years before the date of this Indictment, defendant Wise approached defendant Prentice about "upping the ante." There ensued a disagreement, following which defendant Prentice stopped sharing embezzled funds with defendant Wise, and their criminal conspiracy ended. Defendant Prentice, however, continued to convert city moneys to his own use.

7. On or about April 10, 2003, the Finance Department of the City of Valleydale employed MARY QUILLIAN in the position of staff bookkeeper. From that time until the present, Ms. Quillian, an unindicted co-conspirator, has remained employed by the Finance Department.

8. Approximately 18 months ago, Quillian approached defendant Prentice and told him, "I'm all over this. You and I need to work something out." As a result of their conversation, defendant Prentice offered Quillian $3,000 a month not to report his criminal activity to authorities. He also met Quillian's frequent demands for "treats." Among the items defendant Prentice expended city moneys on for Quillian were expensive clothes, a home stereo, a vacation to Cancun, Mexico, a cruise to the British Virgin Islands, a diamond "tennis" bracelet, a Ford Explorer vehicle, and bail for her boyfriend, who had been arrested on a charge of driving while intoxicated. The total amount of city moneys expended on blackmail and gifts to Quillian is believed to be approximately $130,000.

9. On information and belief, the total moneys converted to his own use by defendant Prentice from the treasury of the City of Valleydale, including payments to Quillian but not to Wise, are approximately four million dollars. An

amended complaint will be filed with the Circuit Court of Blue Ridge when the exact sum becomes known.

The conduct of defendants Prentice and Wise and unindicted co-conspirator Quillian constitute a breach of the Code of Virginia and violate the peace and dignity of the people of the Commonwealth of Virginia.

In the Circuit Court, Commonwealth of Virginia.

Joshua A. Taliaferro
Commonwealth's Attorney

Tori makes some follow-up phone calls.

Trump: By law, I can't discuss grand jury testimony, Tori. You know that.

> Q: Well, may I ask how long ago you talked to the grand jury?

> A: You may ask. I won't tell you. Sorry.

Turpin: Grand jury testimony is secret, Tori. I can't discuss it. Period. That's the law.

> Q: Would this indictment have happened if you hadn't instigated it?

> A: Like I said the other day, every dog has her day. And the other shoe has dropped, if you know what I mean.

> Q: Can I take that as permission to go on the record with your earlier comments?

> A: Yup. As long as you make clear that it was an earlier conversation that was unrelated to my grand jury testimony. Have fun. Bye.

City Directory
Beausoleil, Blue Ridge County, Valleydale

Local Government

Beausoleil

City Council

Mayor	Claudette Peters
Council Member	Daniel Mountain
Council Member	R.D. "Country" Singer
Council Member	Calvin B. "Woolie Booger" Arrington
Council Member	Sarah "Penny" Mays
Council Member	Lafayette Napoleon "Nap" Harris

Administration

City Manager	L.E. "Skeet" Thurston
Finance Director	Eula James
Police Chief	Curtis "Cooter" Wilcox
Fire Chief	Ronald Cox
City Engineer	Hal Stanton
Clerk	Loretta "Etty" Stuart
City Attorney	George W. Wilson

Blue Ridge County

Board of Supervisors

Chair	Penelope Hinds, Cupps Creek District
Boone District	Cleveland McNitt
South River District	Robert "Bobby" Clark
North River District	Will Waddell
Wilson Creek District	James E. "Jim" Jones

Administration

County Administrator	Rufus T. Stallard
Assessor	Patricia Daley
Sheriff	T.E. "Tink" Swofford
Fire-Rescue Chief	Cecelia "Sissy" Baxter
Commissioner of the Revenue	Forrest Greene
Commonwealth's Attorney	Joshua A. Taliaferro
Circuit Judge	J. Meriwether Goodspeed
District Judge	Jenkins "Jinks" Holland

Valleydale

City Council

Mayor	Delmer Hostetter
Council Member	Louise Mutispaugh
Council Member	Eaton Wise
Council Member	T.A. "Tater" Chipps
Council Member	Willie Jefferson
Council Member	Rondah Bullard
Council Member	Leland "Bud" Clark

Administration

City Manager	Ron Allen "Don" Prentice
Finance Director	Luverne Trump
Police Chief	Buford Honeycutt
Fire Chief	L.E. "Skeeter" Wofford
City Engineer	Craig V. Oliphant
Clerk	Horace Culpepper
City Attorney	Phoebe Kerr

Hospitals

Jeb Stuart Memorial Hospital

Administrator	Joy Poindexter
Chief of Staff	Eileen Hunter, M.D.

Schools

Beausoleil

Superintendent	Holly Fairborn
Irland Bromfeld High School	Felicia "Lish" McDonald, principal
Irland Bromfeld Middle School	Lester J. Parsons, principal
Enfield Heights Elementary School	Malcolm "Mac" Foster, principal
King Elementary School	Preston Howe, principal

Blue Ridge County

Superintendent	Howard Fine
Blue Ridge County High School	Leonard Tilton, principal
North River Middle School	Philip Casteneda, principal
Blue Ridge Middle School	Clifford "Zeke" Smith, principal
Central Elementary School	Harry Peters, principal
Ellison Elementary School	Sheryl Potter, principal
Bluefield Elementary School	Gerald Davis, principal
Ridge View Elementary School	Todd Benson, principal
Wilson Creek Elementary School	Mary Prentice, principal

Valleydale

Superintendent	Eleanor Grigsby
Welland Elementary School	Tonya Winfrey, principal
Howard Lynton Middle School	Ray Martin, principal
South High School	R.W. "Fred" Ferris, principal

Listings (addresses are in Valleydale unless noted)

A

AAIX, Casper, Dr. (Evelyn), owner, Blue Ridge Animal Hosp, 219 North River Rd.

ACE HARDWARE STORE, 2110 Sycamore Ave., Beausoleil

ALLEN, Preston M. (Phoebe D., atty.), faculty, SMA, 113 Marshall St.

ALFORD, Dexter (Wendy, hosp tech) owner, Railyard Café, 1280 John Wesley Rd., Blue Ridge County

ANDERSEN, Priscilla, waitress, 1711 Walnut St., Beausoleil

APPLE, George (Ada), Valleydale Public Works dir., 413 Summit St.

APPLE MANUFACTURING CO., K. L. Walton, Pres., 4000 Midland Trail, Beausoleil

ARRINGTON, Calvin B., Beausoleil City Council mbr.; retired, 131 Locust St., Beausoleil

B

BANG, Robert C. (Anne M.), auto dealer, 3889 Royal Ave.

BARNETT, Charles (Addie, nurse), Apple Mfg. Co., 905 Locust St., Beausoleil

BAXTER, Cecelia "Sissy" (Howard, mechanic), county fire-rescue chief, 311 Forbes Rd., Blue Ridge County

BAXTER, Victoria "Tori," reporter, 379 Flower Lane, Blue Ridge County

BEATTY, Effie, asst mgr Valley Bank, 1395 Rebel Dr.

BEAUCHAMP, Ottis (Sherri), pipe fitter, 1912 Sycamore St., Beausoleil

BENSON, Todd (Marya, tchr), principal, Ridge View Elem., 181 South River Rd., Stonewall

BLAND, Talya M., sales clerk, 400 E. Randolph St. #405

BLATCHKY, Martha, 7-Eleven owner, 618 S. Main St.

BLITCH, Iris Fairchild, ret'd. schoolteacher, 181 Walt Faulkner Hwy., Inverness

BLUE RIDGE COUNTY HIGH SCHOOL, Leonard Tilton, principal, 1 High School Rd., Blue Ridge County

BLUE RIDGE MIDDLE SCHOOL Clifford "Zeke" Smith, principal, Brownville Rd., Blue Ridge County

BLUEFIELD ELEMENTARY SCHOOL, Gerald Davis, principal, Bluefield Cir., Bluefield

BOONE, James A. (Twila, tchr), auto salesman, 420 Buffalo Creek Tpke., Culleytown

BOWERS, Randy, student, SMA

BRADFORD, Hermione, potter, 120 Honeysuckle Hill

BRELSFORD, Tiffany Belle student, VPU 137 N. Randolph St.

BROWNE, Aaron W. (Cressida), emp Calhoun Trucking Co., 986 Oak Ave., Beausoleil

BRUNELLI, Melvin "Weasel" (Lorna), private investigator, Rte. 15 N., Blue Ridge County

BULLARD, Amos (Rondah, Valleydale City Council member), evangelist, 390 Thorntree Rd.

BURNSIDE, James W. (Addie), owner Shenandoah Valley Books, 1900 McLaren St.

C

CAMPBELL, Howard D. (Abigail, shopkeeper), owner, Campbell Trucking Co., 19 Forbes Rd., Blue Ridge County

CAMPBELL TRUCKING COMPANY, Howard D. Campbell, owner, McCormack Rd., Bluefield

CAPEN, Vince (Amy, ex. dir. Valleydale Chamber of Commerce), ret'd. Marine Corps sgt., 111 Montevista Rd., Blue Ridge County

CASTENEDA, Philip (Rosa, bank teller), principal, North River Middle School, 711 Hawes Creek Rd., Blue Ridge County

CENTRAL ELEMENTARY SCHOOL, Harry Peters, principal, Central Rd., Valleydale

CHALFONT, Hector (Irma), emp Apple Mfg. Co., 139 22d St., Beausoleil

CHAMBER OF COMMERCE, Valleydale, 28 N. Main St.

CHAMBERS, Helen, asst. commonwealth's atty., 55 Fox Chase Trail, Blue Ridge County

CHASTAIN'S FUNERAL HOME, Lawrence Pearson, dir., 565 S. Main St.

CHIPPS, T. A. "Tater" (Petulia, shopkeeper), Valleydale City Council mbr., mgr., K-Mart, 311 Stonewall Cir.

CLARK, Leland "Bud" (Miranda) Valleydale City Council mbr., auto mechanic, 47 McCann Dr.

CLARK, Robert "Bobby" Blue Ridge County Supervisor, farmer, Scot's Creek Rd., Stonewall

CLARK, Tom, janitor, 990 Farm Rd., Blue Ridge County

CLOTFELTER, Sturgis P., heavy equipment operator, 37 Wilson Turnpike, Zeno

CONNOLLY, Sarah, Valleydale firefighter, 318 Emerald St.

COUNTRY CLUB OF VALLEYDALE, 400 Country Club Dr.

COX, Ronald, Beausoleil fire chief, 311 Camellia Ave., Beausoleil

CULPEPPER, Horace (Donna), Valleydale city clerk, 9 Jackson Ave.

CUPP'S CREEK AIRSTRIP, Airport Ln., Blue Ridge County

D

DALEY, Patricia, Blue Ridge County assessor, 48 Big Bluff Rd., Blue Ridge County

DALRYMPLE, Donald (Jane), emp. Apple Mfg. Co., 567 W. 14th St., Beausoleil

DAPSE, Ernest (Jayne, accountant), prof. VPU, 2414 Rose St.

DARTON, Valjean C., ret'd. tchr., 117 Flower Lane, Blue Ridge County

DAVIES, C.D. "Tarheel" ret'd., former Valleydale mayor, 88 Enright Rd.

DAVIS, Gerald (Betty), principal, Bluefield Elementary School, 788 Timber Ridge Rd., Bluefield

De SHIELD, Wallace N. (Marjorie), Valleydale Police det., 1809 W 34th St., Beausoleil

DIX, Ervin, emp. Berg's Quarry, 1411 North River Road

DOBBINS, Howard F. (Dorcas, weaver), artist, 1910 John Wesley Rd., Blue Ridge County

DOMINICK'S PIZZA, 101 N. Roosevelt St.

DRIVE IT IN DRIVE IT OUT USED CARS, Rt. 50 E.

DUFF, Billy Joe, emp. Apple Mfg. Co., 555 Walnut St., Beausoleil

DURRMAN, Bernard F. (Ramona), owner, The Red Front, 2267 Summit St.

DYNCE, Alvin (Priddie), det., Blue Ridge County, 111 Mole Hollow Rd., Blue Ridge County

E

EASTMAN, Gunnar (Emmalou), consultant, 2001 Old Mill Rd., Blue Ridge County

ELLIOTT, Dale (Cynthia, artist), mgr., North River Manufacturing Co., Scenic Way, Culleytown

ELLISON ELEMENTARY SCHOOL, Sheryl Potter, principal, Culleytown Rd., Blue Ridge County

ENFIELD HEIGHTS ELEMENTARY SCHOOL, Malcolm "Mac" Foster, principal, End Rd., Beausoleil

ESTELLA, Penelope, mgr. Pip's Graphics, 698 Reagan St.

ETERNAL PEACE FUNERAL HOME, 13 Roosevelt St.

F

FAIRBORN, Holly (Zeus, welder), superintendent, Beausoleil Schools, 3314 Magnolia, Beausoleil

FAITH PRESBYTERIAN CHURCH, 379 Birch Ave., Beausoleil

FENDER, Fred, pastor, Grace Presbyterian Church, The Manse, 511 S. Main St.

FERRIS, R.W. "Fred" (Ann, tchr.), principal, South High School, 114 Lime Tree Rd.

FINE, Howard (Patsy), Superintendent, Blue Ridge County Schools, 222 Lewis St.

FINE, Seymour (Fred Robertson, law professor, VPU), law professor, VPU, 211 Walt Faulkner Hwy., Inverness

FIRST METHODIST CHURCH, C. B. Jones, pastor, 114 Magnolia Ave., Beausoleil

FIRST PRESBYTERIAN CHURCH, W.A. Stout, pastor, 782 S. Main St.

FLIES UNLIMITED, Thomas Poindexter, owner, 411 Low St., Beausoleil

FOOD LION, Dale Mutispaugh, mgr., Old Lynchburg Hwy., Beausoleil

FOSTER, Jeff (Dorothy), schoolteacher, 311 Bath Rd., Eden

FOSTER, Malcolm "Mac," principal, Enfield Heights Elementary School, 1911 Chesnut St., Beausoleil

FOX, Christie, teacher, 447 Randolph St.

FRISBEE, Quentin "Twink," prop. The Breeze Restaurant, 330 Lewis St.

G

GEORGE'S BOUND TIMBERS, George Peabody, owner, Rt. 60, Beausoleil

GOODSPEED, J. Meriwether (Ilsa), circuit judge, Little Steppe, 48 Schoolhouse Rd., Blue Ridge County

GRACE PRESBYTERIAN CHURCH, Fred Fender, pastor, 506 S. Main St.

GRAHAM, Susan C., atty., 1515 Lime Tree Rd.

GRANT, Alan W. (Susan E. accountant), Valleydale police off., 1567 Catawba Pl.

GRAY, James D., custodian, VPU, 2060 Monroe Ave.

GREENE, Forrest (Ramona, shopkeeper), Commissioner of the Revenue, 11 High Bridge Rd., Blue Ridge County

GRIGSBY, Eleanor superintendent, Valleydale schools, 419 Myers St.

H

H&M TIRE CO., Martha Hudson, owner, 110 S. Randolph St.

HALLOWAY, Frank (Lily, florist), VPU faculty, chair North Service Authority, 10 Bluebird Way

HARRIS FUNERAL HOME, Lafayette Harris, owner, 216 Hemlock Ave., Beausoleil

HARRIS, Lafayette Napoleon "Nap" (Lisa), owner, Harris Funeral Home, mbr., Beausoleil City Council, 218 Hemlock Ave., Beausoleil

HARRISON, Theodore (Anne), pastor, Randolph Street United Methodist Church, 11 Old Farm Rd., Blue Ridge County

HATCHER, Amy, engineer, 355 Welland St.

HEALEY, Timmy (Suzanne, Blue Ridge County Sheriff's deputy), Valleydale police off., 600 Brownville Tpke., Brownville

HIGGINBOTHAM, G. J. Dutch (Marjorie), farmer, Whirlaway Farms, 3 Parkersburg Pike, Blue Ridge County

HINDS, Penelope, chair, Blue Ridge County supervisors, 4 Stillrun Rd., Blue Ridge County

HOLLAND, Jenkins "Jinks" (Virginia, atty.), district judge, Blue Ridge County, 7 Airport Rd., Blue Ridge County

HONEYCUTT, Buford (Trish, 911 dispatcher), Valleydale police chief, 211 Hooker Pl.

HONEYWELL, Merton B. "Skip" III, student, 22 N. Main St.

HOPE PROJECT, THE 211 Fulham St.

HOSTETTER, Delmer (Treena), Mayor, Valleydale, owner, Sports for All, 119 Lee Ave.

HOWARD LYNTON MIDDLE SCHOOL, Ray Martin, principal, 300 Emerald St.

HOWE, Preston (Nancy, social worker), principal, King Elementary School, 22 Lynchburg Hwy., Beausoleil

HUDSON, Martha, owner, H&M Tire Co., 101 Thorntree Rd.

HUNTER, Eileen, Dr., chief of staff, Jeb Stuart Memorial Hospital, 111 Travis St.

HUNTER, Meriwether Chase "Chip," 1196 Onyx St.

I

INGERSOLL, Matilda, ret'd. U.S. Army, 100 Edmund St.

INN AT HOWLER'S BLUFF, Rt. 22

IRLAND BROMFELD HIGH SCHOOL, Felicia "Lish" McDonald, principal, Irland Bromfeld Rd., Beausoleil

IRLAND BROMFELD MIDDLE SCHOOL, Lester J. Parsons, principal, Middle School Rd., Beausoleil

J

JACKSON, Melvin G. (Ellie), court reporter, 397 W. 37th St., Beausoleil

JAMES, Eula, finance director, Beausoleil, 809 33rd St., Beausoleil

JEB STUART MEMORIAL HOSPITAL, Joy Poindexter, administrator, 111 Foxwood Dr.

JEFFERSON, Naomi, maid VPU, 139 N. Randolph St.

JEFFERSON, Willie, undertaker, Valleydale City Council mbr., 209 Fulton St.

JEFFERSONVILLE HERALD, Blue Ridge County bureau, 411 S. Roosevelt St.

JONES, Betty, exec. dir., Blue Ridge Area Chamber of Commerce, 2344 Old Mill Rd., Blue Ridge County

JONES, Buford. (Darlene, tchr.), prof., SMA, 387 Salt Ave.

JONES, Frederick "Rick" (Janice, nurse), Valleydale sanitation supervisor, 54 Hooper Lane

JONES, James E. "Jim" (Etta), farmer, Blue Ridge County supervisor, 123 Zeno Rd., Blue Ridge County

JUSTICE, Kelly M., mgr., Kentucky Fried Chicken, 144 Summit St.

K

KEEL, Howard, ret'd., 13 Blue Ridge Way, Blue Ridge County

KERR, Phoebe (George, musician), Valleydale city attorney, 87 Johann Bach Rd.

KING ELEMENTARY SCHOOL, Preston Howe, principal, King Circle, Beausoleil

KLEINDIENST, Phoebe, ret'd. schoolteacher, 11 Grouse Run, Blue Ridge County

KOCH, James R. (Mildred, nurse), owner Golden Griddle Restaurant, 3015 Midway Trail, Blue Ridge County

KONDRICKI, Fletcher (Laura, tchr., Ridge View Elementary School), tchr., Ridge View Elementary School, 39 Cedar Lane, Blue Ridge County

KRAMER, Ella, professor, VPU, 31 Salt Ave.

KRAMER, Tom, emp. Va. Dept. of Transportation, 31a Salt Ave.

KRANTZ, Paul, freelance writer, 11 Floral Hill Dr.

KRAY, Billie-Kay, editor, 1319 Freemont Rd., Blue Ridge County

KROGER FOOD STORES, Austin Uncas mgr., Center Square

KRUG, Jon (Molly), president First Union Bank, 27 Country Club Dr.

L

LeBLANC, Meagan, student VPU 137 N. Randolph St.

LINDSAY, Carter L., driver, Campbell Trucking Co., 895 E. 11th St., Beausoleil

LLOYD'S BISTRO, Elton Sowell, owner, 27 W. Adams St.

LOONEY, Mel, reporter, WHIC-FM, 322 38th Pl., Beausoleil

LOWRING, Jason F. (Harriett, maid), Valleydale postmaster, 1178 Cupp's Creek Rd., Blue Ridge County

M

MARTIN, Ray (Cheryl), principal, Howard Lynton Middle School, 5 North River Rd., Blue Ridge Baths

MAYS, Zachary (Sarah "Penny", Beausoleil City Council mbr.), mgr.
Ace Hardware, 788 Nursing Home Way, Beausoleil

McDONALD, Felicia "Lish," principal, Irland Bromfeld High School,
39 Descartes Rd., Wilson Creek

McGEE, Duncan M. (Olivia, dental technician), retired, 880 W. 14th
St., Beausoleil

McLEOD, Anita tchr., North River Middle School, 88 Jordan St.

McNAB, Lewis (Ngwanda, physician), minister Randolph Street Baptist
Church, 237 Fulton St.

McNITT CHRYSLER PLYMOUTH, Cleveland McNitt, owner, 444
Lee Highway

McNITT, Cleveland, auto dealer, county supervisor, 313 Mole Hollow
Rd., Blue Ridge County

MILLER, Melvin (Gloria, masseuse), tchr., Central Elementary School,
18 Fillmore Ave.

MITZENFELDT, Melvin, firefighter, 444 Enwright Rd.

MOORE, Thomas A. (Elise, prof. VPU), pilot, 980 W. 26th St.,
Beausoleil

MOUNTAIN, Daniel (widr. Reba), ret'd. railroad worker, Beausoleil
City Council mbr., 439 Maple St., Beausoleil

MUTISPAUGH, Dale (Louise, Valleydale city council mbr.), mgr. Food
Lion, 480 Wallace St.

N

NESBITT, J.H. "Hoss" (Sarah "Snootie"), surveyor, 678 Possum Rd.,
Blue Ridge County

NEWMAN, Philip, exec. dir. North Service Authority, 477 Buck Terr.,
Blue Ridge County

NORTH RIVER MANUFACTURING COMPANY, Dale Elliott, mgr.,
N. 13th St., Beausoleil

NORTH RIVER MIDDLE SCHOOL, Philip Casteneda, principal, 600
Welland St.

NORTH SERVICE AUTHORITY, Philip Newman, exec. dir., 4
Wastewater Ln., Blue Ridge County

O

OLERUD, Jimmy, photographer, 337 Lee Highway, Blue Ridge County

OLIPHANT, Craig V. (Brenda, insurance sales), Valleydale city engineer, 119 Wells Cir.

ONTOP MOTOR FREIGHT, Sporrin Spruance, mgr., 44 Overlook Highway, Blue Ridge County

P

PAOLI, Dominick (Rosa), owner, Dominick's Pizza, 38 Blue Ridge Turnpike, Blue Ridge County

PARSONS, Lester J. (Lottie), principal, Irland Bromfeld Middle School, 890 Arnolds Rd., Wilson Creek

PASTY, Norbert, janitor, 458 Summit St.

PEABODY, George (Allie), owner, George's Bound Timbers, Eden Pike, Eden

PEARSON, Lawrence G. (Melinda), dir. Chapel of Memories, 779 Lewis St.

PENNEBAKER, Rubelia, deputy, Blue Ridge County Sheriff's Department, 33 Bitterroot Dr., Blue Ridge County

PERROW, Minni (wid. Leland), 617 E. 14th St., Beausoleil

PETERS, Harry (Claudette, Beausoleil mayor), principal, Central Elementary School, 4338 Locust St., Beausoleil

PIERCE, Howard (Sarah, bank teller), auto mechanic, 101 Trailer Park Ln., Beausoleil

PLANK, Harvey (Sally, waitress), cook, 145 Birch Ave., Beausoleil

POINDEXTER, Henry (Joy, administrator Jeb Stuart Memorial Hospital), stockbroker, 58 Salt Ave.

POINDEXTER, Thomas W. (Miranda), shopowner, 195 Trout Ln., Blue Ridge County

POLLERD, Jon (Candace, fisheries mgr.), sergeant, Valleydale Police Dept., 2 North Buffalo Head Rd., Culleytown

PONTEFRACT, Emory W., dir. community relations, Virginia Power, 32 Fillmore Ave.

POTTER, Sheryl, principal, Ellison Elementary School, 3 Covered Bridge Rd., Culleytown

PRENTICE, Ron Allen "Don" (Mary, principal Wilson Creek Elementary School), Valleydale city mgr., 422 White St.

PRITCHARD, Ann Marie, exec. dir., The Hope Project, 45 Cliffs Lane, Blue Ridge County

Q

QUICK, Fred (Beverly, nurse), tchr., South High School, 1575 Carter Rd., Blue Ridge County

QUILLIAN, Mary, bookkeeper, city of Valleydale, 5111 Enfield Ave., #11, Beausoleil

R

RANDOLPH STREET BAPTIST CHURCH, Lewis McNab, pastor, 104 N. Randolph St.

RANDOLPH STREET UNITED METHODIST CHURCH, Theodore Harrison, pastor, 110 S. Randolph St.

RANNEFORD, Jerry (Zita), prof., VPU, 547 Oak St., Beausoleil

RED FRONT, The, Bernard F. Durrman, owner, 123 S. Main St.

REEVES, Lawrence, ret'd. Valleydale city clerk, 44 Stonewall Cir.

REX, Percy J. (Cordelia), Blue Ridge County medical examiner, 321 Skunk Rd., Blue Ridge County

RICHARDSON, Bruce E., prof., VPU, 1913 John Wesley Rd., Blue Ridge County

RIDGE VIEW ELEMENTARY SCHOOL, Todd Benson principal, Hollow Road, Blue Ridge County

ROBERTSON, Fred (Seymour Fine, law professor, VPU), law professor, VPU, 211 Walt Faulkner Hwy., Inverness

ROLLINS, T.D. "Pete" (Carol, clerk), sanitation worker, 510 Spruce St., Beausoleil

S

SANCHEZ-RODRIGUEZ, Teresita L. atty., 911 Salt Ave.

SANDFORD, Harry, firefighter, 862 W. Trafalgar St.

SANTABRIE, Glynnis, education coordinator, The Hope Project, 344 Myers St., Apt. 4

7-ELEVEN, Martha Blatchky, owner, 28 E. Trafalgar St.

SHONEY'S, Dwight Upman, mgr., 144 Chestnut St., Beausoleil

SIMPSON, Gail, city worker, Beausoleil, 111 Magnolia Ave., Beausoleil

SINGER, R.D. "Country" (Oprah, musician), undertaker, Beausoleil City Council mbr., 410 Locust Ave., Beausoleil

SMART, Maxwell, construction worker 14 Old Bridge Ln., Rock Falls

SMITH, Clifford "Zeke," principal, Blue Ridge Middle School, 11 Cyrus McCord Ln., Iron Forge

SMITH, Harold (A.P., educator), prof. VPU, 304 S. Roosevelt St.

SMITH, Patrick L. (Sherri, teacher), Officer, Valleydale police, 107 S. Randolph St.

SMYTHE-WILHOIT, Brittany Davis, student, VPU, 137 N. Randolph St.

SOUTH HIGH SCHOOL, R. W. "Fred" Ferris, principal, Welland St.

SOWELL, Elton (Ronnie, dry cleaner), owner, Lloyd's Bistro, 313 Randolph St.

SPANGLER, H. Merritt Jr. (Sophia, physician), engineer, Chair, North Service Authority, 13 Edmund St.

SPORTS FOR ALL, Delmer Hostetter, mgr., 28 N. Main St.

SPRUANCE, Sporrin, owner, OnTop Freight Co., 333 Elbert Dinkins Highway, Rock Falls

STALLARD, Rufus T. (Zita), county administrator, Blue Ridge County, 311 Bird Rd., Blue Ridge County

STANTON, Hal, Beausoleil city engineer, Old Beausoleil Rd., Blue Ridge County

STUART, Jason (Loretta "Etty," Beausoleil city clerk), banker, 677 Border Trail, Blue Ridge County

SWOFFORD, T.E. "Tink" (Clarice, mgr. Wal-Mart), sheriff, Blue Ridge
County, 77 Little Mountain Rd., Zeno

T

TALIAFERRO, Joshua A., commonwealth's atty., Blue Ridge County,
14 Trent Ridge Rd., Blue Ridge County

TEECE, Gordon L. (Diane), farmer, 1 Balloon Falls Rd., Inverness

THATCHER, Beckley (Thelma), atty., 11 Quail Run, Blue Ridge
County

THE BREEZE RESTAURANT, Quentin "Twink" Frisbee, prop.,
Trafalgar and Roosevelt Sts.

THOMAS, Asa (Alison, bus driver), auto dealer, 55 S. Buffalo Fork,
Blue Ridge County

THOMAS MOTORS Asa Thomas, ownr., Hwy. 50 W.

THURSTON, L. E. "Skeet," city mgr. Beausoleil, 111 Magnolia Ave.,
Beausoleil

TILTON, Leonard, principal, Blue Ridge County High School, 5111
Lee Hwy., Blue Ridge County

TOLLIVER, Billy Joe (Carrie), welder, 113 Red Rock Ln., Bluefield

TOPPING, Courtney Ann, student, VPU, 137 N. Randolph St.

TRUMP, Luverne,Valleydale finance dir., 658 Travis St.

TURPIN, Ed (Alice, Valleydale deputy finance director), art gallery
mgr., 413 Cemetery Dr.

U

UNCAS, Austin A. (Prunella, nurse), mgr., Kroger Food Stores Inc., 209
Falling Doe Rd., Blue Ridge County

UPMAN, Dwight (Cheryl, real estate broker), mgr., Shoney's, 144
Chestnut St., Beausoleil

USTERMAN, Richard (Taylene), laborer, 1911 Elm St., Beausoleil

V

VALE, Gerald (Ernestine), foreman, Apple Mfg. Co., 336 Edmund Ave.

VALLEYDALE PRESBYTERIAN CHURCH, Edwin F. Younts,
minister, Main and Trafalgar Streets

VANCE, Thurgood (Connie), truck driver, 6100 Snake Ln., Culleytown

VINCENT, R. J. (Muriel, tchr.), owner, R.J. Vincent and Assocs., Stockbrokers, 11 Magnolia Ave., Beausoleil

W

WADDELL, Will, Realtor, Blue Ridge County Supervisor, Old Plume Road, Blue Ridge County

WAL-MART, Rt. 15 N., Blue Ridge County

WEDDELL, Sharon, Blue Ridge County dir. of community relations, 12 Blue Heron Lane, Blue Ridge County

WELLAND ELEMENTARY SCHOOL, Tonya Winfrey, principal, McLaren St.

WHEELOCK, Cathy, magazine editor, 448 Travis St.

WHIC-FM Radio Station, 111 Magnolia Ave., Beausoleil

WIGGINS, Robert "Bobby" (Thelma, dog trainer), Sgt., Virginia State Police, coordinator, Blue Ridge Regional Drug Task Force, 44 Marble Valley Rd., Blue Ridge County

WILCOX, Curtis "Cooter," police chief, Beausoleil, 191 Landfill Rd., Blue Ridge County

WILSON CREEK ELEMENTARY SCHOOL, Mary Prentice, principal, School Rd., Wilson Creek

WILSON, George W. city atty., Beausoleil, 1 Balcony Rd., Inverness

WINFREY, Lee (Tonya, principal, Welland Elementary School), hairdresser, 411 Royce Rd.

WISE, Eaton (Dorothy Mae, organist), auto salesman, mbr., Valleydale City Council, 12 Marshall St.

WOFFORD, L.E. "Skeeter," Valleydale fire chief, 2222 Midland Trail, Blue Ridge County

X,Y,Z

YAMASHITA, Sessue, Dr. (Miko, pharmacist), director, Blue Ridge County Social Services, 910 Rebel Dr.

YOUNGMAN, Henry (Priscilla, dental asst.), phys., 4 Enfield Rd., Beausoleil

YOUNTS, Edwin F. (Mary), pastor, Valleydale Presbyterian Church, 590 S. Main St.

ZYSGER, Bob (Kay E.), mgr., North River Bed & Breakfast, 190 Riverwash Rd., Blue Ridge County

References

Anderson, K. A., and B. Itule (1988). *Writing the News*. New York: Random House.

Crystal, D. (2004). *The Stories of English*. Woodstock, NY: Overlook Press.

Fuller, J. (1996). *News Values*. Chicago: University of Chicago.

Gordon, R. *Introduction to spreadsheets: Microsoft Excel. www.ire.org/training/Brazil/xlctybud.pdf.* Investigative Reporters and Editors/National Institute for Computer-Assisted Reporting.

LaRocque, P. (2003). *The Book on Writing: The Ultimate Guide to Writing Well*. Oak Park, IL: Marion Street Press.

Merritt, D. (1998). *Public Journalism and Public Life: Why Telling the News Is Not Enough*. 2nd ed. Mahwah, NJ: Erlbaum.

Metzler, K. (1987). *Newswriting Exercises*. 2nd ed. Englewood Cliffs, NJ: Prentice-Hall.

Index